PELICAN BOOKS

Development in a
Divided World

Development in a Divided World

EDITED BY DUDLEY SEERS
AND LEONARD JOY

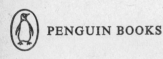 PENGUIN BOOKS

Penguin Books Ltd, Harmondsworth,
Middlesex, England
Penguin Books Inc., 7110 Ambassador Road,
Baltimore, Maryland 21207, U.S.A.
Penguin Books Australia Ltd, Ringwood,
Victoria, Australia

First published 1971

Copyright © Penguin Books, 1970

Made and printed in Great Britain by
C. Nicholls & Company Ltd
Set in Monotype Times

CONTENTS

Part Four: International Development Policies

List of Tables

PREFACE

This book deals with the serious and growing problems of material disparities in the world and what might be done about them.

It was written mainly by the Fellows of the Institute of Development Studies, an independent centre set up in 1966 by the Ministry of Overseas Development at the University of Sussex to undertake research, teaching and consulting work on development problems.*

It is designed for the 'general reader' in the sense that we have avoided technical terms; the problems of poverty and the central issues that they raise can be stated in plain English. But we have taken a fresh look at the subject and we hope that the result will also be of interest to professional colleagues and to students of development, at home and abroad.

One main theme, which is not usually stressed enough, recurs in the book, namely that poor countries today have to find ways of developing, not in isolation, but in the actual world of the end of the twentieth century. This is a world of very big inequalities, where the great majority of the capital and professional resources are in the hands of a small minority of countries, which also hold dominant positions in international trade, enjoy the preponderance of military power, and exercise strong cultural influence. These imbalances create special problems (as well as special opportunities) for poor countries and special responsibilities for the rich.

*While the Institute's Fellows wrote this book, we must not forget the secretaries who typed their way through all its many drafts. Special appreciation, too, is due to Richard Stern and Barry Peters, who assisted with the editing at critical times, and to Raphael Kaplinsky who revised the statistical tables and shared with Susan Purdie Peters the work of indexing.

A great deal of the discussion of development has been vitiated by the failure to take account of the world's economic and political structure. Unless one is fully aware of the context within which governments have to try to develop their countries, it is easy to fall into the trap of assuming, usually implicitly, that analyses and prescriptions derived from the experience of rich countries are also applicable to countries which are not merely poor, but poor in a very unequal world. Development is not only an entirely different task for them; it raises policy problems which have little in common even with those faced by, say, Britain or France in the nineteenth century. It follows that theories, attitudes and syllabuses in the social sciences should reflect these differences; so should development strategies.

To develop even this theme in a couple of hundred pages necessarily involves leaving out a good deal. Little attention is paid, for example, to the world roles of the Soviet Union or China, and none to the internal relationships of the Communist group (although these show, in different forms, some of the same problems of the coexistence of countries at different stages of development). The emphasis is on relations between the Third World and the 'western', or 'capitalist', or 'industrialized' world, with which it is closely linked, especially by trade. These relationships have been intimate ever since the start of the colonial period, and, although they are now in a state of flux, the existence of a Communist bloc still modifies rather than transforms them.

Secondly, we do not try to be comprehensive. Our main aim was not the impossible one of writing an encyclopaedia of development. The treatment and examples reflect, as they are bound to, the personal experience of each author within the very big field of our studies. Our starting point was the expertise available at the Institute in 1968 for a book which was to cover more than just economics; since we needed to cover the main social sciences concerned with development problems and there was no sociologist on the staff at that time – we asked Peter Marris, of the Institute of Community Studies, to join the team. This is, however, more than a collection of essays by experts in different fields. We tried to see that each contribution at least took account of the viewpoint of disciplines other than that of the author. We did this by arranging for the group to meet for the discussion of each draft chapter (except the last one).*

A word on terminology is necessary. We refer to some countries of the world as 'underdeveloped' or 'developing' but we must realize that these descriptions are dangerous evasions of reality. All countries are 'underdeveloped' in various senses, and the most serious problem about the countries usually described as 'developing' is precisely that few of them are successfully doing so. 'Less developed' is perhaps less objectionable, although it carries a faint implication that those at a low place in this ladder should model themselves on those higher up, and this can be positively dangerous as a guide to strategy. What we are really talking about is poverty, and a large part of this book does in fact deal with its meaning and measurement, its causes, characteristics and cure. Anticipating somewhat the discussion that lies ahead, and ignoring a few anomalies, we can take the 'poor' countries of the world as broadly those of Africa, Asia and Latin America. A phrase that is convenient to cover all of them is the 'Third World' but we have also had to use in places the various alternatives mentioned above.

Some of the statistical material is slightly out of date. This is inevitable in view of the time it takes to edit and publish a work by many hands. But in most cases the statistics are merely illustrative and later data would make little difference to the dimensions of the problems discussed.

The book is in four parts. The first deals with the international context. The opening chapter sets the stage by discussing the data, as faced by the governments of poor countries, data which they cannot change, at least in the short-run: the world distribution of income with the associated structure of trade and capital flows, and the accompanying intellectual and political influences. The ways in which the existence of rich countries affects the development of poor countries is then developed more fully in chapter two. Chapter three looks at the international transfer of

*Professor G. M. Meier, an economist from Stanford University, who was then a Visiting Fellow at the Institute, and Hans Singer, now at IDS, also kindly commented on many of the chapters.

technology and discusses how on the one hand it opens up new possibilities of eliminating poverty, but on the other causes great social strains, especially those due to the fact that techniques for controlling deaths have been more effectively transferred than techniques for preventing births.

Part Two shifts the scene to the national level. The opening chapter discusses the nature of poor-country poverty and the following two chapters look at the characteristics of poor countries and the problems they face in the process of development, from social and political perspectives.

The second half of the book deals with policies – Part Three reviews economic strategies which are open to a national government in various fields looking first at domestic policies and then at international policies. There is then a series of chapters dealing with policy issues in the main fields – agriculture, manpower and education, and finance. Part Three concludes with a chapter on planning by the two non-economists, designed to set the discussion on economic strategies in a wider framework.

Part Four discusses what rich countries could and should do, in fields of trade, investment and aid. This takes us back to the international context sketched at the outset, though we now treat it not as datum but as something that could be changed.

This book not merely describes; it prescribes too. We hope it will contribute to the making of policies, national and international, that will reduce the ugly and immoral inequalities in the world, inequalities which do not shock us only because they have become so familiar.   D.S.

PART ONE
THE INTERNATIONAL SETTING

1 RICH COUNTRIES AND POOR*

This book is concerned with human poverty. One can look at this in either 'absolute' or 'relative' terms. Absolutely, there are hundreds of millions of people who are illiterate and inadequately sheltered even from the rain, virtually without furniture or shoes, perpetually undernourished, provided by the twentieth century with little except the growing awareness of their misfortune.

This has, however, always been the case. The striking fact about the world economy today is that tens of millions of people live very differently, and that moreover those with high incomes, high enough (say) to spend a third of them on food, are not scattered evenly over the globe, but are heavily concentrated in a dozen countries bordering the North Atlantic.

There are several reasons for stressing the importance of relative poverty, that is poverty by the standards which are made possible by the application of known techniques. One is that this is simply an immoral situation. But that is not the only reason, nor would some consider it a sufficient one in a book that deals technically with development problems.

Why the heavy concentration of the world's income in a few countries is taken as the starting point here is because this is the context within which poor countries have to develop, and this context creates a new and quite different set of problems from those which these countries would face if there were no such inequalities.

Let us start with some figures on the distribution of the world's income – in table 1.1. The figures are rough and difficult to interpret. The statistics are, in many cases, poor or non-existent.

*I am grateful to Mr David Forbes for preparing the basic data for this chapter.

THE INTERNATIONAL SETTING

Moreover, many activities covered in the national incomes of rich countries, like food preparation, are considered outside the scope of national income estimation in poorer countries. Others, such as travel to work, are really part of the 'overhead costs' rather than the 'income' of richer countries. Moreover, other factors are relevant to 'poverty' – this is discussed at length in chapter two.

TABLE 1.1

Average incomes in different regions in 1965 (excluding Communist countries)[1]

	U.S. dollars per head	
North America	3,110	
Western Europe	1,260	
Average of rich countries (including Japan, Australia, New Zealand and South Africa)		1,760
Latin America	380	
West Asia	360	
Africa (excluding Angola, Mozambique and South Africa)	100	
South and East Asia	100	
Average of poor countries (includes areas not specified)		150
World average		660

Another type of caution is that the average of a region covers very big differences between the countries it contains. The figure for Latin America averages the per capita incomes of countries as far apart as Argentina, with nearly $800 a head, and Haiti where it is under $100. The figure for West Asia (which is rather parochially known in the Atlantic area as the 'Middle East') is pulled up by a few very rich oil states. Even in Western Europe there is a big contrast between a group of really rich countries like Britain, France and Western Germany with about $1,600, and Greece and Portugal ($600 and under $400, respectively).

Regional averages might lead one to suppose quite falsely that Portugal is better off than Argentina. Some obvious adjustments have in fact been made already in the table above. South Africa and Japan have been omitted from their respective geographical regions.

We must not forget either that *within* any country there are also striking differences. This is particularly true of poor countries, where taxation and social expenditures are both low. Such countries are marked by great geographical contrasts; for example, the average income of the State of Guanabara, which includes Rio de Janeiro, is some ten times that of the poorest states of the north-east in Brazil, and in Peru the average income in the jungle areas is less than one twelfth that of the coastal region. In Britain, on the other hand, average incomes of different areas vary only about 10 per cent around the average for the nation as a whole.

Poor countries are also marked by great vertical contrasts. Typically, the richest 5 per cent of the population receive 30 per cent to 40 per cent of the total income before tax – even more in settler countries such as Rhodesia.[2] It would, in fact, be a serious error to assume that all Indians, even, are poorer than all residents of the United States. Those at the very top of the income ladder in a poor country may well receive incomes as high as their counterparts in the industrial countries. Indeed, since they usually pay less tax, they are often better off, especially if one attaches importance to the availability of domestic service and uncongested roads – not to speak of the ease with which they may be able to flaunt national laws.

Nevertheless, when all is said and done, the figures in table 1.1 show differences so striking that they do have some significance. What really characterizes a region with a low per capita income is that the mass of its population lives in conditions of persistent poverty, almost unimaginable now in the rich countries.

While poverty is of course not new – it has been the historical lot of mankind – these contrasts between rich and poor countries have only emerged very recently. In terms of the purchasing power of U.S. dollars in 1960, the average income in 1850 in the emerging industrial countries of the North Atlantic area was probably less than $200, and although in other countries the average was lower than today, the ratio between the average incomes of Western Europe and North America on the one hand, and the rest of the world on the other, was then about two to one;[3] as can be seen from table 1.1, it is now more than ten to one. The increase in world income in the past century has been concentrated in a small group of countries, containing between them less than 30 per cent of the world's population, opening up a very wide gap between the incomes of (say) a messenger in Britain and in Kenya.

Britain, and then some Western European countries and the United States, gained a lead in the nineteenth century. Moreover, once some countries get out in front, they tend to draw further ahead. It is only possible to give a very sketchy treatment here of a problem which has many facets. (A full account would have to explain, for example, the ability of some countries, such as Russia and Japan, to break away from the throng and follow the vanguard.) But one major economic reason for those in front drawing further ahead is the tendency of the demand for manufactures to rise more rapidly than income. This becomes reinforced by other factors. Costs of production are reduced as the scale of output expands, making possible bigger profits for reinvestment, including (especially in the nineteenth century) investment overseas to ensure a growing supply of primary commodities, and a rising inflow of interests and profits. Bigger profits also mean bigger taxes to pay for education, research and military forces; so the industrial leaders acquire political power, enabling them to impose a favourable trading pattern, which further strengthens them economically.

Another feature of this situation must be mentioned. The rich countries of the world, which are growing relatively richer, are predominantly white, whereas this is true of virtually none of the poor. (Even the exceptions, such as Argentina, Chile and Uruguay, are at or near the top of the per capita income table for poor countries.) Moreover, within each country – South Africa and Rhodesia being the most conspicuous, but by no means unique, examples – there is a strong correlation between skin colour and income, with non-whites in multi-racial societies usually holding a disproportionate share of the unskilled jobs.

Statistics on changes in the distribution of income are very scarce, but there is reason to believe that in many countries the incomes of the professional classes are rising more rapidly than those of the unskilled workers, which implies a growing 'gap' within countries between whites and others. Any book on development published at this stage of the twentieth century would be seriously incomplete if it did not refer to the political overtones of the tensions between rich and poor, both between countries and within them.

Development Seen in Historic Perspective

To say this is not to take sides in the rather sterile controversy of whether a country would now be better off if it had never been colonized. The surge forward in world trade in the nineteenth century had beyond doubt a favourable economic impact on many tropical countries. These found growing outlets for commodities which they could readily produce, both foodstuffs and materials, but for which there was no market at home. Thus British imports grew twentyfold in the century following the Battle of Waterloo. New opportunities appeared for the employment of labour in plantations and mines, and new uses for land which had previously been uncultivated. Capital was attracted to the tropics, for ports, railways and roads to facilitate trade, as well as for new mines and land improvements. Between 1880 and 1913 British foreign investments rose (net) about $12 billion, and France's about $6 billion, although in each case less than half went to today's poor countries.[4]

Yet it is an evident fact that the rising incomes in industrial countries did not cause parallel increases in the nations which were being drawn into the world economy. For the latter, exports acted as an 'engine of growth', but not a very powerful one. Many of the reasons for this will be explored elsewhere in this book, but to mention only a few headings – the lack of a market structure for conveying dynamic impulses, the low level of education, class systems not conducive to modernization (often based on land ownership), tribalism (whether of settlers or of indigenous peoples), and the lack of a political system with the power and flexibility to respond to the challenge and opportunity of the scientific age.

There are some offsetting disadvantages, moreover, inherent in this type of growth. The district benefiting from trade often remained an enclave only weakly linked – especially in Africa – with the rest of its country. Here, in fact, is the origin of the internal contrasts, touched on earlier. These enclaves also help to explain the slowness of development. Trade can increase the power of social classes that play a passive or even negative role, such as big landowners; and political alliances between them and importers may make it difficult to develop local industries.

In fact the total effect of the industrial advance of the North Atlantic on the incomes of the rest of the world was limited; national incomes grew from 1850 to 1950 at an average of less than 2 per cent (with, of course, a big difference between countries), and large sections of the population in Asia, Africa and Latin America failed to benefit at all from this rise.

Moreover, the engine weakened in the twentieth century. Food consumption in the industrial countries grew much more slowly than national income, while services (which require very few imports) grew faster. Within manufacturing, the lines that expanded fastest were the sophisticated engineering products with a low metal content. New techniques saved on the use of materials and enabled higher proportions of metals to be recovered from scrap. Synthetics cut into the market for rubber, cotton and nitrates, to quote a few conspicuous examples. Tariffs and subsidies were used to protect farmers in industrial countries, making it possible, for example, to expand the output of beet sugar, and high taxes were levied in continental Europe on imports such as coffee and cocoa. World trade in primary products grew nearly twice as fast as world trade in manufactures in the last two decades of the nineteenth century; but thenceforward, except for the depression of the 1930s, the latter always rose more quickly.*

*The two world wars undoubtedly contributed greatly to this, especially in stimulating production of synthetics. The foregoing four paragraphs are based on a draft by Mr Braun. See also note 5.

In view of all these negative factors, it is rather surprising, at first sight, that, since the last world war, growth rates in poor countries have been unprecedentedly fast: see table 1.2.

An average growth of 4 to 5 per cent a year maintained over more than fifteen years for nations covering the bulk of the world's population is, after all, an historical novelty. For Asia and Africa it means nothing less than breaking out of their traditional stagnation. Although in many respects, as we shall see, their progress has been unsatisfactory and their prospects are gloomy, we should not lose sight of this great achievement.

TABLE 1.2

Changes in income in rich and poor countries[6]: 1950 to 1967

	Average percentage annual increases	
Total income	1950–60	1960–67
Rich	4·0	4·8
Poor	4·6	5·0
Income per capita		
Rich	2·8	3·6
Poor	2·3	2·5

Part of the explanation is that the incomes of the rich countries have grown at a much faster rate than before the war. This was first due to the speed of recovery of France, Germany, Italy and Japan; and, when European growth slowed down in the 1960s, a new impetus came from a long boom in the United States.

Commodity exports however did not benefit by any means fully from this. Primary products (i.e. food, fuel and raw materials) which accounted for 54 per cent of world trade in 1953–4 had fallen to 42 per cent in 1965–6, only a dozen years later. Moreover, *within* the total trade of primary products, the Third World's share has fallen from 45 to 40 per cent.* The counterpart of

*This brings out a significant point: poor countries are not called primary product exporters because they export the bulk of such products (in fact other countries, notably the United States, Australia, New Zealand and South Africa, export much more between them), but because primary products constitute the bulk of their exports.

this has been the rapid expansion of trade in manufactures *between* industrial countries, especially within the European Common Market and the European Free Trade Area, as they lower barriers between themselves.

TABLE 1.3[7]

Trade between rich and poor countries: 1953 and 1969

	$ billions	
	1953	1969
Rich to rich	29	138
Rich to poor	14	36
Poor to rich	15	35
Poor to poor	5	10

Table 1.3 summarizes very briefly the effects on the pattern of world trade. Even in the short period from 1953 to 1969, world trade has become predominantly trade between rich countries. In these sixteen years, internal trade within the bloc of rich countries quadrupled, while trade between rich countries and poor doubled. (These comparisons include of course the effect of price rises, since the table is in current prices.)

What then was the explanation of the relatively fast growth of national income in the Third World in the post-war period? Increased trade among themselves shows a very moderate acceleration, especially in view of the efforts at 'regional integration'. Part of the explanation lies in the increased pace of capital flows. Aid had been very small up to 1955; then it increased sharply, reaching $6 billion (net of repayments) in 1961, and, while this then showed little further increase, private investment rose to more than $3 billion net in 1965; and after falling back temporarily, ran at about $4 billion a year in 1965–7.[8]

But although this is a considerable volume, and certainly helped to sustain economic growth in the 1960s, its significance should not be exaggerated. The majority of aid is tied, in the sense that it can only be spent in the donor country (much of it in fact being spent on surplus foodstuffs), and it is often motivated by a desire for political or commercial advantage rather than to speed the development of aided countries. Moreover the volume of aid and 'hard' loans has led to an enormous burden of debt; the total external public debt of 71 'developing' countries at the end of 1967 amounted to $38·5 billion, more than four times as much as in 1955, and the annual debt service burden amounted to $4 billion.[9] The growth of private investment (much of it in exploration for oil) has been accompanied by a fast growth of profits and interest. In 1966, as can be seen from table 1.3, the value of exports from poor countries only just covered their imports. This means that the net inflow of capital (including changes in reserves) was just enough to pay for the net outlays on insurance, freight and travel, plus the profits and interest on past debt.

More important is the fact that countries which had been colonies were particularly determined to promote development, and to end poverty. Other chapters in this book discuss the range of internal policies which help – in some cases hinder – development. The point that is relevant here is that newly independent countries were now able to pursue commercial policies which were more favourable to their own national interests; for example, they could now make trade agreements with any other country, and they were freer to take measures to protect their own new industries. Import substitution, at least for the products of most light industries, proved quite feasible, especially where markets were large, and the pace of industrial growth has been rapid, averaging 8 to 10 per cent a year for Africa, Asia and Latin America alike.

Yet, just as the averages of table 1.1 covered great differences in incomes inside regions, the growth rates shown in table 1.2 conceal a wide variety of experience, especially among the poor countries. Though few of the twenty rich ones grew at less than 3 per cent, many of the poor showed little growth of national income at all, even over the whole of this period. On the other hand, other poor countries, especially those exporting minerals or petroleum, have been consistently growing at rates of over 5 per cent.

The general acceleration in the rise in income since before the last war has been accompanied by an acceleration in the rate of population increase, which has now risen to about $2\frac{1}{2}$ per cent a year for poor countries as a whole. The consequent failure to benefit fully from the increase in national income is illustrated by the per capita income figures in the lower half of table 1.2. While the *total* income of poor countries grew almost as rapidly as those of rich countries in 1960–65, the population growth was twice as fast in the poor countries ($2\frac{1}{2}$ as against $1\frac{1}{4}$ per cent) so that the income disparities between rich and poor became more marked.

Other explanations for this tendency to increased income disparity have been put forward on theoretical grounds. One implies the necessary long term deterioration of poor countries' terms of trade. However, as there is no clear evidence that the terms of trade of poor countries show any long-period deterioration at all, it is not thought worthwhile to examine these arguments. Such statistics as do exist suggest that trends have been very mixed over the past century.[10] It is possible to find evidence of deterioration of poor-country terms of trade by taking a particular period – for example, comparing the level of prices now with those during the Korean War – or taking a particular country. For such a period or such a country, the effect may be considerable, but, as a general explanation of long-term trends in the world economy, it is untenable.

Another argument which was much used in earlier years has been that the development of exporters of primary products had been hampered by the tendency of these exports to fluctuate excessively, causing uncertainty, and both distortions and reductions in the level of investment, compared to what would otherwise obtain. Recent research has, however, thrown doubt on both the extent of fluctuations in exports, and also on the damage that they do to development.[11] There are of course already agreements which stabilize the prices of some key commodities, such as sugar and coffee, and for others (such as bauxite and petroleum) markets are dominated by a few large firms which find it convenient to peg producer prices. Although certainly fluctuations are severe for particular commodities (such as rubber and cocoa) and therefore for particular countries, their impact on domestic sectors of economies is to some extent muffled by time-lags and by the tendency for offsetting fluctuations to be induced in payments for imports and in remittances of profits. So these are responsible to only a small degree for the opening of 'the gap'.

The lack of evidence for these arguments does not prevent them being used as alibis by those in the Third World who wish to believe them; they imply that poor countries are helpless in the face of inexorable forces from outside. For some members of the Latin American elite, they provide convenient substitutes for the excuse: 'We can't do anything because we were ruined by colonial rule.' What is worse, they are often used as a justification for attempting a rate of industrialization faster than is feasible.

Certainly neither of these arguments is really necessary to explain the widening gap in 'per capita' incomes when one can point to other obvious explanations – including the weakening of trade as a stimulus and the acceleration of population growth.[12]

The Organization of the World Economy Today

An account of the world economy merely in terms of trade can be seriously misleading – it is the counterpart of what Marx called 'commodity fetishism', i.e. concentrating on markets for goods in national economic analysis as a way of evading social realities. Not only are industrial countries richer, they are stronger in various senses, and this too has economic implications. While nowadays, military and political power is kept mostly in the background, its existence certainly has an influence on trade and investment, and therefore on incomes. The trade pattern of French-speaking African countries, for example, still shows relatively far higher trade with France than in poor countries generally. The United States has managed to induce countries in Latin America (although some of them hardly needed much pressure) to cut off trade with Cuba, largely because of the expropriation of U.S. assets there. Aid is at times made conditional

23

on the treatment given to foreign companies. The evidence is naturally slim, but anyone with practical experience knows that governments of rich countries exert some influence – on occasion quite a lot – on the policies, both external and internal, of other governments. (More of this in chapter fifteen.)

There is another way in which these links work. In the post-war world the international company, based in an industrial country, is more important than it was in the past. It takes decisions on exports, investment and other matters which affect profoundly the patterns of development overseas, especially of small countries. It wields considerable economic power in the countries where its subsidiaries are responsible for a high fraction of exports and it usually enjoys access to more professional expertise than the governments with which it deals. In addition, it naturally always receives support from 'its own' government. Its influence is not necessarily harmful, but clearly considerable.

It is of course true that elaborate machinery now exists for regulating international economic relations. This change had its origin in the political and economic settlement at the end of the war. The economic settlement included the International Bank for Reconstruction and Development (IBRD) to provide capital, the International Monetary Fund (IMF) to help countries in foreign exchange difficulties, and the General Agreement on Tariffs and Trade (GATT) to regulate trade.

The philosophy underlying this set of organizations was that of *laissez faire*. Its fundamental assumption was that the free operation of the market would produce satisfactory progress, once the world economy had been reconstructed. GATT forbade quotas in principle and discouraged preferential systems or increases in tariffs;* the articles of the IMF outlawed exchange controls in principle on current transactions, especially discriminatory ones, and also multiple exchange rates; and 'the Bank', like GATT, can only be joined by members of 'the Fund'.

Discontent with this system has been growing. Attempts to speed economic growth led to chronic payment difficulties in

*This is a rather misleading summary. Strictly, contracting members agree to try to observe the principles of certain chapters of the Havana Charter of 1948, which was never actually ratified.

many countries (aggravated, of course, in some cases by mistaken policies), and it seemed that this system tied their hands, especially the rules of G A T T. On the other hand, the system did not stop industrial countries discriminating in favour of each other by tariff reductions (as in the European Common Market and the European Free Trade Association), by imposing quotas on imports of textiles, by protecting their farmers, or by subsidising their exporters. The more sophisticated leaders of the Third World had deep misgivings about whether the rules of the game gave them any chance of catching up – particularly when richer countries were not bound by them. The protection of high-cost beet sugar producers in Continental Europe is entirely contrary to the principles of *laissez faire*, and the very high internal taxes there on coffee, cocoa and tea make rather a mockery of the movement towards lower tariffs.

Moreover, financial help was given by the Bank and the Fund to Western Europe, almost exclusively, in the early years of their operations and – especially in the case of the Fund – this pattern was only modified gradually. The Bank was for some time restricted in what it could do for poor countries by the requirements that projects should be properly prepared and commercially profitable, and that borrowing countries should be clearly capable of servicing the debt. The Fund relates its currency sales and stand-by facilities to each country's 'quota', so that the richest can borrow most.

When the post-war economic settlement was made, very few of the poor countries were independent (in Africa and Asia anyway) so they had little voice in it. The political settlement contained, however, the seeds of an eventual challenge to the economic set-up. The United Nations is 'open to all peace-loving states which accept the obligations contained in this present Charter' and, apart from a few well-known exceptions, new states have joined as they became eligible. It provides, for the first time in history, a forum where the governments of poor countries, which are in a majority, can raise the questions that concern them and force rich countries to take a position; it also collects and analyses information on these problems. Moreover, while in the I M F and I B R D the number of votes each country has at its disposal depends on its financial contributions, in the United Nations General Assembly the rule is one country, one vote.

Why does the United Nations not emulate the governments of the rich countries themselves in curbing regional and social inequalities? The operation of market forces has been increasingly modified inside these countries, notably by heavy taxes on the rich which are used, in part, to finance unemployment benefits, old age pensions and the welfare services of the modern industrial state, including education. Geographical differences have been mitigated by the fiscal system as a whole, not merely by special inducements to encourage industry to build factories, or expand them, in relatively backward areas. Some government action of this kind is inevitable wherever there is true universal suffrage; those who want to achieve (or at any rate hold) political power have to pay heed to the disaffected.*

The United Nations is not in fact capable of mitigating international inequalities. While in the Assembly member countries are numerically equal, the rich countries enjoy heavy representation in key organs such as the Economic and Social Council, as well as being able to count on the support of a number of 'clients' on many issues in any United Nations body. Moreover, in contrast to the national state, there is no power compelling members of the United Nations to comply with its resolutions, even those for which they voted themselves. Effectiveness depends in part on the requirements of foreign policy, but ultimately on the sense of responsibility of the governments of the rich countries, which in turn depends on internal political support for international action against poverty. But the public in rich countries are clearly not prepared to sacrifice a significant part of their existing standards of living. In any case, they know little of the problems of the rest of the world or of proposals for easing them – this aspect of the work of the United Nations receives virtually no attention at all in the world's press.

For the nationalists in the rich countries, moves to strengthen the United Nations and its agencies represent a threat to

*It is very uncertain, however, whether these equalizing tendencies have continued in industrial countries in the past twenty years.

sovereignty. These organizations interfere with the bilateral relations of trade and aid between countries at different levels of development which have, in some parts of the world, taken the place of the colonial link. The United Nations also, despite the veto enjoyed by three rich countries (and the Soviet Union) in the Security Council* and their unwillingness to use its machinery for the settlement of disputes, does restrict somewhat the scope for military intervention, which is still the last refuge of those wanting to exercise political control. It is true that there are internationalists in all countries, but their political power is relatively weak. With the exception of some of the smaller countries, the delegations from North America or Western Europe are therefore customarily on the defensive in international economic discussions, more concerned to sidetrack awkward initiatives than to enter into serious negotiations on ways of altering the economic balance of the world.

Yet it would be wrong to give the impression that there has been no progress. The United Nations has set up 'specialized agencies' in the economic and social field – notably for agriculture (FAO); health (WHO); education, science and culture (UNESCO); and, most recently, industrial development (UNIDO). The creation of the Economic Commission for Europe (ECE) was followed by regional commissions for Latin America (ECLA), Asia (ECAFE) and Africa (ECA). The technical assistance programme, established in 1948, has grown rapidly and been augmented by a Special Fund for pre-investment surveys, now joined with UN Technical Assistance in a Development Programme (UNDP).

Other organizations have responded to the shift in international power and modified their operations in various ways to make their impact less harsh on poor countries. The Bank created the International Development Agency (IDA) in 1960 to make loans which were interest-free (apart from a small service charge); this enabled it to relax its debt-worthiness criterion, and it has been prepared to extend loans in fields like

*The fifth country which nominally enjoys a 'veto', Taiwan (which uses the vote of China), has made limited use of it, for fear of being unseated.

agriculture and education where returns are not very tangible.*
The Fund has lent more readily to poor countries, especially to
meet exchange crises due to commodity price fluctuations, and
with less rigid policy conditions. GATT had allowed them some
flexibility in protecting infant industries; since 1965, the industrial countries have bound themselves to reduce duties and
other taxes on products from poor countries, without reciprocity.

Still, these changes did not meet the demands of the Third
World. A number of resolutions in the United Nations have
focused attention on development problems. One established
the 1960s as a 'development decade', with the target that, by the
end of it, 5 per cent growth rates would be achieved by poor
countries. More significant as an expression of dissatisfaction
with the existing order was the calling of the first United Nations
Conference on Trade and Development (UNCTAD) in Geneva
in 1964. At this seventy-seven of the poor countries of Africa,
Asia and Latin America, combined to put pressure on the rich by
proposing resolutions, *inter alia* setting 1 per cent of national
income as a target for the flow of capital (public and private)
from rich countries, and in favour of commodity stabilization
schemes and preferential trade treatment.

While delegations from rich countries voted for many of these
resolutions, they have not let this influence their conduct very
greatly – though some smaller industrial nations such as Canada,
Netherlands and the Scandinavian countries are notable exceptions. Still, these do not count for a great deal in the whole
picture; the flow of capital has been declining, not rising, in
relation to national income, and – apart from a sugar agreement –
little progress has been made on commodity schemes or on
preferential arrangements. Indeed the 'Kennedy Round' of
trade concessions, which ended in 1967, turned out to be very
largely a mutual swapping of concessions by exporters of man-
factures. In 1968, the second UNCTAD was held in New Delhi,
and since the bigger rich countries were mostly even more pre-

*Previously its strict criteria were understandable in view of its
dependence on floating bonds on the capital markets of industrial
countries. IDA is financed by government subscription and (to a
small extent) out of Bank profits.

occupied with their own problems, virtually no further progress was made on any front. The poor countries then turned their attention to the Second Development Decade, for which they hoped to set economic targets that would carry some degree of commitment.

Intellectual Influences

Nevertheless, too much emphasis is almost certainly placed, especially in the international organizations, on the political and economic aspects of the relations between rich countries and poor. Much more pervasive, and at least as important for development, though less evident, is the intellectual element in this relationship, an influence almost exclusively in one direction – at least if one ignores artistic fashions.

The channels through which articulate influences flow have shown remarkable changes. In earlier periods, the only representatives of European cultures were the missionaries, settlers and traders; later came the colonial services; more recently embassies, military missions, experts and teachers under aid programmes, have been the main agents for transmitting ideas from overseas, augmented in many areas by the officials of foreign companies, and – in some – by tourists. Throughout, one major influence has been education; tens of thousands have come to the famous universities of the industrial world, and even greater numbers have been attending in their own countries universities modelled on older counterparts overseas.

Although the mixture transmitted has also varied, it has hardly ever failed to contain all three of the following: techniques, tastes and beliefs. Thus the mission schools provided skills useful for clerks, and a liking for hymn tunes and ceremonial, as well as religious doctrine. The colonial service – especially the Indian Civil Service of colonial days – introduced administrative order, but also imparted some of their own contempt for the manual worker, even for the merchant and technician, and a stronger interest in the *status quo* than in

29

development. The technical assistant or military expert, like the expatriate company official, lends his own skills and teaches others by his example, but much of his advice is bound to reflect, even if only unconsciously, the ideas current in his own country; all these, not to speak of the diplomatic circle, set a social pace with motor cars and imported drink. The tourist encourages the revival of traditional cultures, even if in an artificial and perhaps debased form; but he brings little of professional value, and the need to attract him and his money may be used as an argument against social change. The medical student on a course abroad learns ways of controlling disease, but he may also pick up techniques that require expensive equipment, and the inappropriate social and political attitudes of students born and brought up in the country where he studies.

Through all these channels, but particularly through the universities, have been flowing the central economic, social and political philosophies derived from the experience of the industrial countries. Whether a political leader in the Third World is a Marxist or a believer in the price mechanism, he probably absorbed this ideology at some overseas university (the Sorbonne or Chicago, for example), or from a teacher who acquired it at such a university. His beliefs have in either event not been derived from a study of the history and structure of his own country, though he may find there what he considers to be supporting evidence, and he may adapt the doctrine so much as to make it almost unrecognizable to Europeans – examples are the 'Marxism' of Haya de la Torre or Castro, the 'socialism' of Kenyatta or Peron.

Since the pattern of economic development depends in very large part on consumer spending habits, on the prestige of different occupations, and on the policies of governments, these cultural influences undoubtedly affect development, but it is very hard to assess their impact. A great deal of the technical assistance provided in specialist fields is clearly of considerable value to the countries which receive it, virtually essential to the development of the really poor countries. Training in science or engineering almost certainly helps the student play a constructive role, especially if he is taught to understand how techniques should be adapted. But is an economist who, *in principle*, favours (or opposes) government intervention likely to give useful advice? And is a knowledge of European history – especially as usually taught – worth a large proportion of the time of a schoolboy in Africa?

We at least know enough to know how little we can generalize with safety on such points: it depends very much on the particular case. One thing we can say with some confidence is that what is harmful is not so much the transfer of ideas (or techniques or tastes) as their *naïve* transfer without adaptation in circumstances for which they were never intended. We also know that the largely unpredictable influences of this kind are very strong indeed, and will remain so as long as countries have to turn to foreign sources of technically and professionally qualified manpower, or to foreign universities, which usually make little effort to find out what would be the most appropriate forms of education for students from overseas. But it is also clear that, in Africa and Asia at least, these influences are not quite so powerful as they were in the 1940s. The availability of technical personnel from a variety of sources nowadays, including international agencies, helps to dilute particular national influences; moreover, overseas universities are tailoring their syllabuses more closely to local requirements.

One particular economic impact we do know something about is the effect on income distribution. We have here in fact one clue to the very big contrasts between rich and poor people inside poor countries. At the time of independence, the 'localization' of the civil service meant, among other things, that local officials took over the salaries of officials who left, salaries which were based on those prevalent in metropolitan countries, and well beyond the means of countries with low average incomes and limited revenues. In countries of tropical Africa, where the public service (including teachers, the armed forces and officials of public corporations) accounts for a large share of those in paid employment, this had a marked effect on the income distribution, an effect which still lingers on. Moreover, another influence has been particularly strong and not only in Africa – the salary levels paid by overseas companies, which also reflect the salaries which these officials, especially at more senior levels, can enjoy overseas.

In the past few years, an additional external force has emerged – the 'brain drain'. The growth of an international market in professions such as science and engineering, and the modification of immigration legislation so as to permit professionals to enter rich countries more easily (but to keep the unskilled out) has meant that growing numbers of those who are badly needed at home are emigrating. This is particularly likely to happen if the education they received was best suited to produce scientists and engineers capable of tackling the problems found in rich countries. Governments which raise their professional salaries to check this emigration find that they cannot easily resist pressures from other classes for higher pay, especially administrators and organized wage-earners, so this too affects the distribution of income, generally in the direction of making it less equal.

Conclusions

One conclusion that can be drawn from the rapid survey in this chapter is that the setting of the development problem today is not at all the same as it was for the industrial countries in the nineteenth century, when they were starting to pull ahead of the rest of the world, especially the tropical areas. It is quite a different matter having an income of $200 a year per head, if this is the highest average income in the world, than if it is a very low income by international standards. In the latter case, the path of future development is bound to reflect the heavy influence of other countries on markets for goods, ideas and men.

This is not to say that the prospects are necessarily worse. There is a great range of techniques to draw on; the problem is to find the appropriate ones and transform them successfully, taking account of the differences in social and political context. There has after all been one very important change in this century. An increasing number of governments in Africa, Asia and Latin America are determined to change their country's structure, not merely economically but socially and politically as well. Despite many false starts and setbacks, the general picture is of slowly accumulating experience and improving performance in policy formation.

2 MORE ON DEVELOPMENT IN AN INTERNATIONAL SETTING

Trade and Development – a Theoretical Excursion

We have seen that it is an essential part of the problem of international poverty today that it coexists with abundance and rapid progress in some areas. Many of the implications of this coexistence relate to the opportunities afforded by international trade and we have discussed its historical significance. We now examine the role of trade in development. Economic theory has looked upon international trade as the instrument for a more efficient allocation of resources through international specialization. The theory of comparative advantage as formulated first by David Ricardo in the early nineteenth century represents an important and distinct intellectual achievement and to point to some of its limitations does not detract from its enormous value. It assumes that all productive resources are fully employed and that they can be devoted either to domestic use directly or to producing exports, which can be exchanged for imports. Trade is beneficial when resources devoted to producing goods for export yield more in imports obtained in exchange than they would by direct production of the imported goods. This implies the re-allocation of national resources in response to changing international exchange possibilities and to new technological possibilities. The analytical and political conclusions of this theory are by no means obvious and are still often ignored.

But in many poor countries certain productive resources – particularly land and labour – can be shifted only at *very* high costs or only after a *very* long time, into alternative lines, either for export or for domestic use. The function of international trade in such a situation is not to promote a more efficient allocation through the international division of labour than would have been possible under autarky, it is rather to provide the demand for the output of the resources which would otherwise lie idle. In such a situation more exports do not reduce domestic production.

The existence of idle resources implies either or both of two conditions: lack of responsiveness of domestic demand for the exportable product, so that even quite large price reductions of, say, coffee or sugar or rubber would not increase domestic purchases; and specificity of resources producing it, so that the land and the labour could not be shifted to alternatives which would be demanded at home. Such conditions prevail in the indigenous smallholder sector for the production of many primary products, such as rubber, tea, cocoa, coffee, sugar, bananas, and coconuts.

The existence of actual or potential surplus capacity in land and labour for the production of certain primary products can work either to the advantage or to the disadvantage of the trading country. If a country is fortunate and there is a large and expanding foreign demand for its exports, the exporting sector might stimulate further economic development. In conjunction with appropriate human attitudes, social institutions and public policies, it can provide, at low or zero costs in terms of forgone domestic opportunities, a source of rising domestic incomes, foreign exchange, savings, fiscal revenue and perhaps the basis for industrialization such as raw-material-based processing. It can thereby contribute to the creation of those flexibilities and mobilities whose absence caused the initial imbalance. Such was the case in the nineteenth century with dairy exports in Denmark, timber exports in Sweden,[1] and coffee exports in Brazil. Today some oil producing (Iraq, Venezuela) and mining countries (Chile) enjoy similar forms of export-led development, though clearly only some resources employed in the production of these primary commodities would otherwise have been unemployed.

But this type of development depends on the existence of market outlets and a state of international demand such that extra exports will increase the exporter's foreign exchange earnings. An increase in the total volume of the exports of a primary commodity may, however, lower its price to such an extent that it leads to a fall in the total value of exports. Thus, although in such a situation a newly exporting country may add to its foreign exchange earnings, it does so only at the expense of established exporters.

This is typically the situation in the world primary commodity markets. It places severe limits on poor countries' abilities to increase the value of their exports – and to give profitable employment to otherwise unprofitably occupied resources – by increasing the volume of their exported production. There may be gain, however, from entering new lines of export: including also, perhaps, spreading the risks of the price of any particular commodity collapsing.

Yet the exploration of market opportunities may not proceed readily. In a rich, more developed economy, there exists an equilibrating mechanism of flexible prices to which producers and consumers respond. If there is a surplus of a commodity, its price falls. This encourages, in the short run, demand, and discourages, in the longer run, supply. Capital, management and labour will move out of the production of this commodity and will seek higher rewards elsewhere. There will also be a wide spectrum of substitutable techniques and goods to choose from, combining factors in different proportions according to price signals and profit incentives. This market mechanism is often weak in poor countries and it may be especially insensitive to international opportunities. The complex system of signals, incentives, substitution and mobility is not, as simple theoretical models sometimes assume, the *cause* of international trade, it is rather its *result*. Only in a developed, complex economy does it become a cause. Lack of flexibility, itself a symptom of poverty, in the face of receding, or slowly growing, international demand and advancing foreign technology, explains the paradoxical coexistence of surplus productive capacity with low incomes in poor countries, which perpetuates poverty.

Factors Inhibiting Development Which Stem from the Policies of Rich Countries

The development prospects and strategies of underdeveloped societies embarking on development are considerably influenced by the prior existence of advanced industrial societies. Some of these influences, and perhaps the most obvious ones, clearly benefit underdeveloped countries. A growing stock of scientific, technical and organizational knowledge has been accumulated, on which the underdeveloped countries can draw. They do not have to go through the laborious process of acquiring this knowledge for themselves and can therefore avoid a number of errors and false starts. The higher level of income in advanced industrial countries and its steady and continuing growth create a demand for the products of the underdeveloped countries and enable them to benefit from wider international specialization than was possible for the pioneers. Private investment, financial aid and technical assistance contribute to the transfer of resources and skills from the rich countries to the poor and thus enable these to draw on a bigger pool of resources. These benefits were not available, or available only to a smaller extent, when the now industrialized countries embarked on their development.

Some authors derive much hope from the economic forces that tend to diffuse technical progress from the advanced countries to the poor. If only the level of demand and employment is kept high and growing, so that the rich economies are forced to search outside their own boundaries for low-cost sources of raw materials and minerals and for manufactured products requiring much labour, if restrictions on the movement of goods, capital and men are removed and if technical assistance and aid are provided on an adequate scale, the progress achieved in the centre, according to this view, will automatically spread to the periphery and the benefits will be widely distributed.[2]

On the other hand, the coexistence of rich and poor countries and the policies pursued by rich countries have a number of drawbacks for the underdeveloped countries. Some of these result from the relationships between countries at different stages of development, others from the fact that rich countries exist. These points are elaborated in different contexts in this book and they are brought together here for convenient reference.

1. The most important difference is that the advanced state of medical knowledge makes it now possible to reduce deaths cheaply and rapidly, without having, at least until recently, contributed to an equally cheap and readily acceptable reduction in births. This has upset the population equilibrium and has caused the large and accelerating rates of population growth, which present the underdeveloped countries with much more difficult obstacles than those the now advanced countries faced in their pre-industrial phase, when the rate of population growth was considerably less and was partly the *result* of successful development and rising levels of living.

2. Although a stock of scientific and technical knowledge is available on which underdeveloped countries can draw, the modern technology is ill-adapted to the conditions and the factor endowments of the underdeveloped countries. Modern technology was evolved in conditions of labour scarcity and its purpose is therefore to save labour in relation to capital. The transfer of these sometimes inappropriate methods, which is encouraged by attitudes towards modernization and by the prestige of Western technology, tends to aggravate the gross under-utilization of labour from which the underdeveloped countries are suffering. When inappropriate technology is transferred and when the labour force grows rapidly, obstacles are created which are fundamentally different from those which the now industrial societies had to overcome in their pre-industrial phase. (These two themes are discussed at greater length in the next chapter.)

3. Not only most available techniques of production, but also existing models of organizations and institutions are ill-adapted to the needs of the underdeveloped world. Modern trade union structure and attitudes, like technology, have evolved in different social conditions and can therefore be damaging if transferred to conditions in which labour is not fully utilized. The demand for

the adoption of social welfare services, which have no or negative impact on development and which were introduced in advanced industrial welfare states at a late stage, has often proved an impediment to development and, far from contributing to greater social justice, has strengthened vested interests and pockets of privilege. Large public expenditure on curative medicine, higher education and indiscriminate subsidies to consumption has absorbed scarce resources and reinforced attitudes and practices hostile to development. Even political institutions, such as parliamentary democracy, are not always adapted to the needs of developing countries and, under the guise of constitutional legitimacy, reinforce the reluctance to touch vested interests and to use compulsion for development.

4. For a number of reasons capital and skilled men, including those of the underdeveloped countries, are attracted to the richest industrial societies. Capital flight is substantial, attracted by higher rates of return and greater political security. Skilled men and professionals, on whose education and training large public funds have been spent, have greater opportunities for emigration, are better and more rapidly informed about them and have stronger incentives to seize them. As a result some of the scarcest, most valuable and most expensive factors of production are drained away from the poor periphery to the rich centre.

5. But the mobility of factors is partial and biased. Whereas in the pre-industrial phase of now-industrialized societies (with the exception of Japan) areas rich in natural resources were still unsettled and were able to receive immigrants, the world has now been parcelled up and immigration of unskilled men and women, particularly if they are coloured, is severely restricted. This, together with population growth, growing under-utilization of labour and the loss of the scarcest and most expensive resources, greatly increases the obstacles to development.

6. As Dudley Seers has shown recently,[3] high levels of remuneration for professional skills in advanced countries raise obstacles to development in underdeveloped countries which go beyond the losses through emigration. By the creation of

an international market in these skills, not only are internal inequalities without functional justification increased in under-developed countries, but obstacles are put into the path of development. International inequality has an impact on internal income distribution in underdeveloped countries which, like the impact of modern technology and modern institutions, impedes development.

7. Systematic scientific research and institutionally built-in innovation, which are reflected in the annual growth of productivity which is characteristic of rich economies, have not only been heavily biased towards products which are not suited for production in underdeveloped countries but they have, in some cases, also led to a reduction in the demand for the traditional primary exports of underdeveloped countries. Technical progress has reduced the need for the imports of the staple products of developing countries

    (a) because synthetics have been substituted for natural products,

    (b) because there has been increasing economy in the use of raw materials, and

    (c) because demand has shifted towards services and products with low primary import content.

For such reasons, as well as because of protectionist policies, and in particular cascading tariffs, rising with the stage of processing, the trade opportunities of underdeveloped countries have been reduced and their ability to diversify and industrialize has been hampered, though their incentive to do so has been increased. These obstacles go beyond the often bewailed, but not fully confirmed, trend in the terms of trade. They are themselves the expression of a desire to insulate a rich and comfortable society from the disturbance of change, even at the cost of some reduction in the benefits derived from international specialization. (See also below point 9.) In any cost/benefit calculus of the impact of research in industrial societies, the disturbances caused to poor growers of primary products are not counted. Recent technical progress in methods of birth control, of producing staple food crops and cheap protein, of transport, desalination and even, on a small scale, of more appropriate industrial technology, has begun to compensate for the earlier bias in research, but it is as yet early to say how effective these compensations will prove.

8. While it is true that foreign private enterprise can help to transfer material resources and human skills from rich to poor countries, it also creates greater difficulties than did borrowing from abroad by industrialized societies in their pre-industrial phase. Then money was borrowed at fixed interest rates of between 5 and 6 per cent and default was not uncommon. Now almost all long-term private capital takes the form of equity at 15–25 per cent pre-local tax and 10–15 per cent post-local tax; moreover, default on loans, whether private or official, is hardly ever allowed to occur. Remitting profits, interest and dividends creates or aggravates the balance of payments problems of underdeveloped countries, partly because of their height compared with the lower interest rates in the nineteenth century, and partly because of inadequate reinvestment.

9. Advance has meant national progress and national consolidation in the industrial countries. The benefits of the welfare state are largely confined to its citizens. National consolidation in rich countries has encouraged nationalism in underdeveloped countries and the attempts of the former to integrate the nation by protectionist and welfare policies have tended to lead to international disintegration.[4] Attempts to maintain full employment, and to insulate the national economy from outside influences have strengthened the forces of protection in the welfare states and reduced the opportunities for trade and migration. Export of capital and scarce skills, and immigration that threatens to upset industrial peace, are restricted by the advanced countries.

In the early enthusiasm with full employment and welfare policies after the last war, it was thought that the achievement and maintenance of full employment would reduce the need for protectionist policies and would restore the era of free international trade and international solidarity. In the event, full employment has created its own strong motivation for restrictions on trade, payments and immigration. First, full employment tended to cause inflationary pressures and balance of payments difficulties to those who inflated faster than others; these led to restrictions. Second, full employment tended to be interpreted as applying to all regions and occupations, so structural unemployment, which some low-cost imports would have entailed, was disliked. Third, full employment was accompanied by the desire to make the fullest use of resources and brought the terms-of-trade argument for tariff restrictions to the fore; in particular, it became important to keep the prices of imported food and raw materials as low as possible. Fourth, the desire to maintain and raise wages constituted a powerful argument against immigration of workers who would weaken the bargaining power of trade unions. Fifth, the need to mobilize savings for domestic objectives set limits to the outflow of aid and private capital. For these and similar reasons, the national welfare state has turned out to be a not very good neighbour to other countries which depended on trade, migration and capital.

10. We have suggested that technical and organizational knowledge are ill-adapted and that their transfer can be harmful to the underdeveloped countries. In addition, Western economic concepts and theories, and policies based on these, are often inappropriate and misleading when applied to current development problems. Economic analysis and policy have tended to focus on investment (whether in fixed capital assets or in 'human capital' called 'education') to the neglect of essential reforms of human attitudes and social institutions; and they have tended to formulate categories of aggregates which obscure the relevant distinctions and neglect the actual behaviour on which the concepts, models and policies are based.[5]

11. Some people have argued that government aid has obstructed progress towards development by supporting and upholding feudal or conservative regimes which are unwilling to carry out the social and political reforms necessary for progress. Aid policies directed at investments and neglecting social reforms are encouraged, intellectually, by the escape mechanism provided by Western economic theorizing and, politically, by powerful vested interests on both the donors' and the recipients' side.

12. While for these reasons the opportunities to develop have been reduced, the sense of urgency among the ruling elites and the still small middle classes overseas has greatly increased. Seeing opulence and rapid growth abroad means feeling the pain of their absence all the more acutely. It is true not only that what you *don't know doesn't hurt you*, which must have made things easier for the now industrialized societies in their pre-industrial stage, but also that what you *do know does hurt*. This clearly reduces the patience with which the development process is viewed by the ruling elites in the underdeveloped world.

It is this coexistence of rich and poor, rather than the intentional or unintentional colonial or neo-colonial exploitation, or even neglect, which can have detrimental effects on development efforts. And it is this coexistence which sets limits to the ready transfer of the lessons of one historical setting to an entirely different one. No analysis can be valid which does not allow for this change in the world setting in which development occurs.*

These considerations also bear on the frequently deplored widening gap between the living standards of the rich and poor countries. On the face of it, it might seem that much more important than the gap is the rate at which the lot of the mass of the people in the poor countries is improving. Should we not all prefer a growth rate of 6 per cent per year in the poor countries combined with one of 8 per cent in the rich to one of 3 per cent in the poor combined with 2 per cent in the rich, even although the former combination would widen, while the latter would narrow this gap? Maybe so. But the rate of progress in the rich countries affects the development prospects and strategies of the poor and it is not obvious that, on balance, faster growth of the rich world is always beneficial to the poor. Many of the difficulties raised for developing countries under the above headings 1–12 grow when international differentials increase, and it may therefore be

*Special problems are created also by the coexistence of poor and poor. The treatment of the Third World as if it were a homogeneous group and the interests of each member in harmony with those of the others is misleading. Some of the opportunities and difficulties created by the coexistence of very poor and not quite so poor countries are discussed in chapter four.

sensible, and not just the result of a dog-in-the-manger attitude, to aim at reducing growing international income differentials, even if this means some slowing down of income growth.

Finally, it follows that development strategies must differ not only, as is now generally recognized, in space, from country to country and region to region, but also in time, from stage to stage. Each stage must be related to the stages reached by other countries. The need to take full account not only of the position in space, but also of the relative position in time, in forging a development strategy greatly complicates the process of planning and reduces the value of lessons from the past and of universal prescriptions. A country, particularly if it is small, must pay attention not only to its own peculiar history, resource endowment and institutions, but also to the events and activities in the countries ahead of it (as well as in those behind it) and must weigh the benefits and drawbacks of outward-looking strategies against those of shielding its frontiers and turning inwards.[6]

3 THE INTERNATIONAL DIFFUSION OF TECHNOLOGY

*The Population Problem – Result of the
Spread of Technology.*

The population explosion of the poor world is historically without precedent, both in its speed and in its lack of economic cause. North-west Europe, during the Industrial Revolution, edged up its population by about 1 per cent each year; and even this small victory of live birth-rates over death-rates came after, and partly resulted from, revolutionary improvements in food production (especially through crop rotation). In Africa, Latin America and South Asia, population growth averages more than 2½ per cent each year. This is because new techniques of death control, developed in rich countries, have spread fast and cheaply throughout poor countries.

Some of the rise in population can be traced to the control of smallpox and yellow fever, the development of penicillin and the sulphonamides, and the improvement of famine control through better transport and United States food aid; millions of Indians died in the 1918–19 famine, but the two *successive* monsoon failures of 1965–6 and 1966–7 produced only a handful of deaths from hunger. Much the most important cause of the population explosion, however, has been malaria control.

Malaria control is typical of the double-edged effect on the welfare of poor countries of techniques transferred from rich ones. DDT, gammexane and other powerful insecticides were developed, and applied to *Anopheles* breeding grounds in many parts of South Asia and North Africa, largely to protect British and American troops from malaria in the Second World War. During and after the post-war independence movements, these irresistibly cheap insecticides almost eliminated malaria in much of the Third World. Ceylon (which has hardly any arable land to spare) is a striking example of the effects. The death rate fell slowly and unspectacularly from 26·5 per 1,000 in 1921–30 to 20·4 in 1941–6; by 1959 it had fallen to 9·1. Why? An intensive anti-malarial spraying campaign reduced the incidence of the disease from 402 per 1,000 population in 1945–6 to only 9 per 1,000 in 1954. That means not only a fall in direct malarial fever deaths, but a rise in the resistance of the average Ceylonese to other diseases. Much of the fall in the death-rate must have been the result of malaria control, as opposed to improved standards of living. Further, the live birth-rate probably rises, both because mothers are stronger without malaria and because they no longer need to take quinine, which tends to act as a contraceptive.* What is more, malaria is usually a killer only if contracted between the ages of six months and four years; therefore the immediate effect of malaria control is more young persons, who have mouths to feed but can seldom provide hands to work. However, this increase in the dependency ratio is transitory, and in part offset by the increased productive capacity of the labour force.

Typically, death-rates in poor countries are now below 20 per thousand per annum (and often close to the rates in rich countries), while the birth-rates have stayed around 40 per thousand. World population, about 750 million in 1750 and about 1,200 million in 1850, reached 2,500 million in 1930, has already passed 3,500 million, and will double by 2010 A.D. at present growth rates. Most of this increase is taking place in the countries with fewest resources to meet it. India (with 560 million people at the end of 1970), Pakistan (130 m.), Egypt (34 m.) and Indonesia (120 m.) have almost exhausted their prospects of expanding the

---

*The most rigorous statistical inquiry so far concludes: 'The anti-malaria campaign ... contributed 60 per cent of the rise in the rate of population growth since [1945], resulting in a population size that, by the end of 1960, was a million larger than it would otherwise have been' – i.e. 10 million instead of 9 million. NEWMAN, P., *Malaria Eradication and Population Growth*, School of Public Health, University of Michigan, 1965, p. 69. See also LIPTON, M., 'Population, Land and Diminishing Returns to Agricultural Labour', *Bulletin of the Oxford Institute of Economics and Statistics*, 1964.

area under cultivation, yet population grows at 2½ per cent or more each year. Even where there seems to be plenty of spare land, as in the Sudan, it is seldom easy to persuade people to move from the overcrowded river-basin agricultures to distant and strange open spaces, lands which grow new crops in new ways and often afford little transport or shelter at first.

Almost every poor country falls into one of two categories: those aware that population is growing faster than cultivable land, and those about to become so aware. Nor is land the only scarce resource that is overstrained as population zooms. More babies surviving mean more diversion of family resources to feeding and clothing small children, and away from saving and investment; hence the supply of capital is retarded at the same time as the demand for it (to build schools and later to provide jobs) is expanded. It is small comfort that the babies who have been saved from malaria *eventually* grow up to become workers; the increasing shortage of land and capital means that their prospects of finding work get dimmer and dimmer as time goes by.

This growing array of jobless persons – the DDT generation – flows to the towns much faster than it can be absorbed into urban jobs. Neither investment finance nor the skill of the migrant work-force suffices to stop urban unemployment growing hugely, checked only by the absorption of immigrants into crime, beggary, prostitution and, above all, functionless public employment – this last creating a severe (but sometimes politically inescapable) strain on the scarce public funds available for development. The threat to social and political stability from the slums is obvious; in a matching of the gloomiest predictions of Marx and Malthus, the income of those at the bottom of the pile is kept down by immigration of the growing surplus rural population to swell the reserve army of unemployed, while the elite of doctors, engineers, and businessmen improves its relative wealth, both by birth-control and by providing services for which demand grows faster than income.

What has gone wrong? It *must* be good for babies to survive where once they died of malaria. Indeed any improvement in health is, *in itself*, excellent. In so far as it raises productivity, e.g. by reducing worm infestation, it may contribute to labour efficiency and to output. In the Dry Zone of Ceylon, uncultivable for years because of endemic malaria, a new and prosperous agriculture is springing up in the wake of D D T. And some of the problems, e.g. the rising dependant/worker ratio, are transitory. However, the total effect of death prevention, especially when introduced suddenly into an environment with little land to spare, is almost certainly to reduce the average level of living.[1]

Can technology, either indigenous or transferred from the rich countries, put right the harm done by technology? We shall look briefly at four possibilities: population control, food production, industrial production (allowing the possibility of exporting in exchange for food) and power and transport (to improve the efficiency of older techniques). We have to remember that new techniques must be tested in the field and must show a convincing rate of return to their users. Harrowing accounts of the wastage of grain in sacks cannot gainsay the fact that for the bin-storage of maize in Nigeria the rate of return on capital is only 16–17 per cent yearly at the research station, probably less for the learning farmer, and perhaps less than the interest he must pay on the loan to buy the storage bin.[2]

New Techniques of Population Control

The addition to income per head in a poor country caused by spending £100 on birth prevention is, at very least, fifteen times the addition to income per head from the best alternative use of £100.[3] For poor countries with population pressure this might suggest the desirability of a massive expansion of birth-control programmes. Yet even in those countries where religious objections are not important and where some expansion has taken place – India, Pakistan, Egypt – total outlay on family planning accounts for below 3 per cent of public development spending. Why so little? Not, certainly, because of a lack of technical possibilities; the oral pill, the Lippes loop and the intra-uterine coil, available since the early 1960s, all have drawbacks but are cheaper, surer and easier to use than any earlier means of contraception. Yet by mid-1970 fewer than 10 million of India's 100 m. couples of childbearing age had been treated (over half by male sterilization). This is not explained by aversion to family planning as such; neither Moslem nor Hindu countries have found religious or social attitudes to contraception *per se* a serious barrier, especially among literate or town-dwelling women. The difficulties in the way of family planning programmes have three sources: shortage of trained medical staff, the consequent initial confidence-destroying errors of some schemes, and the popular wish to have many children (which is not the same as an aversion to contraception).

The shortage of trained medical staff is the most serious obstacle to the expansion of family planning programmes. The total number of doctors in poor countries is small and women doctors seldom comprise even 10 per cent of the total supply; but it is women doctors who are needed to examine village women before the loop or the coil is inserted. Pay, especially for private practice, and conditions, especially for women, are much better in the towns. In India only 11 per cent of doctors work in rural areas, where over 80 per cent of the people live.[4] Junior medical staff, able to carry out routine coil and loop insertions, are almost as scarce and take time to train.

Proper medical precautions in programmes of loop and coil insertion are an essential condition for success. In West Bengal, India, with an acute shortage of women doctors, the Government pushed ahead with coil insertions even though full preliminary checks were not possible. A few women who were suffering from incipient womb cancer at the time of the coil insertion blamed the coil for the disease and discredited the entire programme. It is useless to transfer techniques, however appropriate, from rich to poor countries, unless they are also helped to develop the skills needed to make use of such techniques.

The progress of contraception is further retarded by the wish, not to avoid birth-control, but simply to have more children. European experience suggests that a delay of twenty-five to fifty years normally separates a reduction in the death-rate from a later, responsive fall in the birth-rate.[5] It takes a long time to realize that only one or two sons are needed to guarantee a surviving male heir, when four have been the minimum safe number through many millenia of malaria. In rural South India in 1952, among parents with two or more living sons, 44 per cent of mothers and 60 per cent of fathers still wanted more children.[6] Fortunately, both the move to the towns and rising literacy reduce such figures by reducing the *adaptive lag* between a fall in infant mortality and a consequent responsive fall in childbearing.

We should not leave birth-control with a list of obstacles. The loop, the coil, the pill – the advances in family planning in the last ten years dwarf the advances in the preceding ten thousand. The United Nations, despite religious opposition, has at last begun to give substantial technical assistance in this field. Can we estimate the success of birth-control? In some countries the statistics are weak, because up-to-date information depends on comprehensive registration of births, which is rare; but in Argentina the decline in the birth-rate started some time ago, and in Taiwan, Puerto Rico, Singapore and South Korea, there have been definite signs of a downward trend. Japan's dramatic success – *without* loops and coils, yet owing much more to contraception than to abortion – is another hopeful sign.[7]

Family planning campaigns have not been the only cause of these declines. To estimate causes of changes in social behaviour is very difficult, but one study in depth came to the conclusion that in Taiwan the family planning programme was 'an effort to accelerate rather than initiate fertility decline'.[8] In any case, it looks as if it will be many years before fertility falls dramatically in India and other really poor countries. Even when this happens, the population will continue to grow at a fast rate for some decades, because malaria control really started saving babies at a high and rising rate some ten to twenty years ago – so that now more girls enter the childbearing age-group each year than in the previous one. But a very promising start has been made, and technical progress in rich countries – coils and loops – is largely responsible for it.

New Techniques of Food Production

The main impact of technical progress on food production in the Third World must be through crop production. This is because the real food shortages must be met by items that will reach the *poorest* sections of the population; crop products are, and are likely to remain, very much cheaper than animal, fish, or artificially manufactured foods.

So long as a family needs four to seven times as many acres to feed itself from livestock as from crops, animal husbandry as such is unlikely to be a major source of extra food supply for most hungry people in most poor countries. As people get richer, however, they turn to meat and milk, and these will mean extra cattle, diverting rural land from supplying simple cereals for the rural poor – unless technical changes cause each cow or buffalo to yield more milk. Cross-breeding through artificial insemination is promising, but has lasting results only if the farmer can be persuaded to castrate his low-quality native bulls. Most poor countries have too many cattle, of too low quality, but social constraints – Hindu cow-worship, African regard for cattle as a source of bride-price – inhibit the necessary technical change. While these concerns are less relevant in accounting for the monstrously under-exploited fishery resources of poor countries (though maybe one third of the poor world's 100 million Buddhists* eat neither fish nor meat), the main impact of technical progress on food output in the Third World has to be through crop production.

Here, four main sources of change are revolutionizing agricultural technology, which changed only slowly from the discovery of the waterwheel (about 200 B.C.) to Faraday's discovery of the induction of electric current (1831): new varieties of seeds; the alteration of the soil, mainly through chemical fertilizers, based on soil surveys; electric power, greatly enlarging the scope of

*1966 estimates give the world total at 161·8 m. 1967 estimates for Japan: 65–70 m. Almost all the rest are in poor countries.

irrigation; and the internal combustion engine, drawing both the tractor and the extension worker's jeep.[9]

1. Seed improvements, both to raise yields and to improve resistance to crop disease, have been a major source of agricultural progress in North America and Europe for many years. Recently, progress has accelerated dramatically. But improved seeds are an extreme case of technology needing local adaptation. Many years of field research are needed to develop suitable varieties for tropical conditions; extension services must be equipped to demonstrate and persuade, and credit agencies to lend. Yet in the early 1960s some major breakthroughs were made. Rice yields in Egypt grew by 60 per cent in six years, largely because of a new hybrid variety now covering over 95 per cent of the area. The success story of the Formosan rice hybrids in the Philippines, and the 'Mexipak' wheat varieties in West Pakistan and even more recently in India's 'Intensive Programme', is well-known. These new varieties are quick-maturing and not responsive to day length, so that – given water and tropical sunshine – several crops can be taken each year. They benefit from much more water than traditional strains, though they do not always need it. While they seldom pay without fertilizer, they respond much better than traditional strains to very big doses of it.

The new seeds have spread quickly, and shown some remarkable results. In 1967–8, the Pakistan wheat crop was 37 per cent above its previous record. In 1966–7 $2\frac{1}{2}$ million tons of India's 76 million tons of foodgrain output were a bonus due entirely to these seed improvements – yet they had been introduced barely three years earlier, and 1966–7 was the second of two successive monsoon disasters. These new seeds depend on assured water supply, available to barely one-fifth of Indian farmed land; even here, they pay only the 20–30 per cent of farmers who can afford ample fertilizer, irrigation-water, etc. without recourse to the moneylender's penal interest charges. But with these limitations the 'technical progress' has been remarkable. In India it was achieved by the local development of strains crossbred from imported varieties (Mexipak wheat, Tai-chung Formosan rice) and Indian varieties, and tested in the field. A crude direct import of a technique from another agriculture could never have succeeded so well.

2. Chemical fertilizers are so important in the 'package' comprising the new seeds – which prosper with them but do not pay without them – that we sometimes forget how recently they have begun to supersede traditional organic manures. Commercial fertilizers were introduced to most countries of the world around the beginning of the twentieth century. World fertilizer consumption rose from 4 million metric tons in 1914 to 9 million metric tons in 1938, and will probably reach 65 million metric tons in 1970. But the countries most dependent on agriculture for employment apply least fertilizer to their soils. Thus in 1966–7 the U.K. applied 102 metric tons of nitrogenous fertilizer per 1,000 hectares of arable land, 59 tons of phosphatic fertilizer, and 58 tons of potash. The corresponding tonnages for India were 5·1 for nitrogenous, 1·7 for phosphatic and 0·8 for potash; for Brazil, 2·4, 3·1 and 3·1; and for Kenya 6·9, 9·8 and 1·4.[10]

Partly this reflects poverty – resources are needed to make or import fertilizers. But there are other causes too. Fertilizers demand ample, well-timed water supply. Without it they seldom pay; with very sparse water they can even do harm. But tropical rainfall is unsure; and it is therefore fortunate that peasants take their extension officers' occasional enthusiasm for 'fertilizers before irrigation' with a grain of salt. Further, the three main types of fertilizer are designed to replace specific soil deficiencies, and they may not pay unless a soil survey has been carried out to see what is needed. In Mali, seven years of field trials were needed to discover the combination of fertilizers best suited both to the cotton crop and to the food crop that follows in rotation.

Fertilizers, then, have their drawbacks. Under the right circumstances, results can be sensational; but they tend to go to bigger farmers (who obtain easier credit) for cash crops, even though the small farm, which can use 'free' idle family labour instead of hiring workers, is more likely to support the fertilizers by uprooting the fertilized weeds! Irrigation, field demonstration, and advance knowledge of soils are costly, but often necessary if fertilizers are to be worthwhile. Often, too, a better use of manure (including human manure), especially by composting, can obtain most of the benefits of fertilizers without the risks, strains and costs. But there is no doubt that enormous expansion of fertilizer use would pay many of the farmers of the Third World.

3. Improved seeds seldom pay without fertilizer; fertilizer may be wasted without *reliable* water supply; conventional tank and shallow-well irrigation is not reliable, since the sources dry up if the rains fail. Reliable irrigation is thus closely linked to the spread of electric waterpumps, and thus of electric power, even though artificial water supplies are at least 2,000 years old. Irrigation is discussed more fully on pp. 188–9; here we consider the links to electricity, which turns out to be a major (if disguised) new farm technique.

The main effect of electricity on agricultural production in the Third World has been indirect. Electric milking machines, etc., are a costly irrelevance in countries so starved of capital; but dams are not, and the fact that dams now yield hydro-electric power for industry *as well as* agricultural irrigation has pushed many projects over the border into viability. The Roseires-Sennar complex of the Sudan, which provides electricity to Khartoum, also irrigates the Gezira cotton scheme; the great international water schemes of Mekong and Indus have a similar dual function. This is politically crucial; in India or Kenya, the millions of tiny farmers, having less political weight than the organized urban businessmen and union leaders, need the 'hydel' side-effects to make the case for big irrigation schemes. In India, however, this has had one unfortunate result: the emphasis from 1956 to 1966 on huge dams, to the neglect of maintenance operations and small well schemes. The latter often yield a higher rural payoff – but no electricity output.

Less indirectly, electric-powered pump-sets (often privately distributed), in support of a major tube-well network, have permitted a big expansion of the irrigated, fertilized area under new seeds in West Pakistan.

4. In Africa and South Asia, over 90 per cent of the power on farms is generated by human beings and animals. The back-

breaking work of turning the hard earth by hand hoeing is an evil in itself, and in the African heat is a sure cause of lethargy. Scrawny animals, otherwise useless, retained solely to draw the plough, have made it a platitude that India is a land where cows eat up men.

Tractors have obvious advantages; where there is a land shortage, they enable hard soils to be brought under the plough; where labour is scarce, they conserve it. But, especially in East Africa and Western India, there is a serious drawback. Tractors almost always pull iron ploughs, which can crumble the thin topsoil and render it an easy prey to wind erosion. Even where tractors are clearly desirable – where benefits exceed costs by a greater percentage than for alternative uses of funds – potential users may be too poor or own too little land to buy a tractor, so that an intermediary is required, usually a credit cooperative or a private hirer; or plots may be too small for the tractor; or the necessary training may be lacking. While there are some success stories, the consensus of expert opinion is probably that tractors are a low priority for most tropical agricultures.

New Techniques in Industry

For agriculture, we listed the main types of innovation that were important for poor countries. For industry this is impossible; the diversity is too great, the enlargement of technology too huge and too fast. More fundamentally, both the industries where new techniques have clustered and the processes themselves have been specially tailored to the needs of rich countries. Big international monopolies or cartels, with a relatively small and highly skilled labour force, massive resources of both physical and financial capital, and enough scale and power to keep the benefits of their innovations and to ensure big, stable markets – these are the firms where large-scale research and development are most likely; steel and petrochemicals are typical of such 'research-intensive' industries (though there are occasional examples of advanced small-scale steel technology). As for recent technical changes, those that dramatically enlarge the spectrum of technology – nuclear power, complete automation of factories, high-speed giant computers – demand both skilled specialists and numerate generalists, not only in installation but also in operation and management; use much capital and little unskilled labour; and involve major financial and technical tasks in the initial stages. In short, neither the radically modern technique, nor the firm with the resources to introduce it, is normal in very poor countries.

Nevertheless, the huge acceleration of industrial innovation plainly gives the poor countries great opportunities. Poor countries today can choose from a bigger 'shelf' of techniques, in almost every operation and industry, than could their European forerunners. Unfortunately the enlargement of choice is not always as big as it looks. A poor country may well find it more economic to produce steel by old-fashioned, labour-intensive techniques; but where can it buy the equipment? Nor is there a universal panacea in 'intermediate technology', which is often an unsatisfactory halfway house, not saving much equipment by comparison with a traditional technique, yet holding back the development of industries into genuine maturity. In India, small-scale power-loom weaving uses not only more labour per unit of output than large-scale processes, but also more capital.[11] Compromise may achieve the worst of both worlds.

For a poor country, then, the main points about new industrial technologies are: some of them provide opportunities for innovation; they have usually been designed for rich companies in rich countries; and the enormous range, both of industries and of 'underdeveloped' environments, precludes the construction of any complete book of costed blueprints, in which the government of India, Peru or Dahomey might find guidance as to the most suitable technologies for industrial development. Yet almost every poor country seeks to increase the share of its output and employment that is provided by modern industry. The search for general technological guide-lines is fruitful in two areas: transfer of industrial technology from rich countries, and balance of research-and-development efforts among industries in poor countries.

The diverse ways in which the transfer of industrial technology happens are illustrated by a hypothetical example: a new £10 m. chemical complex in India. Of the cost, 'perhaps 5 per cent would be the cost of licences and know-how, 1 per cent the cost of training technical personnel in India and abroad, 15 per cent the cost of [mostly imported] design and engineering.... The plant might be financed by private foreign investment or [aid]. The conclusion of the contract would be preceded by [the consultation of learned papers published abroad].'[12]

The various methods by which technology is transferred all have their limitations for poor countries. Books and articles are limited in their usefulness; vital information is kept to preserve monopoly. International migration *from* poor countries, initially for study purposes, has a distressing tendency to become permanent; and if the technologists do return it is too often as the commercially indoctrinated salesmen of Western products. When Western technologists move *to* poor countries, they are seldom the best men in their companies, or willing to stay long enough to understand local conditions. Aid, foreign investment and technical assistance also have their limitations (pp. 316–21). As carriers of self-sustaining technical progress they can succeed only if the overseas experts train indigenous counterparts to replace them.

Oldham, Freeman and Turkcan thus argue that much more attention should be paid to the transfer of techniques through the sale of licences, patents and 'know-how agreements' to governments and companies in poor countries. At present these countries are almost certainly involved in less than 3 per cent of all world transactions in these fields. A major problem is the strain on the balance of payments from such arrangements; by their very nature, poor countries are likely to be net buyers for the foreseeable future.

The discussion of 'transfer of technology' often concentrates on sensational (and usually unsuitable) instances. For India the nuclear reactor at Trombay may well make long-term sense. India has 3 per cent of her 190 m. workers employed in factories with either power or over 50 employees, or both – an enormous 'modern industrial sector' by underdeveloped standards.[13] But

57

in most countries the 'technological shadow' of long-established Western innovations is much more important. Typical are tools, jacks, vices and other standard workshop equipment, following the innovation of the motor car into Asia and Africa; or, in the field of low-cost construction, building-block presses and the variations on stabilized earth mixes that have followed them.

With such simple equipment, the obstacles are seldom technical (inability to acquire new skills) or economic (an inadequate rate of return compared with alternative projects). More usually it is the social innovations that encounter resistance. The continuous, timed discipline of the assembly line has to be learned by workers with rural backgrounds. Factories are pressed to segregate, wastefully, Luos and Kikuyus in Kenya, cobblers and priestly castes in India. The very notion of scientific method – experimental variation, as opposed to the view that if a seed improvement is followed by a drought then the new seeds 'caused' the rain to fail – is new and foreign. Responsive, shrewd and commercially-minded Indians, right up to Board and Cabinet level, commonly consult astrologers to decide the best date to start a project. In rural Africa, the success or failure of an innovation may be attributed to witchcraft. The current switch of emphasis from capital aid to technical assistance (pp. 319–20), especially the training of local counterparts, is justified; but 'training' as wider implications than is often recognized. The demand for a Westernized technological elite for poor countries is not always a neo-colonialist strategem.

But a Westernized culture, or the imitation of Western techniques, is much less desirable for a poor country than a Western scientific methodology. Top scientists and technologists in poor countries are largely trained in the West, or in institutions and from textbooks modelled on the West. The special prestige of pure theory and the contempt for mere technology, damaging enough in Britain, is far worse when allied to the Brahman traditions of India. Western influences also divert technologists in poor countries from local problems to more fashionable, prestigious ones, like those dealt with in the great research laboratories of Cambridge, Massachusetts. This diversion of effort – an insidious relation of the brain drain – is the more serious because industrial research is a very recent development in most poor countries; the indigenous institutions therefore have little accumulated wisdom for handling local technological problems, and are easily diverted to European ones.

This badly balanced approach to Western technology, combined with the technological elite's familiarity with Western consumption patterns, has very damaging results. Very many poor countries have television stations and airlines, making big losses and absorbing many scarce engineers but serving less than one per cent of their people, long before they have a serious programme of fertilizer manufacture or food processing. Yet it is in such 'agro-industry' that technology must make its main contribution. A start has been made here. Mechanical grain drying has proved to be much more efficient than traditional sun-drying in removing, from harvested grain, the moisture that assists deterioration; it is in use in many parts of the Indian Punjab. Polythene food-packaging lowers transport and storage costs and is resistant to extremes of climate; it has been used for milk in East Africa. Food technology institutes have been set up in India, Brazil and Egypt.

Much more consideration needs to be given to the priorities for industrial research and development in poor countries. It is natural for new steel plants to take twice as long to attain full production levels in India as in the U.K. This lag is much shorter in 'agro-industry', where widespread and long-established sugar refineries and cotton mills carry a good deal of experience in assimilating new techniques. The trade barriers erected by Western countries against processed imports (pp. 303–8), and the tendency of aid to be tied to sophisticated but unsuitable Western machinery exports, are partly to blame for the technological imbalance in poor countries. It is easier, if less efficient, for Brazil or Colombia to persuade United States businessmen to erect a steel mill than to get them to import soluble coffee. It is also easier, for similar reasons, to get new plant than to obtain maintenance of existing plant.

Other problems come with new techniques in power production and means of transport. For thousands of years these have been provided by the bullock. Today the big dam, providing at once power and irrigation, is the symbol of the energy revolution which is capable of transforming both agriculture and industry. However, most new fuels go to the big cities. We must see how the services provided are relevant to the rural masses.

'A high level of fuel consumption is not a prerequisite of development but a result of it.' In very poor countries, yearly consumption of commercial energy (converted to 'hard-coal equivalent'), in kilograms, is about the same as yearly income in dollars; a very rich country consumes about five times as many kilograms of commercial energy as it produces dollars' worth of income.[14] The explanation is the rapid adaptation of industry to new sorts of energy in rich countries and the eagerness of business, faced by dear labour, to replace human power.

Rich countries are also adaptable countries, in energy as elsewhere. The switch from non-commercial fuels – wood and dung – to coal, oil, gas and electricity is almost complete in rich countries; imitation in poor countries raises problems. The new fuels are produced with much more capital and less labour than the old. Possibly more technological energy should be devoted to improving traditional techniques; cow-dung gas plants, enabling the dung to be used for fuel while leaving a valuable manurial residue, are a possibility.

In the last twenty years, a succession of new techniques has appeared on the scene. 'Lurgi' conversion of coal to gas, and nuclear reactors feeding directly into the national grid, are famous, large-scale and very expensive of capital. Such projects, especially in electricity, require a smooth loading by users over the year, and may not fit countries where seasonality in agriculture (and inexperience with night-shifts) impose irregular loads. The less sensational new energy techniques may be more appropriate to meet small, peaked demands. It might sometimes, for example, be economic to use solar batteries or wind energy or gas turbines to supply electricity to small food-processing factories in villages remote from the national grid. Bottled calor gas has an analogous role.

Similar considerations affect the development of transport. Most countries, except very small or very mountainous ones, have some sort of rail links. These usually served the security needs of past colonists, or the marketing requirements of pre-war export agriculture. Very seldom can they meet the needs of an expanding population, and growing exchange between factory and farm, without expansion. Track doubling, greater speed, and the use of operational research to improve turn-round in marshalling yards are the main enlargements of technology possible here. The first two need a lot of capital, the last scarce skills; but rail capacity, like electricity, is a sector where the wastage from 'too little' (i.e. spare capacity in all the user industries) is greater by far than the wastage from 'too much'. Both sectors tend to be publicly owned, and under the usual pressures to charge too little (see pp. 254–5), so that chronic shortages are common.

In Argentina, as in several other countries, the general inadequacy of the transport system has again and again held back development. In 1957–9, Indian coal and steel output were held back by shortage of freight capacity. In 1967–8, the Sudanese cotton crop deteriorated seriously for want of transport to Port Sudan. The Sudanese case exemplifies the inflexibility of rail freight capacity. Safety factors and marshalling yards do not take kindly to sudden big rises in the number of wagons running. Roads are much more flexible. A fleet of lorries does not provide anything like the scale economies of a railway system; but it can be more *easily* enlarged. It is hard for a Western reader to think of surfaced all-weather roads as a new technique, but in much of the world they are just that.

Technology and the Reduction of Poverty

Thus, in each of the various fields we have considered, we have been able to identify possibilities of applying new technologies to increase average incomes in poor countries – both in relation to controlling population growth and in relation to increasing output.*

*Elsewhere we look at a more general concept of 'technology'. New techniques of economic planning (national income analysis, input–

But to consider the problem as one of selecting and transferring rich countries' technologies, suitably amended, misses the main point. We are worried about the growth of population in poor countries because we fear that it will make them even poorer and harder to develop. New technologies can indeed contribute to development and the reduction of poverty; but they will be wrongly selected and wrongly applied if we assume that, in less developed countries, people are poor only because of technological backwardness.

Let us look at the problem another way. The number of hungry people in the world is increasing every year. They need food, but cannot afford it; thus, despite severe and growing malnutrition, world *demand* (as opposed to physical *need*) for food rises so slowly that no general increase in world food grain prices is forecast. If anything, prices seem likely to fall. In south-east Asia, where new grain varieties are bringing yield increases, importing countries may soon have surpluses for export which they cannot sell. This transformation has already happened in the Philippines. Even if it spreads, there will still be hundreds of millions of Asians – millions more every year – who cannot afford an adequate diet. Indeed, the new farm techniques (while they create jobs in the short run) will lead to an increase in farm size and the displacement of labour by machinery. The income inequality of poor countries (p. 15) means that need for food does not produce effective money demand for food. In such an environment, unplanned technical change may well produce both more food and, by aggravating unemployment and being confined to rich farmers, more hunger too.

Thus, to a large extent, the problem of poverty is a problem of the distribution of income, jobs and land, rather than of the average productivity of labour. If new technologies are to contribute to the solution of poverty, it will help if they can be applied in

output tables) and public administration (critical path analysis, Macnamara-style cost–benefit analysis) are important in today's interventionist world – as they could never have been when European countries developed, in 1780–1890. 'International technology' has been transformed by aid and the international private company, and affected by new bargaining arenas like UNCTAD and GATT. See pp. 24–8.

ways which lead, directly or indirectly, to an increase in total employment.*

Investment in improved technologies implies the existence or creation of an effective demand for the increase in output. For this, the poor countries would be greatly helped by increased access to markets in rich countries and by the reduction of protection and subsidy of competing products of the rich countries. British aid – we believe rightly – has done much to improve the technology of sugar-cane growing in the Caribbean and Mauritius. It makes no sense in the long run for Britain to subsidize her own farmers to grow beet sugar, thus making it artificially competitive with cane sugar. That way British housewives get needlessly costly sugar, British farm resources are diverted to systematically inefficient uses, and only fragile international price agreements permit any livelihood to tropical growers.

Finally, if the problem is to improve the distribution of output, at least as much as to increase total output, the deliberate choice of high-employment, low-output techniques may in some circumstances be appropriate. A major factor in such a decision is the extent to which further employment (and further output, rather than inflation) is created by the spending of those to whom new investment has brought increased incomes (see pp. 241–6). There is clearly a range of 'technology mixes' and investment strategies possible in any situation. There is a great need for further study of the consequences of adopting different strategies.

*The tax and transfer systems of most poor countries are in no state to compensate for, or insure against, unemployment caused by technical change.

PART TWO

POVERTY AND DEVELOPMENT – NATIONAL PERSPECTIVES

4 HOW POOR ARE THE POOR COUNTRIES?

Countries are neither poor nor rich. It is *individuals* that are well-fed or hungry, sick or healthy, literate or illiterate, happy or miserable. This is so obvious as to be hardly worth saying, were it not for the fact that we often speak, write and act as if we had forgotten it. The ultimate purpose of production, trade, migration foreign investment and aid is to improve the lot of individuals. When we speak of poor countries we are using shorthand, and we must not be misled by our metaphor.

By a poor country we therefore mean one in which the people are poor. The simplest and commonly used way of expressing this is to divide the total national income by the number of people in the country and to arrive at a figure showing income per head of the population. Most underdeveloped countries turn out, by this criterion, to be low income-per-head countries, though there are some exceptions, like Kuwait (see table 4.1).

TABLE 4.1

Gross National Product per Head (U.S. dollars) approx. for 1967

	GNP PER HEAD ($)		GNP PER HEAD ($)
UNITED STATES	3,670	FRANCE	1,950
KUWAIT	3,490	NEW ZEALAND	1,890
SWEDEN	2,500	NORWAY	1,860
CANADA	2,380	GERMANY, FED. REP. OF	1,750
SWITZERLAND	2,310	BELGIUM	1,740
LUXEMBOURG	2,000	UNITED KINGDOM	1,700
AUSTRALIA	1,970	ICELAND	1,690
DENMARK	1,950	FINLAND	1,660

	GNP PER HEAD ($)		GNP PER HEAD ($)
NETHERLANDS	1,520	GUYANA	330
GERMANY, DEM. REP. OF	1,300	SURINAM	330
AUSTRIA	1,210	ALBANIA	320
PUERTO RICO	1,210	GUATEMALA	310
ISRAEL	1,200	COLOMBIA	300
ITALY	1,120	MALAYSIA	290
CZECHOSLOVAKIA	1,110	TURKEY	290
JAPAN	1,000	IRAN	280
U.S.S.R.	970	SWAZILAND	280
IRELAND	910	EL SALVADOR	270
HUNGARY	900	DOMINICAN REPUBLIC	260
VENEZUELA	880	ALGERIA	250
ARGENTINA	800	BRAZIL	250
TRINIDAD & TOBAGO	790	CHINA, REPUBLIC OF	250
CYPRUS	780	JORDAN	250
POLAND	780	BRITISH HONDURAS	240
LIBYA	720	HONDURAS	240
RUMANIA	720	IRAQ	230
GREECE	700	IVORY COAST	230
BULGARIA	690	KOREA (North)	230
SPAIN	680	RHODESIA	230
HONG KONG	620	MAURITIUS	220
SINGAPORE	600	OCEANIA	220
SOUTH AFRICA	590	PARAGUAY	220
MALTA	570	ECUADOR	210
PANAMA	550	TUNISIA	210
URUGUAY	550	GHANA	200
YUGOSLAVIA	530	ANGOLA	190
LEBANON	520	LIBERIA	190
MEXICO	490	MOROCCO	190
CHILE	470	SENEGAL	190
JAMAICA	460	PHILIPPINES	180
BARBADOS	420	SYRIA	180
PORTUGAL	420	ZAMBIA	180
COSTA RICA	410	BOLIVIA	170
GABON	410	CEYLON	160
MONGOLIA	410	KOREA (South)	160
NICARAGUA	360	UNITED ARAB REPUBLIC	160
PERU	350	SIERRA LEONE	140
CUBA	330	CAMBODIA	130

GNP PER HEAD ($)		GNP PER HEAD ($)	
CAMEROON	130	PAKISTAN	90
MAURITANIA	130	SUDAN	90
THAILAND	130	DAHOMEY	80
YEMEN, SOUTHERN	130	MALI	80
CENTRAL AFRICAN REP.	120	NIGERIA	80
KENYA	120	TANZANIA	80
VIET NAM (South)	120	AFGHANISTAN	70
INDONESIA	100	BURMA	70
MALAGASY REPUBLIC	100	CHAD	70
TOGO	100	HAITI	70
UGANDA	100	NEPAL	70
VIET NAM (North)	100	NIGER	70
BOTSWANA	90	ETHIOPIA	60
CHINA (Mainland)	90	LESOTHO	60
CONGO, DEM. REP. OF	90	MALAWI	60
GAMBIA	90	RWANDA	60
GUINEA, REPUBLIC OF	90	BURUNDI	50
INDIA	90	SOMALI REPUBLIC	50
LAOS	90	UPPER VOLTA	50

Source: *World Bank Atlas of per capita production and population*, IBRD, 1969.

Problems of Measuring Poverty and Income

But the procedure of dividing total income by the number of heads may be misleading unless there is a fair amount of equality and not very great deviations from the average. One would not wish to call a community rich in which one man had all the money while all the others had nothing.

Perhaps the reason why we feel that it is all right to speak about *countries* as being rich or poor, as shown by their income per head, is that we tacitly assume that countries set up institutions and pursue policies which aim at correcting extremes of inequality, through taxation, subsidies, social services, etc. Such institutions do not exist to even out inequalities between nations. Thus if we had two entirely separate and sovereign nations with the same population, one with income per head of £100 and the other with income per head of £1,000, it would not be meaningful to say that the average income of the two is £550.

Yet something like this is true within many underdeveloped countries. They are deeply divided societies. Even brief and superficial visits to these countries show the existence of extreme inequalities in many spheres: air-conditioned Cadillacs or jet planes next to bullock carts; luxury skyscrapers towering over shanty towns. There is inequality not only in income and wealth, but also in technology and productivity, in education and health. A distinguished international civil servant used to say that you could tell the poverty of a country by the size and luxury of the limousines in which its delegates would arrive.

The split between the few rich and the many poor is reinforced by differences between urban and rural levels of living, between large foreign companies operating in mines, oil, or plantations and small-scale indigenous activities, between modern industrial enterprises and primitive crafts, between luxurious residential universities and rural illiteracy, between the most modern hospitals and village traditional healers. The dualism is often further reinforced by a division along racial, ethnic or religious lines, so that the small enclave of the privileged oligarchy is largely or entirely recruited from one community. While some of these divisions reinforce one another, some of them run across social groups, so that those who are deprived in one respect may be privileged in another. Where the status and position of women is low, even the women of rich families suffer from discrimination. The same is true of racial or religious minorities who are confined to certain activities and barred from others. Though the rural sector is poorer on average than the urban, the misery of the unemployed inhabitants of the shanty towns matches that of the sharecroppers.

Such social and economic divisions greatly increase the difficulties of using low average income per head as an index of poverty or its rise as an index of development. For the question 'Who benefits?' can no longer be put aside, as it sometimes can in a country like Britain or America. It goes to the heart of the matter. This is not to say that development is advanced only when everyone, or the poorest, or the majority, benefit. For when profits accrue to a small minority who save and reinvest them, the process may lead to greater benefits for a larger group later. The difficulty created by a dualistic society is not simply the prevalence of inequality, but the absence of interaction, at any rate positive, mutually beneficial interaction, between what are sometimes described as two sectors but what may often be two distinct societies, built on different institutions and regulated by different rules – though particular individuals may participate, permanently or temporarily, in both and although some transactions take place between the two sectors. It is the absence of spill-over from the modern, often export-orientated but sometimes import-replacing, industrial enclave into the stagnating, indigenous, partly subsistence economy which makes aggregation of income and division by heads illegitimate. Income per head may grow as a result of a rise in world prices of the metal mined and exported by the modern enclave, which results in higher profits and perhaps also higher wages and tax receipts. Even so-called development projects can remain confined to a narrow area. We should not speak of development as having taken place in circumstances where poverty has not, either directly or indirectly, been relieved.

A better guide than average income per head would be the median income if reliable figures were available. If we arrange all family incomes in ascending order from the smallest to the largest, the median is the value halfway up this order. Or the mode, which is that income earned by most families in the community, could be used as an index.

In addition to income per head, one may wish to measure the rate of encroachment of the money economy on the traditional sector. The reason for this is not that there is anything particularly wonderful about cash, but that it provides a rough index of increasing differentiation, specialization and, given certain assumptions, of rising levels. What we are after is an index of the lot of the mass of the people, their level of living, their poverty or prosperity. That part of income which contributes to current consumption is one component of this level, but it contains others such as the amount, unpleasantness and conditions of work, life expectancy, availability of medical services, the certainty of employment or threat of unemployment, and others.

71

Different societies set aside different proportions of their income for such purposes as defence, which adds neither to current nor to future consumption, and to investment in capital, which, if wisely selected, directed and used, raises future consumption. One of the important differences between advanced and underdeveloped societies is that many consumption expenditures which do not raise production in rich countries, do so in poor ones. More and better food for an under- and ill-nourished labour force reduces apathy and raises ability to work; so does better health, sanitation, education and housing. Much of private and social consumption can therefore be productive, while the mere erection of structures, even though labelled 'investment', need not raise future consumption.

Apart from the difficulties already discussed, a new set of difficulties arises when income indexes are required for the purpose of international comparisons of consumption or income per head. Conversion of national income at exchange rates, the method used by the United Nations (see table 4.1) is unsatisfactory, for these do not reflect purchasing power equivalents. They lead to such incredible results as that the average Ethiopian has an income of only eleven cents a day and yet manages to survive. To avoid this anomaly one would wish to compare incomes, using a common set of prices. But this method can give widely varying results according to which country's prices we use; for the things which are plentiful and cheap in America are scarce and dear in Ethiopia, while some of those which are cheap in Ethiopia are dear in America. This is the result partly of different factor endowments, so that products requiring much capital and skill are relatively cheap in America, and partly of different preferences, so that the Ethiopians enjoy local products which would be dear in America.

Quite apart from pricing problems, however, the available statistics provide only a very frail basis on which to build our comparisons. We depend largely on guesswork for transactions in the large traditional sector of the economy. Good agricultural statistics are not only expensive to collect, but accurate information is difficult to extract from an illiterate and suspicious peasantry, hostile to central authority. Figures for the rest of the econ-

TABLE 4.2

Some economic and social data about groups of countries with different annual incomes per head (1955–60)

	Group					
	I	II	III	IV	V	VI
Annual income in $ per head	1,000 and above	576– 1,000	351– 575	201– 350	100– 200	100
Total population in millions	275	340	165	320	270	1,390
% of the national income from agriculture	11	11	15	30	33	41
Expectation of life at birth	71	68	65	57	50	45
Inhabitants per doctor	885	44	1,724	3,132	5,185	13,450
Infant deaths in first year per thousand live births	24	34	68	75	100	150
% of illiterates	2	6	19	30	49	71
Consumption of energy per head (1,000 kilogrammes of coal equivalent)	4	2·8	1·9	0·7	0·4	0·2
School attendance (%)	90	83	75	60	43	37
Caloric consumption per head (in 1,000 units)	3·2	2·8	2·8	2·5	2·2	2
Carbohydrate content of food (%)	44	52	60	72	68	82
Annual domestic letters sent per head	186·8	110·1	47·3	46·6	13·6	4·8
Stock of road vehicles per head	0·2091	0·0720	0·0306	0·0157	0·0073	0·0021

Source: Jan Tinbergen, *Development Planning*, Weidenfeld & Nicolson, 1967 and Wilfred Beckerman, *International Comparisons of Real Income*, Development Centre of the OECD, Paris, 1966.

omy are somewhat easier to get and less unreliable, which tends to reinforce our general bias in favour of the enclave. Foreign trade figures are often the best.

People have tried to get round this difficulty by using non-monetary indicators such as the stock of telephones, energy consumption, steel consumption, cement consumption, the number of vehicles, the stock of doctors and dentists, daily newspaper circulation, post-primary school enrolment ratio, quality of diet, meat consumed, letters posted, stock of cinemas, etc. Dr Wilfred Beckerman has recently correlated many of these non-monetary indicators with real income and consumption for a large number of countries for which reliable data were available and suggested ways of 'predicting' the latter from the former, where they are not.

The main reason for experimenting with this method is the relatively much greater availability of data for non-monetary indicators than for national income or consumption (see table 4.2).[1]

Although Dr Beckerman's observations do not contain as many low-income countries as high-income countries and would be improved by the addition of further very low-income countries, he achieves strikingly high correlations between private consumption and some non-monetary indicators. With all its limitations, the method suggested by Dr Beckerman of using the number of letters sent per head, steel consumed per head and the stock of telephones per head provides a cheap way of getting at international income or consumption comparisons.

But these comparisons themselves suffer from certain faults. Thus, although urban workers enjoy a multiple of the income of peasants and sharecroppers, a part of this should not be counted as income but as an expense necessary to earn income. Housing and transport costs are necessary expenses in urban employments, while they are lower in the country without an equivalent loss of welfare. So are shoes and clothing. The price of food in towns is higher than in the country, not necessarily because the quality is better, but because the price must cover costs of transport, storage and retail distribution. The urban worker must therefore earn a higher income in order to buy the same food (although it is less fresh) as the peasant who grows it in his plot.

In addition to consumption per head, there are other indexes of social welfare, such as rates of infant mortality, life expectancy, literacy rates, unemployment rates, etc. Again, many of these variables are correlated with one another and with income per head, although no simple uni-causal explanations can be derived from these correlations. There is, normally, mutual causation, higher literacy rates or longer life expectancy causing higher incomes, which in turn raise literacy and life expectancy. The expectation of life of a newly born baby boy in the advanced North is between sixty and seventy years, while in the underdeveloped world it is between twenty-five and forty-five. Only poor countries have infant mortality rates greater than 6 per cent, while in developed countries they are less than 3 per cent. Illiteracy rates vary from 2 per cent in advanced countries to 70 per cent or more in the least developed countries.

Any index of poverty and development is bound to contain, implicitly or explicitly, value judgements, for development means change towards a social state judged desirable. It is important to make the value judgements explicit by showing *who* enjoys the incomes.

Not only the aggregation of heads but also the aggregation of a bundle of commodities and services into a composite 'income' presents difficulties. In countries where land is not plentiful and food production cannot easily be increased, a further disaggregation is necessary. Not only do we have to distinguish between what happens to income per head in the sophisticated money economy and what happens in the traditional sector, but we must also distinguish between the growth of food per head, which is essential to the mass of the people, and other goods and services. Even this may constitute too much aggregation if there are serious transport difficulties, storage problems or political obstacles to the distribution of food surpluses to areas where food is deficient. A 10 per cent rise in the production of bicycles, accompanied by a 2 per cent fall in food may show up as an increase of income, but it will, in conditions of extreme poverty, mean a rise in poverty.

In using income per head as an index of poverty, and its growth over time as an index of the rate of development, we must, then, beware of two logical traps. First, in a society rent into at least two separate components, one traditional, rural and stagnant, the other specialized, modern and often export-orientated (though it can also be import-replacing), the crucial question is: income and development for whom? Second, gross inequalities of income would not matter if we were looking at the production *potential* of the economy. Thus it might make good sense to ask: how much would there be per head if incomes were equally distributed? In attempting to answer this question we convert different goods and services to a common measure by using their prices. But this procedure assumes either that all goods and services are potentially consumed by all people, or, if different income groups demand different things, that the factors of production could be switched from producing, say, luxury flats for the rich to producing food for the poor. These assumptions are warranted in a rich country but not in most poor ones. For the factors of production used for luxury building, four-lane highways and personal services could not be switched to the production of more food, though foreign exchange could. To equate one block of luxury flats with so many tons of wheat is therefore economically meaningless. We must examine separately what is happening to food production and what to construction and industrial production, even if we are concerned only with *production* and entirely ignore actual distribution.

The Relation between Income and Development

We have seen that low income per head cannot be used as an entirely satisfactory index of poverty, nor its rate of growth over time as an index of the rate of development, because of the dual structure of underdeveloped economies and because of the different products and factors necessary to meet the needs of the people in the two parts of the economy. Even if we had a satisfactory index of real incomes to measure the change in the extent of poverty, its use as a measure of development would still miss a great deal that is conveyed by that term.

Development is both more and less than rising real incomes. It has become a platitude to say that development means modernization and modernization means the transformation of human beings. Development as an objective and development as a process both embrace a change in fundamental attitudes to life and work and in social, cultural and political institutions. The difference between economic *growth* in advanced countries, which, of course, is reflected in faster 'development' as measured by growth of income per head, and *development* in so-called 'developing' countries is that in the former attitudes and institutions are, by and large, adapted to change, and society has innovation and progress built into its system, while in the latter attitudes and institutions and even policies are stubborn obstacles to development.

But the transformation of a tradition- or authority-bound society into a modern, innovating, experimenting, progressing one *may* be successfully achieved without registering for a considerable time any growth in income or income per head. Institutional and human reforms, like building an educational system; land reform; recruiting and training an efficient and honest administrative service; nursing an entrepreneurial class interested in saving, working, risk-taking and large-scale producing; laying the foundations for national, political unity; these and other measures take time and may not be accompanied initially by increasing consumption. The most important measure is often an effective population policy which aims at raising incomes per head by reducing the number of heads over which future income has to be spread. But, although some economic benefits of population control are noticeable very soon, the full benefits accrue only after one or two generations and rapid development can occur without a substantial rise in current income per head. Just as there can be economic growth without development, there can be development without economic growth.

We may conclude therefore that development is certainly not synonymous with rising income or income per head and care must be exercised if these concepts are to be used as rough measures or indicators of development. An ideal measure would need to account for such factors as the rate of encroachment of the modern sector on traditional ways of life and work, and embrace so-called non-economic factors such as human attitudes and social institutions. Pseudo-precision, expressed in single indexes of income per head and growth rates, often reflecting habits of thought acquired in the advanced industrial North, can be misleading if used in isolation. Above all, it is important to remember that such measures cannot but imply value judgements about the aims of development about which there will be no universal agreement.

Characteristics of Poor Countries

While poor countries differ from one another in many respects – some are densely, others sparsely populated; some are humid, others dry; some have been independent for long, others have emerged only recently; some are small, others large; some have been populated by Europeans, others not, etc. – they have a number of common characteristics.[2]

It is easier to enumerate these than to say whether they are causes or effects of poverty or both, whether they are caused by a third factor or whether they are just coincidences.

Perhaps the most striking fact is that most underdeveloped countries lie in the tropical and semi-tropical zones, between the Tropic of Cancer and Tropic of Capricorn. Recent writers have too easily glossed over this fact and considered it largely fortuitous. This reveals the deepseated optimistic bias with which we approach problems of development and the reluctance to admit the vast differences in initial conditions with which today's poor countries are faced compared with the pre-industrial phase of more advanced countries. But a hot and humid climate reduces the efficiency of men, cattle and land. Work generates body heat and is clearly more difficult in a hot climate. In addition, land erosion of the top soil, through wind and rain, is much more serious in tropical countries. So is leaching (the washing downwards by the action of water of essential ingredients in the soil) which is particularly serious in tropical areas with high rainfall and is one cause of rapid loss of fertility. In other areas inadequate or uncertain rainfall is often severely limiting. Moreover, high rates of evaporation mean that irrigation aimed at overcoming water scarcity can lead to soil salination unless extra care, and investment, is provided for meticulous control of water applications, or unless drainage is installed to carry away surplus water. It is, of course, true that the growth of science and technology has created a prospect of prodigious technological advance with respect to such matters as the control of tropical diseases and pests affecting cattle and plants, the scientific introduction of improved strains of crops and livestock and the improvement of methods of production, storage and distribution. But much scientific research has been applied to solving agricultural problems in temperate zones and much of the knowledge gained cannot be directly applied to the different conditions of tropical agriculture. Many of the problems of tropical agriculture have had to be tackled afresh and much remains yet to be done.

Yet a feature common to all the poor countries is the large proportion of the domestic product that is generated in agriculture, even when compared with such 'agricultural' countries as Australia and Canada (see table 4.3). In India, for example, the

TABLE 4.3

Percentage distribution of gross domestic product average 1966–67

Country	Manufacturing and construction	Agriculture and mining	Services
Tanzania	9	55	36
India	17	52	30
Peru	24	24	53
United Kingdom	41	5	54
United States	33	9	62
Average Low-income (9 underdeveloped countries)	18	43	39
Average High-Income	55	7	38

proportion contributed by agriculture and mining is 52 per cent. Moreover, unlike the advanced countries which display a rough correspondence between output and numbers employed (in Britain the 5 per cent of the work force in agriculture contribute 5 per cent of the gross domestic product and the 44 per cent in manufacturing contribute 41 per cent), the poor countries display a marked disparity (see table 4.4). Thus India's agricultural and mining contribution of 52 per cent is produced by 73 per cent of the work force, while the 17 per cent contribution of manufacturing is generated by 11 per cent of the workers. Hence the disparity in personal income between agricultural and industrial workers is much greater in a poor country than in a rich one.

TABLE 4.4

Structure of the Economically Active Population

| Country | Year | Percentages * | | |
		Manufacturing and construction	Agriculture and mining	Services
United Kingdom	1951	44	9	47
France	1962	35	21	44
United States	1960	33	8	59
Canada	1961	30	14	56
New Zealand	1961	35	15	50
Australia	1961	36	12	52
Argentina	1960	31	20	49
Brazil	1960	12	53	35
Mexico	1960	17	55	38
India	1961	11	73	16
Egypt	1960	11	57	32

*These percentages are only very rough because figures for occupations are difficult to collect, partly because the same individual may follow several occupations. The conventions used to attribute only one occupation to each individual are not always the same for different countries.

Source: *Yearbook of Labour Statistics*, I L O, 1966.

So far, only a few of the many characteristics of poor countries have been touched on. We have, however, set down a list of a number of these characteristics as they relate especially to the backward indigenous sector of a poor country.[3] The items selected may to some extent be disputable or at least in need of qualification; their grouping is to some extent arbitrary for the economic and social system is a complex and interrelated whole. No moral or other judgements are implied by this presentation.

1 ECONOMIC INDEX
   low output/worker
   low income/population

'Economic' forces operating on output per worker and income per head

2 CONDITIONS OF PRODUCTION
    small industrial sector
    absence of economies of scale
    primitive and crude techniques
    absence of specialization
    little capital per worker
    scarcity of products requiring much capital
    small savings per head of the bulk of the population
    little enterprise
    inadequate physical and social infrastructure
    low output per acre, particularly of protein foods
    concentration of exports on a few primary products
    low volume of international trade per head
    low labour utilization:
        low participation
        short duration
        low efficiency

3 LEVELS OF LIVING
    large proportion of expenditure on food and necessities
    under-nutrition
    malnutrition
    high mortality rates
    bad housing and overcrowding
    bad hygiene, public health and sanitation
    inadequate medical attention
    inadequate cultural facilities

4 APTITUDES
    absence of training facilities
    inadequate education
    illiteracy
    ignorance, false beliefs and useless or harmful knowledge

'Non-economic' forces operating on output per worker and income per head

5 ATTITUDES TO WORK AND LIFE
    poor discipline
    no punctuality

caste, religious or racial prejudice
superstition
lack of foresight
lack of ambition
weak acquisitive motivation
apathy
lack of adaptability
unwillingness to bear risks, venture, innovate
inability to cooperate outside the family or tribe
contempt for manual work
submissiveness
low standards of hygiene
work-spreading attitudes
absence of birth control and high fertility rates

6 INSTITUTIONS
land tenure hostile to improvements
uneconomic division of plots
poor markets for labour, credit, capital
poor marketing facilities for products
poor information
weak government (national and local)
political uncertainty
corrupt, inefficient and inadequate administration
rigid class, caste system
inequality
absence of opportunities
arbitrary legal administration
non-enforcement of contracts
prevalence of child labour
inferiority of women's status
weak or absent middle class

7 POLICIES
soft state: unwillingness to enforce law and to legislate for
   development
concentration on 'economic' action to escape painful institutional reforms
ineffective taxation

The possible links between these characteristics are numerous, but a few can be indicated by way of illustration:

1   low income – low savings/income ratio – low investment/income ratio – low income;

2   low income – poor health – less vigour and ability to sustain work – low income;

3   low income – absence of economies of scale – low productivity – low income;

4   low income – weak government – poor political and business confidence – low income;

5   low income – reduced democratic consensus – reduced effectiveness of government – reduced ability of government to promote development – low income;

6   low income – strong caste or religious prejudice and weak administration – low income;

7   low income near subsistence level – need to avoid risk – impossible to innovate – low income.

Not all characteristics of poverty are to be found with equal strength in all poor countries. Some quite poor countries have high rates of literacy or high standards of hygiene or do not treat women as inferior or do not suffer from dietary deficiencies or have a high life expectancy. But most of these characteristics tend to be found together and tend to act upon each other, thus contributing to the perpetuation of poverty and to the stability of the low-level equilibrium.

5 SOCIAL PERSPECTIVES

Long ago, a Kikuyu soothsayer predicted the coming of an iron snake spitting fire. The snake would bring a strange race, whose skin was the colour of a pale frog, and their dress like butterflies' wings. These fierce strangers, with the lethal magic sticks, would rule the Kikuyu until a certain giant fig tree died. The tree has duly withered and fallen, and the white rulers have gone. But the snake – the East African railway – remains, linking the highlands of Kenya to Lake Victoria and the Indian Ocean, carrying tea, cement, bags of maize, bacon and cotton cloth – goods unknown in the soothsayer's time – to countries he could scarcely have imagined. In less than one man's lifetime, the civilization of western Europe – in its greed and idealism, curiosity and aggressive nationalism – thrust itself upon the small-scale, self-sufficient societies of eastern Africa, destroyed for ever the traditional boundaries of their lives, and surrendered its responsibility. It brought a wealth of knowledge and technical skills: and their counterparts, awareness of ignorance and poverty. The colonial experience was both liberating and humiliating, denying what it seemed to promise, and profoundly disruptive – not only of ideas and relationships, but of the ecological balance of populations.

Nowhere else, perhaps, has the transition been as abrupt or recent as in tropical Africa. Elsewhere an earlier history of trade or colonial settlement had established states or empires, sometimes created a more sophisticated aristocracy of landowners, a unifying religion, or washed a community of international traders on to the shores of an agricultural hinterland. And even within Africa, the scale of effective social organization varied – from the city states of the Yoruba to the Ibo villages, from the kingdom of Buganda to the intimate hills and valleys of Kikuyu country. But for all the diversity of their history and traditions, the possibilities of nationhood in a technologically sophisticated world seem to impose on all societies the need, for their own survival, to achieve a much larger scale of social organization than ever before. And those countries most conscious of their backwardness, where the need is most urgent, are also those where the obstacles are greatest.

Even to maintain the present standard of living of their people, many of the poor nations of Asia and Africa must exploit their resources more intensively, since their populations are growing by 2 or 3 per cent a year. At the height of her industrial expansion, Britain never faced so hectic a growth: nor did the children born in the slums of Manchester or London expect the rights which every nation now tries to promise to its children – education, medical care, protection from the exploitation of their labour. In the new nations schools and hospitals, humane industrial laws, have preceded the industrial growth that might sustain them. To educate and feed and care for this abounding population, to fulfil, even within a generation, some of the promises of nationhood, these poor countries have no choice but to expand their resources at a far higher rate than has ever been achieved before. And they cannot do this, unless they also reintegrate their societies upon a much wider scale.

Economic growth cannot, for the most part, be realized by extending the traditional manner of cultivation: there is now little idle land to bring into use. It depends upon specialization in marketable crops, the aggregation of land-holding, mobility of labour, diversification of occupation, the establishment of industry. And none of this will be possible without creating a pattern of social relationships far more wide-ranging, differentiated and complex, than those which served a society of peasant farmers, craftsmen and cattle-keepers. This specialization and diversification has to take place within a system of economic exchange international rather than national in scope. It means flying out-of-season strawberries to Fortnum and Mason, turning grazing land into tourist hotels for viewing wild game, mass-producing craft goods for shops in New York, London and Frankfurt. It means that those who can no longer subsist on family farms travel to sell their labour and their skills hundreds of miles from home, learning new trades, starting new businesses. There must be, too, a political and administrative structure wide enough in scope to gather and redistribute the product of this enterprise, allocating schools, hospitals, roads, development capital: and powerful enough to defend its trading interests in a competitive international community.

But the new nations face far more daunting obstacles than the industrial empires which set their aspirations, and established the system of international exchange through which they must realize them. Many of them are made up of heterogeneous populations of different language, race, culture and very unequal resources, contained within arbitrary boundaries. A tribe may be split by frontiers, while each part is expected to identify with fellow nationals who are wholly alien to their traditions. In Europe nationhood grew out of awareness of a common language and culture; linguists and collectors of folk-tales were the first heroes of the nationalism which broke up the Austro-Hungarian empire and remade the map of Europe. In Africa and Asia it was imposed from without, by the accidents of conquest.

The political boundaries of new nations do not, then, usually correspond with any tradition of social organization on so large a scale. Even where, in the past, an indigenous people have built an empire – as the Inca in South America or the Fulani in West Africa – they have seldom bequeathed much more than a romantic memory, or more insidiously, an essentially feudal structure incompatible with the development these nations are now seeking. Political leaders, especially in Africa, have sometimes appealed to the traditions of their society, seeing in customs of cooperation an example of the socialist principles they hope to establish: but the appeal is to an analogy, rather than a model. To translate the quality of village relationships to a nation, altogether new institutions will have to be created to embody them: the traditions of a tribe can be of little direct guidance.

The institutions of the colonial period are often unsuitable too, since they were not designed to promote a progressive economy under indigenous control. Until the last few years, most people in colonial Africa were discouraged or forbidden to take part in political life, education was preoccupied with training junior administrators, clerks, and technicians; economic policy was pre-occupied with a few primary products of value to the imperial power; and the administration was an alien bureaucracy, owing its first loyalty to the colonizing nation. Few new nations can find, either in their recent or more distant past, relevant models for their present needs – especially since older nations, too, as the inventiveness of technology carries us towards strange opportunities and strange problems, are less than ever confident of their own principles of organization.

The profound social changes which the poor countries of the world are now undergoing arise from the progress of a transition from small scale peasant societies to nations with a specialized but diversified commercial agriculture, feeding a complex of industrial production; where the pressure for quick results and the obstacles to be overcome are equally formidable; and where there is little experience to guide them. At the same time, these pressures generate their own reaction, as people seek to escape the demands of new and complex relationships they cannot handle. Tribalism, linguistic nationalism, nepotism, racialism all seek to limit involvement, to reduce the scale of life once more to manageable proportions, however crippling the economic cost.

In the pages which follow, I have tried to explore some aspects of this tension between the compelling need to expand and diversify the range of social relationships, and the desire to retreat, to simplify and guard oneself against its disturbing implications. The circumstances of poor countries of course vary greatly. Most of tropical Africa is free of any inherited caste or class system to constrain mobility, but unlike Asia has few traditions of highly developed crafts. The Caribbean has complexly intermingled race and class antagonisms, a legacy of slavery, but a longer experience of modern institutions. The states of Latin America are older than many in Europe. No general discussion can take account of all these differences. My examples are mostly taken from Africa. But the theme, I believe, is universal, and the struggles of emerging nations centre on it.

The Range of Economic Relationships

The changes in the conception of social relationships that must accompany this transition run very deep. In an African society of the past, for instance, where the economy was based on subsistence agriculture, economic, political and social organization were characteristically determined largely by lineage. A man's place amongst his kin, in one way or another, decided his entitlement to land, the authority to which he was subject, the women he might marry, his rights and duties. Even where no ties of blood or marriage were traced, terms of kinship often served to define relationship: by virtue of his age grade, or his clan, a man would salute as mother or brother members of his community outside his family. Elaborate – and very varied – systems of relationship structured the whole society, so that while some might be enemies, none were strangers; and every relationship embodied familiar rules of behaviour. Some of these rules seem to us bizarre – like the ritual hostility of 'joking' relationships, the acting out of kidnap when a bride (after months of negotiation between the families of the couple) is carried by force from her father's house, the avoidance of personal names in address. But they symbolize an understanding of the nature of society – of the balance of conflict and cooperation, the ordering of power and responsibility, the cross-cutting of allegiance – within which everyone could know his place. At the same time, the rules expressed through conventional behaviour were reinforced by myth and ritual, representing more abstractly the order of the universe and the legitimacy of the social order which reflected it. The system of thought and behaviour formed a whole. This tribal life is now disintegrating, sometimes only gradually, sometimes wholesale.

If the people who subsisted on this land are now to exploit it more intensively for national and international markets, they will have to master a far more complex social organization, extending to include more different kinds of people towards whom a person must behave with competence. They begin to form part of different systems of relationship which may have little in common, and may even be based on incompatible principles. In different situations, they may need to act from quite different conceptions of the nature of social organization.

Farming itself comes to involve cooperative societies – with registered members, committees, accounts, audits – marketing boards, produce inspectors, cesses, compulsory spraying, bye-laws, land titles, planned investment and calculated returns. To manage his affairs, the farmer has to understand, and react appropriately to, strangers as well as neighbours, and an elaborate hierarchy of specialized institutions, each with its own system of permits, forms, regulations and personnel. As a member of a cooperative society, he has to vote in accordance with a constitution, guard his interests against fraud and appeal to courts of law or a government ministry if he is dissatisfied. It matters to him what happens in international crop auctions, what his government can negotiate at trade conferences. The relationships that govern his life are not only far more wide-ranging, but more limited to particular purposes, and more impersonal. And the same process of differentiation takes place within his family. Brothers and sons leave home in search of education and jobs, and become part of different occupational structures with different styles of life. Kinship is no longer the basis of society, but one strand amongst the many which draw people together or twist them apart. Behaviour is determined as much by the employment structure, the commercial network, the hierarchy of educational qualifications, the systems of justice, administration and political authority – each with its own pattern of relationships, values and institutions. This increasing scale and complexity of society means, too, that people have to react regularly to people whom they have never seen before, and may never see again; whose familiarity rests only on the position they hold – and who may be of other tribes, races, languages and cultures.

To master this new social environment, people have to be able to distinguish the behaviour appropriate to one system from another, even when the actors are the same – as when a nephew applying to his uncle for a public post must be treated simply as a candidate. And they have to agree on the nature of the relationship, and the expectations which should govern it. At the same time, since the transformation of society is continuous, they need to be quick to identify new kinds of relationship, establish their form, and to abandon those which no longer serve.

Consider, for instance, the progress of a village carpenter, as by shrewdness and determination his business grows. He may never have been to school, but learned his craft by casual apprenticeship from a friend of his father. He begins by selling to his neighbours, and buying his timber from local pit-sawyers. At first, his business is bounded by the village community, his commercial relationships contained within a familiar world. But if it is to expand, he outgrows the resources of this narrow circle. He needs capital which only a bank or government agency can provide, skilled employees, wider markets, machinery imported from abroad. These new assets are no longer provided informally within a system of intimate personal relationships, but by contract between strangers. He has to establish these commercial relationships on a basis of mutual trust, though his wholesaler, his employees, his bank manager may be of different tribes or races. At the same time, for his own protection, he has to segregate these commercial relationships from the claims of kinship. If now he agrees to oblige a friend or relative by employing his son, he risks a loss through bad work which may ruin him. Wasted wood and broken machinery cut his profit, raise his overheads, and land him in debt or without money to buy timber to fulfil his contracts. As a businessman, he has to treat kinsfolk as he would strangers, just as, in his commercial transactions, he has to treat strangers with the same sense of obligation as he bears towards his family. If the business grows still larger, the structure of relationships may change again, as personal ownership gives way to a limited company, with a formal directorate, audited accounts, shareholders' meetings, and the search for new markets.

The change implied by economic growth is not then, simply a change from one set of values to another – from love of cattle to love of money, from respect for seniority to respect for education, from faith in customs to faith in science – but a more profound change in the nature of social skills. Instead of absorbing, throughout childhood, a conception of the social world as static, bounded, and governed by principles which intermingle in every aspect of life, men and women grow up into a social world continually evolving, whose limits vary from situation to situation, whose principles are ordered differently for each kind of relationship, and change as functions are differently rationalized. To survive, they will need to be endlessly adaptable, to abstract underlying principles of organization from any particular time or place or purpose.

Reactions to Uncertainty

The older order was, by its nature, adapted rather than adaptable. Its conception of life was expressed through specific acts, rituals, myths, externalizing and particularizing its understanding. It could have little immediate resilience in the face of new circumstances. The intrusion of alien institutions – schools, hospitals, money – at once shook its foundations. Education began to offer to a few young men authority and wealth which affronted the political rights of elders, and challenged the accepted meaning of seniority. Money changed the nature of control, substituting a fluid resource for a fixed asset. Where, for instance, bride-wealth was traditionally paid in cattle, it served as a bond between two families, guaranteeing their concern for their children's marriage. For if the young bride behaved badly, her parents would lose the cattle they had received for her, and if the fault lay with the husband, his family stood to lose both daughter-in-law and the bride-wealth they had paid for her. But once money was substituted for cattle – or cattle became readily saleable – the bride-wealth became hard to reclaim: it disappeared into someone's pocket. And the same with means of livelihood: if a wife was entitled to land, for cultivation, from her husband and his family, she was secure in her possession. As this became instead a right to support from her husband's income, she was much more at his mercy. She could turn for redress only to the alien system of courts and maintenance orders, which lay outside her experience – and were as likely as not unenforceable.

But though schools, money, taxes, trade goods were at once

disruptive, they did not put any viable alternative in the place of the relationships they were undermining. They formed part of the social system of the colonizing nation, but they intruded upon the colonized piecemeal, as fragments of an alien society, whose consequences were scarcely considered. Children went to school to discover the powerful secrets locked in written words: no one foresaw, or even wanted, perhaps, the overthrow of the whole basis of tribal authority. The new institutions existed side by side with the old, eroding them but not replacing them, creating a growing confusion and insecurity.

This uncertainty about the nature of relationships is very hard to tolerate. In order to survive, a man must be able to predict how others will react to his behaviour, and how they expect him to react to theirs. Unless he can do this, more or less successfully, his behaviour disintegrates: he becomes increasingly withdrawn, or frantic, ultimately becomes apathetic and even dies. In the Nazi concentration camps, for instance, the administrators deliberately created a capricious and unpredictable social environment, to destroy the personality of their prisoners: very few could withstand for more than a year or two this relentless social bafflement. Life becomes a nightmare, once the obligations and expectations of relationships cannot be foreseen with any confidence. An African farmer, on trial for murder before a colonial court, cried out 'For God's sake kill me and have done with it, I can't stand any more of this': the artificial procedures of British justice were to him incomprehensible, and therefore cruel, even while they attempted to protect his legal rights. The new and unfamiliar therefore generates profound anxiety, which must quickly be contained, either by avoidance or by assimilating these relationships to something intelligible from the stock of experience. However great the potential advantage, however stagnant or crumbling the old order, change is a threat to the integrity of personality: nor are those who have most to gain necessarily the same as those whose confidence in their mastery of the social situation will be most painfully disrupted. The reaction against change is obstinate and continuous, arresting and distorting the process of evolution.

At the outset, a society may refuse altogether to respond to the demands of economic development, protecting its traditional ways – as, for instance, amongst the Masai of East Africa. The cost is isolation, increasing relative poverty and political impotence. Any member of the society who rejects this conservatism can no longer find a place within it, so that a way of life becomes a policy of resistance, unable to meet the forces it opposes on any common ground.

But more common, and more insidious, is a kind of conservatism which tends towards rigidity. It does not reject new institutions, but in the anxiety to re-establish stable relationships, emphasizes their formal structure at the expense of their purpose, and clings obstinately to them. Schoolteachers resist changes in teaching methods and curriculum; administrators perpetuate the conventions of colonial bureaucracy; professionals and technicians trained abroad follow the practices they have learned without re-examining them in their home environment. This displacement of concern from the ultimate aims of an organization, to the preservation of the organization for itself, is the universal disease of bureaucracy. But the newer and more insecure these organizations are, the greater the risk that routine will become an end in itself – a brace to hold up the fragile confidence of the insecure official, and free him from the burden of personal decision. Policy, interpreted in organization, quickly becomes ritual. An Indian agricultural training centre, say, intended to give practical guidance, dwindles into a course of irrelevant formal lectures bounded by the classroom, and no amount of encouragement will get the teachers out into the fields, demonstrating their techniques. Institutions which may be neither appropriate nor efficient obstinately survive.

Most damaging of all, people may give up the attempt to integrate their behaviour on a scale large enough to sustain development, restricting their concern to some smaller and more homogeneous group. The group may be an elite, seeking to pre-empt educational opportunities and the best jobs; a race or privileged class; a tribe or a family. Even nationalism itself, where it retreats from the need for international cooperation, frustrates the chances of economic growth. This tendency towards secession has been the most obvious threat to new nations – in the Congo, Nigeria, the break-up of the Caribbean Federation, linguistic nationalism in India – and it represents, best of all, perhaps, the social dilemma of people in new nations. For tribalism, in this broad sense, is both a rejection of the wider society, and a means of defining one's place within it.

Tribalism as Adaptation and Rejection

In an account of his father's life, a Nigerian Ibo writer has described the career of a village pioneer of change.[1] His story shows very clearly how tribal loyalties can adapt under the stress of change to fulfil new functions, and how tribal membership begins to acquire a new meaning within the framework of a nation. But the recent history of Nigeria also shows how disastrous the consequences can be.

This village pioneer was the first child of his community to seek an education from the missionaries. He met strong disapproval. His parents refused to support him, and he was driven to cultivate tabooed bush to feed himself while he studied. With courage and determination, he withstood the hostility of his family and the ostracism of his age-mates, and learned enough to become in time a post office manager. So, as a young man, he fought the prejudices of his community, willing to become an outcast rather than abandon the promise of new ideas. But later he began to see how these ideas, and the administrative changes of the colonial regime, were threatening to demoralize his people. Respect for traditional authority was giving way as chiefs became corrupt, and colonial government distorted the former basis of their legitimacy. Disputes which had once been settled by discussion now went into litigation. And as people left the village to settle in cities like Lagos and Port Harcourt, they neglected home affairs. So he, and local leaders like him, set out to re-establish the unity of their community – to restore its ability to handle conflict, overthrow corrupt authority, and bind together those who stayed at home and those who had gone in search of new opportunities in the towns. In the 1940s they formed an association, to which every villager was to belong, whose aims were both integrative and progressive. It forbade anyone to take disputes to court, without first submitting them to the association for settlement, and instituted a 'general return home' every third year – when everyone, whether he was working in Lagos, Enugu, Port Harcourt or the north was to return with his family, or face a substantial fine. The association also promoted a market and postal agency in the village, raised money for scholarships, and contributed several thousand pounds towards a cottage hospital. Its branches sprang up in every major city, meeting regularly, attending to the welfare of its members, and collecting contributions for development at home.

Tribal unions of this kind grew up all over Eastern Nigeria, and became an important basis of organization, not so much to conserve a cultural tradition as to meet a variety of new needs. They served to integrate city and village, to mediate between colonial institutions and traditional ways, and to recruit resources to exploit new opportunities for education and health. But their very success tended to forestall the possibility of integration on a larger scale – not because these unions were intrinsically hostile to national unity, but because the effectiveness of their organization seemed to threaten that they might dominate the whole of Nigeria. The adaptability of their sense of community, which had been so powerful an advantage, also stamped that advantage with a tribal mark, and made them tragically vulnerable.

Tribalism, as a sense of identity with people of the same language and culture, or local patriotism, can in itself be integrative and constructive – though it seems that only some peoples, whose traditions of social organization were always relatively individualistic and flexible, are able to exploit it as effectively as the Ibo. But it has also a more negative aspect: the rejection of outsiders. In this sense, tribal membership no longer defines the structure of relationships within which a person acts out his life: rather, it defines an aspect of his relationship to others in a social environment which includes many different tribes. When a newcomer arrives in a city, in search of work and shelter, it provides an immediate frame of reference by which to find his place. Where is he to stay? Who can he approach for help? Where should he inquire about a job? The obvious answer is his countrymen. At the same time, he can make at least a crude adjustment to the strangers about him, in terms of tribal stereotypes.

Stereotyping seems a universal device for structuring an unfamiliar environment. It enables one to make assumptions about a stranger's behaviour from the most casual acquaintance. Accent, dress, race, language are taken to imply a whole range of characteristics, arranging others in degrees of acceptability. But these stereotypes are always more or less hostile, since their purpose is to rationalize avoidance: other tribes eat disgusting food, follow dirty practices, are lazy or lying or thieving. The stereotypes can therefore be very tenacious. People cling to them to excuse their inability to establish relationships of mutual understanding with people who speak different languages and follow different customs. The unsophisticated may never make enough acquaintance outside their own people to challenge their prejudices. But even amongst the most educated, every frustration – quarrels at work, disappointment in promotion, being cheated of a bargain – is likely to revive them. This pervasive latent hostility to strangers, once it becomes associated with tribal or racial classification, is profoundly dangerous. In the face of insecurity and disappointment, people project the threat outwards, so that the danger is no longer within themselves – an inability to meet the demands of their environment – but from outside. Tribal stereotypes provide ready-made enemies against which to turn. Contempt becomes anger, and people begin to see other tribes – often quite irrationally – as the source of their difficulties. The appalling atrocities committed on the Ibo in Northern Nigeria were possible partly because the northerners saw the Ibo as scarcely human: their stereotype had been distorted into something that no longer deserved ordinary human decency.

Even so, the tragedy might never have happened if the Ibo had not also been conspicuously associated with a position of advantage. They held many of the clerical and administrative positions in the north, pre-empting jobs which the northerners felt should be for them. In the same way, the Asians of East Africa were vulnerable because of their control over commerce. Where an economic grievance can fasten, with more or less justification, on a tribal or racial group, the combination can easily lead to a violent outburst so disruptive that it destroys the very economic opportunities at issue.

The Ibo experience illustrates both the value and risks of tribal identity as a principle of adaptation. Confidence in and respect for the culture in which he grew up helps a man to master new situations without feeling that his essential personality is going to pieces. And there are aspects of life to which this identity remains appropriate within a wider society – the economic progress and welfare of his home district, local politics, the introduction of newcomers to city life. But if it extends to become an all-embracing principle of organization, it turns into separatism. Whenever an inherited structure of relationships successfully adapts to new functions, there is a risk that some kinds of activity will become restricted to the racial or cultural group from which this structure arose, and sharpen group antagonisms. Tribalism has to be contained by cross-cutting loyalties based on other principles. The evolution of a society able to carry the demands of economic development depends, then, on the ability to discriminate the system of relationships appropriate to each activity, and find your identity within it – as a member of a tribe, as a professional responding to the principles of a vocation, as an entrepreneur responding to the demands of a commercial system. The danger is that people will be unable to handle the strain of these multiple identities, and try to merge them. The danger is all the greater, because their past has handed down to them so little in common.

The Disjointedness of Change

So far we have discussed the transition to a larger scale of social organization in terms of the insecurity it generates. But the defences against perplexity and disintegration – withdrawal,

97

rigidity, separatism – are compounded by the disjointedness of change. Innovators are always adapting to a society not yet created, at the risk of making their situation untenable in society as it is. The farmer who plants crops for sale may stand to earn more. But he may also thereby opt out of a traditional system of exchange by which people supported each other in times of want. In times of distress, he finds himself without friends. Even his prosperity may generate so much jealousy that his plans are defeated. The risks of innovation can, then, look very different to the agricultural planners in a government ministry, and the farmers who are expected to implement them. As chapter nine describes, traditions of cultivation are a subtle and expert adaptation to the circumstances which govern a subsistence farmer's life, and he will not abandon them lightly for the advice of an agronomist who does not know his community or understand the constraints under which he takes his decisions. The planners are thinking of yield per acre in the long term: the farmer has to consider what will happen if his crop fails next year, or if envious rivals burn down his grain store.

Nor are the risks of innovation always borne by those who choose them. A sophisticated couple who marry across caste lines may live happily enough in a Bombay suburb, while their families at home are ostracized. Between city and village, between economic systems and systems of social insurance, the unevenness of change leaves incompatible principles of organization unreconciled.

Just as vainglorious governments sometimes build pretentious monuments to their modernity, which stand incongruously amongst the shacks and rutted lanes, waiting for the nation to catch up with them, so the institutions of the state may be sharply at variance with the prevailing standard of life. In most African nations, the salary and privileges of the civil service remain those of the colonial regime, and within that salary structure, conform to a continuous gradation of reward. In the context of African society, they represent not two or three times the average wage, but ten or twenty times. The disparity between the style of life of the urban elite, who govern and educate the future governors, and those they govern is profound; and in future generations there will no longer even be the bond of a common childhood experience. For those in power, like everyone else, herded their father's goats, and walked barefoot to the village school between their mothers' plots of maize and beans. But there are children growing up in Africa now, to whom it is natural to go to school in a Mercedes-Benz, and to come home to cake and Coca-Cola on the drawing-room carpet, watching television. These privileges have not grown up from a selfish exploitation of power, however self-interest may help to sustain them. They arise because different parts of society are framed in quite different orders of value. A university graduate who enters the civil service, works with foreign advisers, prepares reports for representatives of the World Bank, attends international conferences, does not see himself as privileged, but only as living the life of government servants anywhere in the world. To deny him this is an affront, implying that he is not as worthy as his international colleagues – and a humiliation for his country too, that it cannot sustain a sophisticated modern bureaucracy. The values against which he judges his self-respect, and what is due to it, have only the most tenuous links with the world of a peasant farmer. Each conceives life in different terms, and though they work for each other, their behaviour may be mutually unintelligible.

The Range of Language

Most of these problems of change are not peculiar to new nations. Bureaucratic rigidity, racial antagonisms, separatism, conflicts over redundancy and growing disparity of incomes are familiar enough in the most industrialized countries, and seem to arise from a similar reaction against the growing scale and complexity of the economic system on which society is based. The difference lies partly in the abruptness of the transition. The son of a village elder represents his country at the United Nations: in one generation, the scope of relevant relationships breaks out from a circle of hills, a plain, to cover the whole world. There is a crippling shortage of people with knowledge or experience to master the problems of transition. Some countries faced independence with scarcely a single university graduate trained to take over the responsibilities of administration. But there is one crucial handicap, characteristic of these new nations, which makes the problems of integrating a national society very much more difficult. Unlike the industrial countries, they lack an established common language which everyone can read and write.

Unless most people are literate in a national language, it becomes much harder to communicate ideas at every level, and much more expensive. If a farmer cannot read the instructions on a tin of insecticide, an agricultural officer must call and explain them – and this might be an assistant who cannot read them himself and who, in the process of memorizing them translated into his own language, has got them wrong. The quality of what is communicated becomes distorted by translation, cruder and more fragmented, and more readily misunderstood. Once the scale of society outgrows the range of personal relationships, written words become the vital link between individuals and the institutions of their society. And these words must embody, not only practical instructions but the conception of the social order which the nation is struggling to evolve. It would be virtually impossible to convey these through the language of any small-scale society, let alone communicate them in several languages at once. For the language of the nation must express, not only new ideas, but a different logic from the languages of the past.

In tribal society, the principles of life are conveyed through ritual and conventions of behaviour, not abstracted from them. In a relatively static society, with familiar boundaries of experience, proverbs, myths, the natural environment provides elements of argument from which a skilled orator can elaborate a subtly structured speech. But the logic of this structure can scarcely be grasped by an outsider, even when the literal sense is translated. The juxtaposition of the elements of the argument are meaningful only within a particular world of experience. The language lacks the kind of abstract concepts which can be universally applied, irrespective of a familiar situation. But it is impossible to interpret the principles of life in a large-scale, complex, changing society except in these more abstract terms. Even the ideas of political independence and freedom themselves could often be conveyed in the languages of the people who fought for them only in a sense which profoundly distorted their meaning. And conversely, if different tribes are ever to understand each other, their different cultures will have to be interpreted in terms which make sense to them all. Thus the language in which people communicate becomes one of the most powerful forces binding or dividing groups, making intelligible their structure and variety, and defining their limits.

But to achieve a society literate in a common language, there must be competent teachers with a relevant and adaptable curriculum, and therefore good colleges to teach them, and able administrators in the ministry of education. The more urgently schooling is extended, the worse its quality is bound to be, while talent is so scarce. If untrained teachers, unable to master their role, reduce their classes to a ritual incantation, if success in formal examinations of artificial knowledge become the accepted ladder to positions of power, then the conservative rigidity we discussed earlier can cripple the progress of society as well as ignorance itself. Educational policy is caught between the need for an intelligent elite, able to guide society through its evolution, and the risk that such an elite may be unable to communicate or even sympathize with the mass of the people they are leading. All the frustrations and promises of change converge upon education, so that who should get schooling, for how long and in what language are passionately debated.

The Search for National Integration

Throughout this discussion, we have tried to trace the social implications of an economic logic which impels poor countries towards a larger, more complex, more differentiated and adaptive structure of relationships, where in the recent past there existed neither common institutions, nor even the words to conceive their present situation. This structure cannot help but be at first very fragile and disjointed. Its uncertainties and unfamiliar demands generate powerful reactions, which can stultify progress, or break the nation into pieces, as people seek refuge in a more manageable world of experience. In the face of these threats, there are essentially two conceptions of how an integrated national society can evolve. One concentrates on unity, the other exploits the conflicts of diversity, and each largely excludes the other. Each derives from a different aspect of the problems we have discussed. There is a need for a common language, a common set of principles by which to articulate the relationships of society as a whole: there is also a need to differentiate the conventions and interests proper to each activity, to separate the loyalties which should govern one kind of relationship from those of another. In styles of government, in argument and development strategy, one or the other aspect seems to preoccupy attention. So, for instance, Tanzania and Kenya, though their problems have much in common, approach them with a consistently different emphasis. Tanzania stresses a common language and an articulate national ideology, impatient of tribalism, sectional interest, independent trade union pressure or the claims of an administrative elite. All activities are ideally subordinate to an over-riding party which embodies the national purpose. Kenya pursues the politics of coalitions of interest, encourages private enterprise, tolerates the independence of trade unions, and is moving towards vernacular teaching in its primary schools. Not that either nation, by its history and the complex of its political circumstances, could freely have chosen to follow the example of the other. But in each of them, the sense of how the nation should evolve seems to be dominated by a different principle, with strengths and weaknesses the other lacks.

The preoccupation with national unity leads towards the ideal of a radical transformation of every section of society, based on common principles. Such a policy assumes a national ideology persuasive enough, and backed by sufficient sanctions, to bring about a fundamental reconstruction of social relationships. Its boldness is attractive, especially in former colonies where so much of the accretion of recent history can be seen as a humiliating alien imposition. And since it is seldom possible to make fundamental changes in one aspect of life without parallel changes in many others, its universality promises escape from the interlocking constraints of accepted ways of life. But it has also serious drawbacks.

If the nation is to be integrated by pervasive ideology, nothing that formerly defined relationships can any longer be taken for granted. A new, comprehensive code of behaviour extends to every aspect of life, and people must redefine their part according to it. New rules are needed for husbands and wives, parents and children, for the arts and sports, as much as for economic and political relationships. If people are to understand each other these rules must be propagated explicitly and unambiguously, and everyone must accept them, just as they must accept the rules of language. Any radical social reconstruction, undertaken consciously as a coherent whole, is necessarily dogmatic and intolerant. Otherwise it claims to invalidate all past experience, without replacing it by any sufficiently predictable code of behaviour to govern relationships.

But there are all kinds of issues which cannot be solved by any dogmatic prescription – centralization or decentralization of organization; priority for agricultural or industrial development; mass participation or the training of an elite. Society has to alter course as it runs into difficulties. The dogmatic style of a unifying ideology makes these adjustments difficult. The need to replace the certainty of the familiar with a corresponding certainty of doctrine makes for a rigidity which adapts awkwardly and abruptly to its mistakes. A definition of social relationships, explicit enough and enduring enough to give their citizens a secure sense of their own identity within the system, also imposes a constraint which handicaps adjustment to circumstances and experience.

The pursuit of national integration through a common language, a common framework of ideas leads on towards an authoritative ideology. It centres the structure of relationships on a core of master principles which, if they are not viable, bring everything down with them. The alternative is to integrate society through the cross-cutting loyalties to which everyone is subject, and ally him now with one grouping, now another. As a member of an occupation, a man is loyal to his trade union; as a churchgoer, loyal to his denomination; as a tribesman, loyal to his compatriots. So long as each brings him into association with a different group, the potential disruptiveness of the conflicts into which any one such loyalty may draw him is checked by his need to maintain his ties also with others. The conflicts themselves then become integrative rather than disruptive, because the over-riding need to reconcile them creates means of arbitration. And acts of arbitration are amongst the most sensitive means of evolving pragmatically the principles of a social order.

As a conception of how a national society can evolve, this alternative calls for a great variety of formal associations – professional bodies, tribal welfare societies, trade unions, student groups, chambers of commerce, cooperative unions – each concerned with a specific aspect of life; and secondly facilitating agencies, such as advisory services, to help people understand the demands of unfamiliar relationships. It is little help to a man to be formally a member of a trade union, a shareholder in a company, a cooperative farmer, if he does not understand how it can serve his interests, and how to exercise his rights. And he must understand too what interests it cannot serve – that it concerns him only as an employee, a shareholder, a farmer, relating him to society in that aspect of his life alone. The gravest danger to this whole conception of integration arises when these various interests converge. So long as the tribe, for instance, is only one amongst many groups which lay claim to loyalty, it is no more disruptive than religion, class, politics or profession. But if tribe and religion, or tribe and occupation, come to coincide, if political loyalties are based on ethnic ties, or members of a tribe are identified with a privileged class, then too many conflicts, rational and irrational, are drawn together in a single confrontation.

There is a risk, too, that a society integrated through the cross-cutting loyalties of functional groupings will correspondingly lack means to sustain faith in its underlying unity. Because its manner of integration is structural rather than ideological, and emphasizes the arbitration of conflict, its symbols of national unity and purpose may be poorly articulated and unimpressive. Impatience with the frustrations of conflict and compromise may provoke a reaction towards more authoritarian rule. Indeed, the evolution of society seems likely to proceed at first by violent swings between the stress on over-riding unity, and the encouragement of autonomous institutions representing the diversity of interests and functions. But in the long run, as the mediation of conflict creates over-arching principles of law and constitution, or a revolutionary movement settles into an established division of functions, the two approaches to integration must converge. Otherwise, either remains precarious.

If this is so, we can begin to see the kind of social criteria which should be most relevant, in assessing a country's chances of sustaining economic development. Is there a common language, and how many people can read and write it? Are there means of communication – newspapers, radio, advisory services, political discussion – which reach the villages, and can they also carry the villagers' response? Within an income group, an occupation, how well are the different tribes, races or religions of the society represented? Do associations representing different activities and interests exist, and if so, are they genuinely differentiated and autonomous, or merely instruments of an extraneous, more powerful interest – political, perhaps, or tribal? Are there means to resolve conflicts by principles and procedures independent of personal political authority? Is education open to children irrespective of their class or region? Is recruitment to occupations governed by criteria relevant to their performance, or by some other standard of acceptability? And finally, we can ask just the same kind of questions about the institutions of international relationships, on which the chances of development equally depend.

6 POLITICAL PERSPECTIVES

Few would disagree that increasing wealth is a central objective of development. Yet a preoccupation with economic development can be misleading in a number of ways, and can even be self-defeating.

In the first place, economic development is not pursued as a sole or even a prime objective by people in poor countries to the extent that writers on development have often assumed, and strategies which ignore this are unlikely to work. To plan effectively for economic development a first essential is to understand (a) what 'economic development' means to the various groups and categories that make up the political system, how far different forms of growth seem to hold out benefits or risks, to justify sacrifices in order to obtain them or resistance in order to prevent them; and (b) what other, generally competing, objectives are being pursued by the political leadership of poor countries.

In the second place economic development cannot occur without sympathetic developments in other spheres of life, among which the political system is obviously of key significance. Any serious development strategy for a given country must be based on an analysis of its political structure and political culture, the influences that make them what they are and also those which are working to change them. (It must equally take into account the social system, of course; this is discussed in chapter five.)

Economic Goals are not Necessarily 'Paramount'
To take the ordinary man or woman first, we have been far too prone to accept the stereotype implied by phrases like 'the rising

tide' (or 'revolution') of expectations, and to think that, after centuries of fatalistic acceptance of their lot, people in poor countries now give as much priority to the goal of increasing their incomes as people like the authors of this book think is necessary. But for many reasons this is not true. Not that ordinary people in poor countries do not want to earn more and live better. But, in the first place, men do not live by bread alone even in the poorest countries; they have other ambitions that may well be equally or more important. In India, building a temple for the village often evokes more enthusiasm than building a road; in Africa, more local resources may be invested in pursuing a clan boundary dispute than in building a cooperative store.

Secondly, people may be justifiably sceptical of the actual measures proposed to them for improving their incomes. Some of these have been simply wrong, as in the examples given in chapter nine below; others have been impossibly onerous, like the agricultural rules introduced in the East Lake area of Tanganyika after the Second World War, which included the requirement that people working entirely by hand should apply 3 tons of manure annually to every acre of land (the point is not that it *can't* be done, but that either the return hardly compensates the drudgery involved or it is less than could be achieved from some other investment of equivalent effort). Even where the measures urged upon them are technically sound they often have the effect of increasing output but also of increasing risk – i.e. they make the farmer who adopts them more vulnerable to accidents such as drought or flooding, or even to a fall in crop prices. This is all very well for farmers who can rely on efficient insurance and famine protection arrangements, but not for producers whose families have no protection but their own foresight and wisdom.*

Thirdly, even when the measures proposed would indeed raise incomes at an acceptable risk, they may entail other costs which

*These facts are, however, no reflection on the unique contribution which agricultural extension workers have made to development. Because they have grappled directly with the real problems, their mistakes are as instructive as their successes. A much fuller discussion of the problem of risk may be found on chapter nine.

cancel out the advantage. This is especially true where the measures involve breaking with some aspect of the existing social structure. They may mean, for instance, giving up leisure, during which a man can cultivate friends and acquire respect and standing, for the sake of a few extra pounds on a cash income of perhaps £30 a year, or they may mean refusing to give money to relatives for marriage dowries, to invest it instead in a new plough, when this means that one's own sons may be unable to marry when they are ready to.

In general, the new behaviour required for 'development' often seems to mean the sacrifice of something tangible for something intangible; with the virtual certainty of family dislocation, uncertainties, risks, disappointments, and snubs that innovation so often entails. For a poor peasant who makes sacrifices to improve his income cannot usually hope to win through to the status, security, equality, etc. of a farmer – or even a farm-labourer – in Europe, even though in certain exceptionally favourable conditions the most successful individuals may prosper greatly. He will usually be embarking on a long period of uncomfortable, anxious, and perhaps lonely transition; of humiliating dependency on a host of (generally) young 'change agents', offering him advice and homilies or even threats; with, perhaps, the attendant fear of the ultimate disaster of losing his land as a result of debts incurred in unsound innovation. It is not surprising that such people should often be ambivalent about what economic development means to them. And, of course, there are important groups – for instance landlords – whose interests may be directly threatened by it.

But even if it is conceded that the ordinary man is not necessarily committed to economic development, and may not even understand what it requires, it is almost always assumed that political leaders and civil servants not only understand these things but assign them the utmost priority. Development is pictured as the result of a partnership between politicians who want to accelerate economic growth, technicians who show them how, and aid donors. This view of the matter has been encouraged, it is true, by political leaders who naturally and quite properly emphasize to all representatives of donor countries and aid agencies their earnest desire for economic growth and their need for assistance.

Yet this view depends on a highly unreal conception of politics. With very few exceptions the political systems of poor countries, no less than of rich ones, hold up *some* sort of a mirror to the perceptions and attitudes of the people who live in them. There may even be a well established system of elections, as in India, making the political leaders directly sensitive to popular views. Elsewhere a single party, maintaining itself in power by manipulating elections or by abolishing them, may itself constitute an arena for intense factional politics in which the support of local followings is keenly sought by the leaders, who must, therefore, once again take local feeling closely into account. Even military governments are not an exception; although they can often install themselves easily in power by a mere show of force, they usually find they can only exercise power effectively by catering at least partly to the aspirations of the very groups whose influence they aimed to abolish. A political leadership dedicated above all to economic growth, willing and able to pursue this goal at the expense of all others and able to rely on the party, the bureaucracy and the army to contain the resentment and reaction that will be entailed, is to say the least highly exceptional.

Of course, political leaders normally (though not invariably) want a rapid rate of economic growth. But it is only one among many objectives which they *want* to pursue. The word 'want' is used deliberately, rather than 'must'. Exasperated economists in planning ministries not infrequently come to view the situation as follows: 'their' minister (the Minister of Planning) genuinely *wants* to do what is needed to secure an improved rate of growth. But he is *obliged*, by reason of the need to stay in power, to compromise with all sorts of conflicting political interests – to agree to wage settlements which destroy the income assumptions of the plan; to build more than the planned number of schools; to locate industries, or roads, in economically far from ideal places and so on.

When this process is very pervasive, and hardly any of the things needed to implement the plan are actually carried through, the planners are apt to conclude that, in spite of the politicians' presumed *desire* for planned growth, they fundamentally lack the moral fibre to do what is necessary to achieve it; the problem is pictured as one of the 'will to develop' – 'a great glittering generality retrieved from abstractions of nineteenth century psychology, political philosophy and metaphysics.'[1]

Of course, politicians do vary in determination, honesty, singleness of mind, and so on. But, speaking generally, political leaders do not *want* one particular goal beyond all others. Like the ordinary people whose affairs they try to manage, they have a multiplicity of goals they want to achieve and most of the time they are pursuing them all more or less simultaneously. It is only if one presupposes that economic goals (or any other kind) are the only *really* legitimate ones that one is driven to such feeble interpretations as that politicians, of all people – in this toughest of all political contexts! – are systematically lacking in will.

Experience shows that few people in rich countries are easily convinced of the truth of what has just been said. In the spirit in which Stendhal imagined that all the ordinary man wanted in Europe before the French Revolution was '(*a*) not to be killed; and (*b*) for a good warm coat' we tend to project onto people in poor countries our idea of what *we* would think most important if we were (suddenly) to be reduced to their level of poverty. We find it hard to believe that their whole being is not focused, as in that event ours certainly would be, on how to become less poor and we are fortified in this misconception by the keen interest in personal wealth exhibited by most of the poor countries' elites. This perhaps helps to explain why people – and not least development planners themselves – find it hard to give up the idea that economic goals *are* somehow 'paramount', 'basic' or 'ultimate'. Even when they are confronted by some extremely obvious example of resources earmarked for planned productive investment being used to achieve some social or political goal – for instance, extending school or hospital building programmes to politically restive districts – they tend to see this as a merely tactical diversion – as still indirectly, 'ultimately' aimed at making it easier to accelerate economic development at some later date. In a sense this is true – the one may well help the other – except that at the later date, the experience will almost certainly repeat itself in a new form. The moment when everything is ready for the untrammelled pursuit of those 'basic' economic goals somehow never arrives. The view that all other goals are pursued as instruments to achieve economic ones turns out to be the fallacy of economic paramountcy in yet another new guise.

The next section considers some of the other problems and goals which politicians in poor countries have and which compete for resources and attention with economists' development goals. It should be obvious that, in the last analysis, all are of equal legitimacy. Yet, if there are sacred cows in politics, general economic development is very rarely one of them, *least of all in poor countries*; and the basic importance of this paradox is so great that one is tempted to speak of politics, not economics, as somehow 'primary', although this would be an equal and opposite distortion. It comes to this: the politics of a country does comprise the interests, the conflicts, the aspirations and the capacities for collective action of its people as they actually are at any given time. These things are not immutable, but neither are they easily changed; on the whole they provide a fairly firm set of constraints to which any plan for economic development must be subordinated if it is to have any hope of success. The social structure normally associated with poverty, however, does tend to produce a particular type of politics, which is the type least likely to set a high premium on so generalized an objective as national economic development, or to undertake programmes of 'forced' social transformation to achieve it.

This point is of enormous importance and obviously cannot be left in this sweeping and abstract form. It is, however, really a summary of the central argument of this chapter, and so an attempt to state it more clearly is left till later.

To sum up: there are political leaders of poor countries, such as Batista or Sukarno, who are *not* really interested in economic development. Most, however, desire it; but most are pursuing other goals at least equally keenly and seldom hesitate to subordinate economic development to these other ends. Their commitment to development is strictly instrumental and far from occupying a paramount place in their priorities, it is apt to have a fairly modest one. Those anxious to help the cause of economic development cannot do so intelligently unless this is grasped; otherwise they will almost inevitably find themselves proposing policies that assume a far higher degree of priority for economic development than is actually attached to it. The resultant failures of development planning may be correspondingly large, setting back development instead of helping it on.*

Other Problems and Other Political Goals for Political Leaders

Many of the problems characteristic of poor countries are described in chapters one and two. One group can be summed up under the heading of 'poor integration': the linguistic, cultural, racial and religious differences discussed in chapter five; the wide gap between town and country, and the often growing gap between economic classes; the uneven spread of development and services; the insecurity and unpopularity of many frontiers; all these place exceptionally heavy burdens on the governments of poor countries. In Uganda in 1964 the federal government faced: a secessionist guerilla movement in its western province, due to inter-tribal conflicts; a threat of violence encouraged by the government of one of the federal states to frustrate a federally instituted referendum concerning that state's boundary with another; fighting between the nomadic tribes of its eastern border with those in Kenya; a massive refugee problem, resulting from political persecutions in Rwanda and the southern Sudan; and a serious risk of military conflict with the mercenaries operating against the Lumumbist regime in the eastern Congo, with whom the Uganda government was in sympathy. At this time critics could be heard condemning the government for devoting scarce resources to broadcasting the news – *its* news, certainly – in eleven of the thirteen major languages of the country; a measure which, viewed in this perspective, appears as the most elementary

---

*This is only one form – though a common one – of the dangers that can arise from a failure to recognise the relationship between politics and development. It is particularly damaging if it leads to a discrediting of planning itself.

act of national self-preservation. The slogan of 'national unity', like all slogans, frequently cloaks activities which are hard to justify by any criteria of public interest: it nonetheless refers to a problem which is entirely real in many poor countries.

Another set of problems faced by governments in most poor countries are those of 'legitimacy'; the fact that it is by no means taken for granted that the government – the police, the agricultural officer, parliament – have a right to do the things they do and ought in general to be obeyed, let alone positively helped by sacrifices of any kind. This has diverse causes and takes many forms. The most persistent and dangerous challenge to legitimacy comes from 'primordial sentiments' – the bonds of kinship, language and locality which far outweigh the 'civil ties' which govern the citizen's relationship with other citizens generally and with the civil authorities.[2]

In many poor countries – especially the recently created states of Africa and Asia – there has been too little time to create those 'civil ties'. There is not much shared experience of central government. National institutions have little visibility in rural areas; taxes are collected by local officials, order is kept by local police; the agricultural assistant, with his all too often misleading textbook formulae, his youth and his lack of experience, is often the most tangible symbol of the central government, and not one calculated to inspire the loyalty it requires. The party in power usually commands some loyalty. This, however, is much more limited than was once supposed. Professor Zolberg has recently examined the electoral support secured by the most powerful west African 'mass' parties at the height of their popularity and shown that it amounted to from one-sixth to two-fifths of the adult population.[3] After independence, of course, this support began to disintegrate, most evidently in India, where free elections clearly reveal the facts, but actually everywhere. Dominating, 'charismatic' leaders such as Sukarno or Nkrumah succeeded for a time in evoking feelings of enthusiasm but few of them were able to sustain these feelings or transfer them to the institutions of the state. Most of these leaders have now disappeared.

In a rich, old-established country such as Britain there is a tendency to take the legitimacy of the government and the

113

constitution entirely for granted. As a result, people sometimes find it hard to conceive what an immense asset this phenomenon is and how its absence limits the scope for effective, government-directed change and increases its costs. In a study of five countries carried out in 1960 to 1961, Professors Almond and Verba showed how exceptional Britain is in this respect even among rich countries: and how one poor country (Mexico) contrasted sharply with the rich ones covered in the survey. Four out of five people in Britain thought the national government improved conditions, compared with only two out of three Mexicans: one Mexican in five thought Mexico would be better off without the national government; more than half of them felt that they were not themselves affected by either national or local government activity and nearly a third expected that, in any encounter with the civil service or the police, their point of view would be ignored. These things are not evidence that Mexicans do not regard their government as legitimate, but it is reasonable to guess that its legitimacy is less strongly or broadly based than that of the other countries in the study.

The extent to which governments depend on being regarded as highly legitimate can be exaggerated but the ease with which civil governments have been displaced by the armed forces throughout the Third World is not solely due to the power of a few hundred armed men where no rival forces exist. It is at least as much due to the fact that relatively few people even see the civil authorities as uniquely entitled to exercise power – let alone being willing to organize or take risks to defend them, as the Spanish were in 1936 or the French in April 1961.

These problems of integration and legitimacy are also present in some rich countries, of course, and they do not necessarily threaten the stability of government in poor ones. But they tend to be present in unusually severe forms in poor countries. They are also very much harder to cope with when the government itself is not rich and when politically powerful groups or classes are voicing demands – which they expect to be listened to – for services, jobs and other economic benefits that were scarcely thought of – and certainly could be largely disregarded – during the early economic development of today's rich nations. (Another manifestation of the difficulties of 'late' development in a world dominated by rich nations.)

These problems demand solution. In addition to the aspirations which leaders – both as individuals and as a group or a class – carry with them when they enter political office, and which may also include so much else besides economic development,* national integration and the establishment of legitimacy pose continuous problems the solution of which must be a major goal of political leadership.

Political Structures

To understand that non-economic goals are usually at least as compelling as economic ones, and what sort of goals they are, may be the beginning of wisdom in development. The next step is to examine the political frameworks within which all such objectives as are selected must be pursued. But can anything general be said that is both true and worth saying? The political diversity of the poor countries is almost their most dominant characteristic. Considered as entire regimes, they range from the largest open democracy in the world – India – to miniature dictatorships such as Nicaragua or Togo. This diversity does not greatly diminish when one narrows down the range of states to a particular area or particular aspect.†

In many cases there is a similar diversity of political structure *within* the state itself, especially where smaller-scale traditional

*We should recall the passion with which Sekou Touré replied to De Gaulle's threat – later carried out with complete ruthlessness – to withdraw French economic aid from Guinea if she opted for independence: 'We prefer poverty in liberty to riches in slavery.'

†As Professor Lieuwen put it, before trying to classify the twenty Latin American states according to the political functions of their armed forces: 'At one extreme is Costa Rica, which abolished its army; at the other is the Dominican Republic with its absolutist military dictatorship. In between there are eighteen gradations.' LIEUWEN, E., *Arms and Politics in Latin America*, Praeger, New York, 1963, p. 157.

political structures are still important. Thus, for instance, to get a system of village wells sunk may in one area be a matter of making it attractive to a large number of extremely local leadership groups; in another area it may be a question of inducing a single leader to command it to be done because in that area there is a strongly hierarchical system of political authority; while in a third it may be impossible to get wells sunk at all without a local revolution, because control of access to the existing limited supplies of water is the basis of the local elite's political power.

In spite of this, several writers have attempted to relate the 'types of regime' of poor countries to levels of economic development; table 6.1 is an example.

TABLE 6.1

Political Regimes and Economic Development

(a) Latin America

'Rank' in economic development	Competitiveness of political structure		
	Competitive	Semi-competitive	Authoritarian
1	Argentina		
2	Uruguay		
3	Venezuela		
4			Cuba
5	Chile		
6		Panama	
7		Mexico	
8	Costa Rica		
9		Colombia	
10	Brazil		
11			Paraguay
12		Peru	
13		Ecuador	
14			Dominican Republic
15			Nicaragua
16			El Salvador
17			Bolivia
18		Guatamala	
19			Honduras
20			Haiti

(b) Asia and Africa

'Rank' in economic development	Competitiveness of political structure		
	Competitive	Semi-competitive	Authoritarian
1	Lebanon		
2	Malaya		
3			United Arab Republic
4	Philippines		
5	Turkey		
6			Iraq
7	Ceylon		
8		Morocco	
9		Jordan	
10		Tunisia	
11			Libya
12		Ghana	
13			Iran
14		Thailand	
15		Indonesia	
16	India		
17		Malagasy Republic	
18			Saudi Arabia
19		Burma	
20		Cambodia	
21		Camaroons	
22		South Vietnam	
23		Nigeria	
24			Pakistan
25			Laos
26			Liberia
27			Sudan
28		Togoland	
29			Ethiopia
30			Afghanistan

If – a very big 'if' – one accepts the system of political classification, such tables seem to suggest some positive correlation between the level of economic development and the 'degree of democracy' or 'competitiveness' exhibited by the political

117

system. However, the relationship is not very pronounced; two or three *coups d'état* can significantly change it and have done so since the table was compiled. In any case, it tells us nothing about the causal connexions between the economy and the politics which might assist the economic planner. Furthermore, an attempt to correlate *rates* of growth with democracy in Latin America found no positive correlation at all.

It is difficult not to conclude that this line of inquiry is premature and tells us little we did not know before from more casual evidence. What is of much greater importance is to understand some of the particular processes and structures through which political and economic factors interact with each other in particular cases. First, we will consider some widely distributed factors which are at work in poor countries and see how they influence the structure of their politics. Then we will focus slightly more systematically on some of the main elements into which their – or any country's – political systems can be analysed.[5]

1. '*Traditionalism*'. In rich countries, the logic of social mobility and occupational specialization leads people to see themselves and others in categories: as 'youth', old-age pensioners, workers, middle-class, home-owners, parents, etc. The law looks on people in this way too: what applies to one car-owner applies to all. It makes sense for people to organize politically to secure advantages for themselves in alliance with people in the same category, and the performance of politicians is judged by what they are seen to do for such organized groupings – for car-owners, for unskilled workers, etc. There is also a general realization that everyone will lose if politicians manage to build support on the alternative basis of purely personal followings, whether on the *Führer-prinzip* or via the pork barrel.

But people brought up on a small-holding in Uttar Pradesh or a *latifundio* in Peru – or in any small-scale, relatively closed community – are prepared from childhood to rely on personal, especially kinship, relations for literally all purposes and this is carried over into their political behaviour. With the beginnings of economic development, social mobility has increased but the dominant relationships are very often still those of the rural majority. Most people are still born to a station in life, or at least a limited range of stations. The idea that people enter specialized roles, strictly separated from others, is not strongly established; people in official roles, in particular, are not expected to perform them as though none of their other roles were relevant to it at all. Thus a policeman is expected to deal less severely with a fellow clansman than with a 'stranger'; a minister is expected to see that his own district, where his support lies, gets a second secondary school even if the next district has not yet any. If a man improves his lot, it tends to be taken for granted that it is because he has the right connexions; those in powerful positions are expected to share the benefits with their relatives and other personal supporters. People may for some purposes see their individual interest as bound up with that of their region as a whole, over-riding local divisions; what is rare is that they can be mobilized to support any grouping that does not have at its centre the core of immediate personal ties into which they have been born.*

The influence of this factor is felt in politics in both behaviour patterns and attitudes, and this becomes especially striking when it happens in countries where some, at least, of the elements of 'modernity' are quite strongly established. The Philippines are a case in point. They are not among the poorest of the poor countries, are highly Christianized, and have a fast-growing industrial sector: the political system established by 1916 is very closely modelled on the American and includes a nation-wide two-party system. But the basis of party support is strictly an extension of the social relations governing life at the village level: people do not group themselves with others according to some specialized interest which they all share as a group – as farmworkers, for instance, or sharecroppers – but put their vote at the service of a local patron in return for material rewards – jobs, loans, intervention with the police, etc. The political consequences of this are far-reaching.

Clear norms of conduct according to function are absent. Voters judge the men they elect to office on the norms of social life, how well

*Some institutions, such as cooperative societies, may succeed in combining an appeal both to 'Traditional' and 'Modern' orientations and as such be valuable, if delicate, instruments of transition from the one to the other.

they deal with local problems, how careful they are of others' *hiya* (face), how approachable they are. . . . The Legislative performance of political candidates, except for their fiscalizing activities, are seldom, if ever, referred to in their political campaigns. Indeed, members of Congress have been strong advocates of land reform even though their legislative record is one of consistent opposition to land distribution proposals. . . . Politics is the trading of votes for jobs on public works projects or in return for school houses or roads.[6]

The result is the extreme looseness of party discipline, the constant changes of party labels by politicians and ideological or even policy differences within the parties that characterizes Philippine politics; laws that are habitually honoured more in the breach than in the observance; the routine institutionalization of illegalities (known as 'anomalies') and the plundering of public funds which everybody accepts as the main business of politics – but never entirely openly. There is a word for this too – '*delicadeza*'.

The implications of such a state of affairs for economic development, at any rate for planned development – are obvious. A very wide gap exists between development theory and practice; the civil service is elaborate, but formalistic and corrupt; large programmes of public works are undertaken before elections solely to enable government candidates to give jobs to voters; budgetary controls are virtually impossible; large rake-offs to contractors are commonplace. Although the Philippines are a somewhat extreme case – extremely frank, at any rate – they do illustrate very well a connexion between 'traditionalism' and a style of 'modern' politics that is very widespread in poor countries. Even where the results are much less dramatic, a significant consequence that is almost always present is the fact that ministers will devote a great deal of their time to *politics* – to a constant round of interviews and tours and bargaining – rather than to the urgent policy files placed on their desks by the planners.

2. *Inherited or externally determined institutions and cultural patterns*. The problem is not the importation of the 'wrong sort' of institutions. The closing of the sterile debate as to whether the 'Westminster model' was or was not well suited to African or Asian needs is one benefit, at least, of the various *coups* which

have, with fine impartiality, replaced presidential and cabinet systems alike by the authority of the single party or the army. It is on attitudes that colonialism (both neo- and paleo-) has left a more significant mark: in the amateur tradition of recruitment to the higher civil service, in the political power of conservatively-orientated ministries of finance, in elite- and urban-oriented school systems. These influences might be summed up under two headings: conservatism, and acquisitive individualism. Latin America exhibits the power of both most vividly but their influence in Africa and Asia is scarcely less profound. This leads to the third factor of general importance.

3. *The novelty of the 'new nations'*. Many African countries have only become independent in the 1960s, often with very little preparation by the Colonial powers. In such cases a civil servant may well become a Permanent Secretary within three or four years of leaving university; and in this case he is obviously exceptionally dependent on precedent – on what he can find in the files, and on what he has learned from a succession of expatriate superiors in the course of his hectic rise to the top. He is, in fact, much more likely to be *plus royaliste que le roi* than to be an innovator. Not surprisingly, it is the old and venerated Indian administrative service which has produced a few of the bureaucratic reformers and experimenters which development requires (even if it has not made very much use of them as yet).

One consequence of novelty is, therefore, conservatism. Uncertainty is another. In general, unfamiliar political structures are risks to be insured against. The party in power insures against defeat (which might land them in jail) by electoral manipulation and, as a double insurance, by making private fortunes for banking abroad. The opposition, considering the days of competitive politics numbered, look for allies in the army or police, try to store arms and send young men outside the country for military training. The individual voter insures by looking for a protector – a local leader, who can have his vote in return for keeping him in a job or, more generally, insuring that the locality is never excluded from the government pork barrel. Civil servants insure by passing on as many decisions as possible to the minister and by a retreat into formalism. The forms of reaction to political uncertainty parallel closely those described in the social and economic spheres in chapters four and five and have similarly dangerous results.

Lack of confidence in the new structure is self-justifying. Constitutionalism, already discredited by the rapid succession of pre-independence 'preparatory models', seldom develops around the formal structures of the state and the gap between the political system as it works in theory and in practice is widened.

4. *Poverty itself*. The demands made on governments are not necessarily lighter in poor countries than in rich ones; yet the resources that can be applied to meeting them are small.

TABLE 6·2[7]

Government revenue and extent of radio ownership in countries of different income levels 1960

No. of countries	U.S. dollars mean GNP per capita	Mean central govt. revenue as percentage of GNP	Mean no. of radios per 1,000 people
11	56	17	12
15	87	13	20
31	173	22	57
36	445	25	158
14	1330	27	352

Table 6.2 suggests that in 1960 the governments of very poor countries had to take an average 17 per cent of national income to get revenue equivalent to about $10 per person. A slightly less poor group of countries – though still extremely poor – took 13 per cent of national income to get revenue equivalent to $11 per person. The richest group of countries by contrast, were taking 27 per cent of GNP in revenue: but this produced $358 per person, and still left nearly $1,000 per person in private hands. The poor countries tax themselves hard to produce little and there is seldom anything in hand to cope with political emergencies. The temptation to raid – in effect – the funds needed for development (e.g. by reducing the contribution from recurrent revenue to the so-called capital development budget) is ever-present and not always resisted. Pressure groups cannot be

bought off by concessions if there are no resources to concede; when resources become very scarce, politics increasingly becomes a game in which winner takes all, and correspondingly tense and even violent as the stakes rise. The absence of a substantial private industrial sector in many poor countries has similar consequences: jobs can often only be obtained on the government pay-roll; loans can only be obtained from public or local authorities; the building of a road in the district assumes immense economic significance, attracting correspondingly great political pressures. The political bitterness of the depression years is perhaps the nearest analogy which the experience of the rich countries provides.

The figures on radios in table 6.2 above are an equally striking manifestation of poverty and are hardly less important politically. Even in countries with fifty radios per thousand people, the vast majority of the population in the countryside will be without one although there will be a few sets, in the local store or the school, listened to by many. Very few people will read a national newspaper. In these circumstances the problem of communicating new ideas becomes extremely complex and a shared public view of daily events as they affect the nation as a whole – such as has been a basic fact of politics in most rich countries for a hundred years or more – cannot be assumed. Yet, without such a foundation of common national experience, the ability of governments to 'sell' new national policies is severely reduced.

Although these factors are frequently encountered, their precise effects on politics in any particular country – and through politics on development – depend on a host of others: the historical starting-point of the 'modernization process'; natural resources; the nature of the colonial experience; the sequence in which new external influences, or the presentation of new group demands, make themselves felt; and so on. To take a simple example: where personal political ties correspond to traditional and linguistic ties, the result may be to make an entire region highly responsive to economic innovations, provided they are sponsored by the regional leadership – but it may also result in communalism or even secessionism, at a severe economic cost. By contrast, where personal ties form the basis of factionalism within a large governing party, as in the Indian Congress Party, they usually cut across purely communal (and in that case, caste) loyalties. In this way personal ties may help to integrate the nation, though often at the expense of weakness or even paralysis in economic policy-making. They may also hinder the development of specialized interest organizations of a modern kind.[8]

We must now examine a few common characteristics of political structures in poor countries. Some parts of the political process are more directly related to economic policy-making than others: political elites, institutions for registering demands on the government, and institutions for dealing with demands. This is an abstract way of putting it; and it is tempting instead to refer to institutions like 'parties', 'pressure groups', and so on. But we must guard against the assumption that the functions performed by these institutions in developed countries are necessarily or always performed by them elsewhere. In India as in Britain there are farmers: but whereas in Britain there is a strong farmers' union which presses the farmers' interests on politicians and the Ministry of Agriculture, farmers' organizations in India are relatively weak, in spite of the far greater importance of farming in the economy. But farmers' interests do not go unrepresented in India; the richer farmers get a good deal of what they want through their local influence on the member of parliament and state assemblies in their areas; the poorer ones try to protect their interests on an individual basis by personal ties with richer ones. Similarly, it does not follow that, just because a military junta has abolished parties, no further popular demands are registered with the government: the representative function must sooner or later be assumed by some other 'institution' – perhaps the civil service, perhaps a system of go-betweens, (lawyers, chiefs, scribes – someone who 'knows his way round') etc.[9]

1. *Elites.* The political and bureaucratic elites of poor countries vary greatly in social background but they seldom come from the poorest strata of society. When they do (as did, for example, a proportion of the leaders of some African 'mass' parties) there is some tendency for them to be assimilated to the middle and upper strata. Recruited by patronage, or from an educational system

which itself reflects elitist values, the political and bureaucratic elites in non-communist countries are rarely eager for measures which would entail redistribution of wealth or any threat to their own status or prospects. In the worst cases they can play a selfish and parasitical role in relation to the rest of society. This is, of course, true of elites in all countries. What distinguishes those of poor countries is that the institutions which can hold these tendencies in check and make the elite give the public value for its privileges – parties, interest associations, free elections, an independent press and radio – are so often feeble or non-existent. In many cases military leaders have justified *coups d'état* by the need to replace selfish or corrupt leaders, but owing to their own dependence on the old bureaucracy, if not to lack of good faith, radical economic reforms very rarely materialize. Of course, there is a wide range of variation and there are some notable counter-examples. Presidents Nyerere and Touré are both distinguished by their consistent attempt to prevent the new political elite from trying to institutionalize its own privileges; some civil services – e.g. Pakistan's and India's – stand out as relatively hardworking and incorrupt.

The usual conservatism of the elite does not mean, however, that they will not promote economic development at all. In the first place, economic progress is likely to play a significant part in their ideology, which is usually closely identified with 'modernity'. Secondly, they are seldom monolithic groups; there are generally rifts between politicians and civil servants, between younger and older politicians, or younger and older bureaucrats; and in many countries there are increasingly important counter-elites, who cannot be assimilated by the incumbents because, for instance, there is no money to provide them with jobs in the civil service or because the incumbent elite has an inflexible value-system or inflexible criteria of entry. All these factors provide opportunities for innovation which must be exploited by those who want to accelerate economic development.[10]

2. *Institutions for registering demands*. The weakness or absence of institutionalized structures is itself a major problem. We have already considered the rather common situation in poor countries where specialized interest associations fail to emerge and interests

are promoted individually through personal ties. We have also seen how political parties can fail to serve as vehicles for representing the needs of broad social groups. These situations make the task of economic policy-making more difficult. When general policy is being formulated, no easy direct test can be made of its acceptability among various general interests whose support or acquiescence will be required; explicit bargaining with crucial categories of the public is made much more difficult; party leaders cannot be relied on not to sabotage by innumerable 'anomalies' policies they have publicly agreed on.

This situation also puts an excessive premium on the 'brokerage' skills of the leadership, who must be constantly on the move, keeping in touch with individual lieutenants in all districts, correctly assessing the strength of feeling lying behind new issues and deciding what responses to make. This has two obvious drawbacks in terms of economic development. First, the leaders who excel at this, from Shastri to Akintola, are unlikely to be equally good at grasping and championing economic policies which almost invariably hurt some while benefiting others. Second, failures in the system are liable to feed communal or sectarian feelings, lending support to political groups which are essentially antagonistic to the regime itself.

The weakness of political parties has internal causes as well as those derived from the social structure. This was particularly clear in the case of the African 'mass' parties, which aimed to embrace the whole population but mostly lacked the organizational skills, the financial resources, the ideology and the programme to fulfil this aspiration after independence. Two broad types of governing party emerged – the 'rally' and the 'machine'. The former was normally characterized by a forceful leader appealing directly for mass support, on the basis of an ideological bond between leader and led (such as Sukarno's 'Manipol USDEK' or Nkrumah's early African Socialism) reinforced by a carefully fostered personality cult, ritual and symbolism, parades, public monuments and vigilantes. The latter was non-ideological, and conformed more or less to the type considered above, with its unending round of pledges of support and promise of rewards and a pattern of public policy reflecting the payment of political debts and the nice balancing of political pressures. Most of the West African parties corresponded more or less to this type.

Each type had its own particular weakness. The 'rally' lost support when the interests of different sections of the population diverged after independence, when the ideology proved not to symbolize an effective strategy of development and when the party cadres were absorbed into the government (to ensure political control over the bureaucracy and to provide the cadres with salaries and status). The 'machine' lost support when it could not reconcile all the conflicting claims, and especially when the spoils of office came to be treated as personal perquisites by the politicians and were too sparingly distributed to followers. Both types increasingly substituted suppression of opposition for the support they had lost. This in turn meant bringing the police and the military into the centre of the political arena and neither type proved more resistant than the other when the colonels decided to supplant them.

3. *Institutions for dealing with demands.* This discussion raises another question, the mechanisms through which demands are handled in poor countries. These mechanisms are extremely varied. In Peru, Ecuador, Columbia and Paraguay, landlords on the *latifundia* may often play the role of an absolute ruler. In Pakistan, the bureaucracy accepted the main burden of authority from the army. In Northern Nigeria, the State Government bureaucracies share authority with the army and the native authorities (that is, largely with the traditional ruling group of emirs). In Burma, the army has retained a much larger direct share in administration. In Tanzania, the division of authority is between the bureaucrats and the single party.

Clearly the composition of the ruling elites – their skills, their relationships with other elements in the social and political systems, and their ideologies – will be different in each case, and lead to very different ways of handling the problems of government, but there are some fairly common structural features of particular types of governmental machinery which deserve a brief discussion: in particular, civil services, the single party, and military rule.

Civil services still tend to reflect in their organization and conventions something of the 'night watchman' conception of government which still largely prevailed in the metropolitan powers a hundred years ago, and in many colonies as late as the 1930s. The ideal of the non-technical, 'generalist' administrator still persists overseas; very low levels of economic understanding are encountered at the top of the hierarchy in key ministries, including finance ministries (a problem not unknown in 'developed' countries either); and methods of recruitment and training are rarely designed to attract the entrepreneurial, executive personalities on which the successful management of development projects so largely depends.*

The relative autonomy of ministries, corresponding often to the real political independence of powerful ministers, tends to make the theoretical hegemony of planning offices unreal. Where the procedures of annual budgeting are left largely undisturbed, especially, the 'planning process' tends to become, literally as well as metaphorically, an academic exercise leading to the production of a plan document which is largely unconnected with the real processes of government. At the same time, the lines of responsibility between the field officer and the top of the bureaucratic hierarchy are long. While this befitted a service geared for the sifting out of answers to new problems emerging gradually from a largely autonomous process of change, it does not suit a situation in which change is being engineered and in which field officers are responsible for major projects and need direct access to prompt, high-level support. When their requirements must travel slowly up a long communications pipeline, being more or less unimaginatively re-interpreted by a succession of minute-writers along the way, they become utterly frustrated.

The single political party makes up for some of the characteristic shortcomings of public services as an organization for managing economic change. Its cadres are rarely selected on educational criteria and they usually include many energetic activists. The party's basis in popular support, however imperfect,

*Where there is a strongly based manufacturing sector, as in India, men of enterprise and talent can also earn much more in the private sector than in the civil service.

tends to give those cadres access to local elites and an under-standing of how to secure their cooperation. And, as a rule, party organization can be easily adapted to new needs: party constitu-tions can be revised or simply ignored, party personnel have no formal career ladder and can, within limits, be deployed as needs dictate. The limitations of parties, however, are equally plain. Civil servants can, to some extent, insulate themselves from the pressures of special interests by taking refuge behind their code of impartiality, impersonality, fixed jurisdiction and discipline. Party personnel, on the other hand, are constrained by the bonds, whether ideological or material, which tie the party's supporters to the party. They cannot easily resist pressure for more social services in less well-provided regions when greater regional equality is a major theme of party propaganda, nor can they turn away new applicants for jobs when the local party leadership's support rests on the understanding that their followers will be found employment. Party personnel also tend to lack some of the skills that development requires; in cartoons in the Soviet press the pompous but baffled party secretary, ludicrously out of his depth in some problem of collective farm management, is a stock figure of fun; and the point could be applied with at least equal force to many of the party personnel in the single party regimes of poor countries.

Considering that some kind of military rule is the most widely distributed form of government in poor countries our know-ledge of it is still relatively slight. Before the spread of military rule in Africa, there was much speculation that it would be a modernizing force, on the following grounds:[11]

    (a) armies had both modern technological skills and mo-dern technological attitudes

    (b) armies, and especially their officer corps, were often drawn from relatively lower social strata, and hence were apt to be socially radical

    (c) the units of armies were regionally integrated

    (d) army leaders were bound by a strong patriotic ethic

    (e) armies are disciplined, accustomed to doing things on time, etc.

These speculations, reasonable in themselves, were based on

superficial knowledge of the armies in question. The army in Dahomey has made three coups, without, so far, showing a greater tendency to promote economic development, or, for that matter, any other social change, than the governments it dismissed. Where the military do seem to possess the qualities mentioned above, and also display an interest in economic development, the general tendency of the army to withdraw from direct involvement in government is very marked. This, undoubtedly, is because the distinctive qualities of the armed forces – their discipline, professionalism and their position 'above politics' – are apt to decline very quickly as soon as they become deeply involved in non-military affairs. The most significant form of military rule, therefore, is likely to be what Professor Finer has called 'indirect' or 'dual', in which the military are, in effect, setting the limits within which either politicians or civil servants determine policy goals.[12]

The conditions under which the military are likely to intervene in politics, and the forms which their intervention is likely to take in given circumstances, have been much better explored than the consequences for economic development of military rule. Are some forms of military rule more conducive to rational economic policy-making than others? What distinguishes the decision-making process of juntas from that of other kinds of oligarchy? Does the experience of military rule shed any light on the question whether 'dictatorship' is more efficient than 'democracy' in securing economic development? What makes some military regimes economically more progressive than others – the social origins of the officer corps, the political experience of the commanders, the degree of sympathy shown towards the army by civilian bureaucrats, or what? This is, in fact, an area for research in which political scientists have an obvious contribution to make.

What Can be Done?

The emphasis in this chapter has been on political difficulties in the way of high rates of planned economic growth, partly because of the urgency of competing goals and partly because of the incompatibility of many features of the political framework in poor countries with effective economic policy-making and implementation. This does not mean that growth cannot occur. Some countries may be fortunate enough to secure rapid economic development through largely unplanned enterprise; Japan and Mexico are examples. Others are bound to be more dependent for development on government economic policies: but even when the political system is far from ideally orientated to economic development, it is possible for progress to be accelerated provided that as much trouble is taken with the political and social factors involved as is noramally taken with the economic.

For this to happen we still need a major conceptual or imaginative breakthrough in connexion with the concept of *interdependence* between the economic, social and political systems. While planners recognize from bitter experience that social and political 'factors' have an important bearing on the outcome of economic policies, they accept the idea in the spirit that these factors are so many irksome 'obstacles' which, once they have been pointed out, the politicians should somehow remove. But, while there certainly are areas within which politicians have real choices, and while some politicians are more far-sighted, hardworking and interested in reform than others, the major political 'obstacles to development' are deeply rooted in the structure of society. It is this structure too which largely determines the kind of politician that emerges and the conceptions which politicians have of what is possible and desirable.

It is necessary to grasp the basic idea that the 'economic system' is, after all, an abstraction: it is only one set of roles, (having to do with producing, consuming, trading, saving, etc.) which are played by *people* who are also playing roles in other systems – in a social system of kinship, locality, class and other relations, and a political system of group, competitive and authority relations (to mention only two of the simplest). The behaviour of people in any one of these systems is intimately affected by their involvement in each of the others and, consequently, the working of each system as a whole is in a constant process of adaptation to changes in the others. The way this happens is largely through 'role conflict'. Thus, for instance, population pressure leads to the fragmentation of land holdings down to a size below which men can no longer bequeath viable holdings to each of their sons; their roles as farmers now conflict with their former roles as family heads; their adult sons cease to accept their authority as they start looking elsewhere for economic independence. The decline of the father's role and the enforced new independence of the adult son's role has still further implications for politics, for instance, in making available a new generation of 'young men' who look to 'modern' political leaders for help. This in turn affects the political system in various ways: by altering the type of support it may alter the type of leader who comes to the top and the kind of economic policy that the leadership adopts; and so on back through the economic system.*

Seen in this light economic development implies that sympathetic changes can be made to occur in the social and political systems to permit or stimulate the necessary changes in the economic system. Political leaders are, of course, usually in a position to initiate some changes in each system; but it is very rarely that they are in a position to break a whole range of behaviour patterns at one fell swoop, even after a successful revolution, as Latin American experience shows very clearly.

More usually, politicians are trading resources they have accumulated in one system, so to speak, for resources they require in another. ('Resources' in this sense may be virtually any scarce thing they need – e.g. votes, money, time, prestige.) To get resources in the economic system (say, more revenue) through economic growth, they must consume resources in the political and social systems; e.g. the good will of the trade unions must be used up in wages control, the payment of political debts deferred, sacred cows slaughtered (even literally), new privileged classes created ('emergent farmers'), social unrest accepted. At other

*General systems theory, introduced into social science principally by Talcott Parsons, has been carried farthest in political science by David Easton; for a short statement see his *A Framework for Political Analysis*, Prentice-Hall, Englewood Cliffs, 1965.

times, the trading goes in the opposite direction, with resources from the economic system being consumed in order to acquire social and political ones.

It cannot be emphasized too strongly that no politicians have unlimited credit in any of these 'banks'; and it is particularly unlikely that politicians in very poor countries will have the sort of credit which will allow them to give consistent priority to policies leading to economic development. It should by now be clear why this is so: it is because the social and political structures which are well-adapted to low levels of production are small-scale, particularistic and personalized; and the mechanisms of adaptation to change, when it begins, often reinforce these characteristics, which are directly reflected in the basis of the support enjoyed by political leaders and the kind of political skill which brings them to the top. (An obvious example of this reinforcement process is the use of the tribe as a basis for political action. Tribes have actually been *invented* by certain mixed urban communities needing a basis of solidarity in the face of insecurity and competition from other groups; the 'Bangala' of Congo (Kinshasa) are perhaps the best known.)

This is likely to be the fact of the matter, whatever the leadership's economic aspirations; their political and social 'credit' will usually stand only minor and piecemeal sacrifices among any part of their network of support, whereas rapid economic development is likely to call for extensive and sustained ones. The art of the possible in this situation is to see what changes – social and political, as well as economic – are within the politicians' 'means', and what are not; and what patterns or sequences of change, among those that are practicable, will carry the process of economic development farthest and fastest at the least cost in the politicians' resources.

What is clearly not adequate is to think that merely pointing to social and political 'obstacles to development', followed by an implied invitation to politicians to remove them, is the extent of what has to be done; or that there are organizational panaceas (such as finding the 'right place' for the planning office in the government structure); or that there may be a change of heart ('fundamental administrative reforms' – which somehow never materialize – are a favourite version of this hope); or that, making the best of a bad job, the only thing to do is to 'measure' the 'lack of political will to develop' and put some extra costs to cover it into the economic calculus, adding some percentage to the costs and some extra time to construction periods, and so on.[13] The only constructive answer to the multifaceted problem of development is to start thinking analytically and strategically about political and social change.

This line of thinking implies that other kinds of social scientists beside economists need to be added to the professional planning staff working for governments in poor countries. In the early stages, their contribution will not usually be as neatly compartmentalized or as quantified as that of economists, although their work may well develop rapidly in this direction with greater involvement in practical problems of policy. There is, however, no shortage of tools already available to political scientists and sociologists embarking on this kind of work. Apart from some impressive general work on systems theory and development generally, there are many particular areas in which analysis can be made with some confidence and which are of the utmost importance for development.

A simple illustration comes from a study of cooperatives in Uganda undertaken by a mixed team of social scientists working at the University of East Africa. The cooperative movement in Uganda now handles virtually the entire crop exports of the country and is thus vital to economic development. Yet, like other countries in Africa, Uganda has experienced severe difficulties in getting the cooperatives to work efficiently and honestly, and there is no doubt that this exercises a serious drag on production. The answer to this problem clearly does not lie primarily in economics; part of it is the province of administration. But the most illuminating insights to the nature of the problem came from the work of a political scientist and a political anthropologist – the former working at the level of the cooperative unions, or associations of primary (growers') societies, the latter at the level of, in fact, one particular primary society. Both found a number of critical political factors at work in determining the performance of the cooperatives. The primary society, in particular, had run at a loss for most of its career; and the fundamental cause was that the leaders who originally started it had been interested in politics. The then colonial administration worked to insulate the co-operative movement from politics, however, so that these 'spiralists' (men working their way up out of the local community) shifted their energies into party activity. Their abilities and business sense (most of them had commercial incomes of one sort or another) were thus lost to the society and their place was taken by the traditional leaders of the locality, who used the society as an arena for factional conflict and left its management, which they did not really understand or care about, to dishonest and incompetent appointed officials. They were, however, experts at the game of patronage and fixing elections, and they effectively resisted threats to their control of the society until its affairs were so desperate that in 1965 the cooperative union finally threatened to withhold the usual credit against the coming season's crop, and, in 1966, even to liquidate the society. By this time the opportunities for political 'spiralling' had been severely reduced and there was once again a pool of capable people interested in holding office. In face of the crisis, democratic procedures finally prevailed and a new and competent management committee was elected. The society stopped running at a loss.[14] Understandably, it was just at this time that the government had become prone to step in and replace elected committees of management by appointed managers and secretaries. Thus, many societies retrogressed to a system of control by officials just when the conditions for advance – lessons of experience plus people capable of applying them – were at last available.

The analysis described here related to an extremely small unit of economic organization and was not designed as a contribution to planning, but its potential for large-scale policy-making is obvious. There seems to be no reason why, in preparing a development plan, a practical analysis of the cooperative movement in terms of its political and social context should not be prepared – with policy recommendations appropriate to the various types of society and union and their environments and stages of development – for incorporation in the plan. Nor is there any reason why the same principle should not be extended to other sectors and indeed to the social and political systems as a whole.

Political science may also have a contribution to make to the whole process called 'planning'. Everyone knows that planning needs to be a continuous process of analysis, goal-setting, more analysis, action, feedback, re-analysis, resetting of goals, etc. indefinitely. But few countries really tackle development in this way and, while many plans are drawn up, few are successfully implemented. We have already seen how the administrative machine rarely conforms to the procedures that would be required and waiting for it to do so will usually mean a very long wait indeed. From a political point of view, aiming for 'comprehensive' planning before the policy-making of individual ministries is subject to planning is often a clear case of trying to run before you can walk. It may, however, be necessary to establish a central ministry or office of planning first in order to illustrate and champion the whole idea of planning among the administration generally. An effective system of continuous reporting, evaluation and policy-revision might, however, be more easily established within the framework of a single ministry. In a single sector, the true costs of alternative policies can be more easily analysed; the interdependencies are more specialized and, indeed, better understood by politicians.

Obviously, what should happen is that the available professional planners should be distributed in a sensible balance between the central office charged with overall planning, and a number of ministries and other agencies responsible for priority areas. As things are, there is a tendency for all the professionals to be engaged on overall planning, while the ministries whose actions the plan is supposed to coordinate follow their own devices. If a choice has to be made it might well be better, once the initial idea of planning has been effectively established, to concentrate the planners in a limited number of priority ministries.

Another aspect of the planning process that needs attention is the business of 'choice' itself. The situation in which political leaders are asked to choose the major targets of the plan is one of the few in which political life appears to resemble daily life in the matter of choosing, and as we have seen, the results are often quite unreal. Political systems, or even just central government machines, are not as well integrated as individuals, and the process of 'choice' rarely consists of an explicit 'moment' at which some appropriate person or committee reviews the alternatives, weighs their pros and cons and consciously selects one of them. It is, generally, a continual process of options foregone, through the passage of time, and through the taking of other decisions which have the often unforeseen consequence of closing off possibilities in spheres not considered at all in the context of the decision.*

Planning, however, is a process of choice above all else; and it needs to be designed in such a way that the processes by which decisions are really made in a given society do not remain entirely outside its scope. 'Documentism' (the preparation of an impressive plan document to which no organ of government is committed and without fairly elaborate machinery for ensuring that policy-making and action conform to it) is fundamentally due to a failure to grasp this central feature of governmental decision-making.

A final precept under this heading seems too obvious to mention were it not so commonly ignored. This is to devote as large a share of resources – of personnel and time – to making certain of political support for planned policies, as to drawing up the document which contains them. Indeed, speaking generally, the process of planning needs to be designed to fit the political and administrative structure of the country. It must reflect the sanctions and incentives that the government actually commands and the people will tolerate, the traditions and career structures of the administration, the range and penetration of the changes which it is supposed to bring about. This seems obvious but it has not usually been done. Very little thought has been given to it, in fact, and some highly incongruous systems have been imported (it has been a great field for post-colonial institutional importations), with consequently disappointing results. Above all, most planning structures devote too large a share of resources – of personnel and time – to making plans, and too little to ensuring

*And such decisions taken by officials and politicians will often be thought of as having somehow 'nothing to do' with economics or planning at the time they are made.

that what is in the plans will be assured of enough political support to ensure that it will be carried out. Discovering what political strategy will secure the necessary minimum of support, and helping politicians to put it into effect, should be a major, if not the principal function of a planning agency.

PART THREE

NATIONAL STRATEGIES FOR DEVELOPMENT

7 ECONOMIC STRATEGIES

The Ideal Plan

In attempting to design a strategy for economic development, it is natural for a tidy-minded person to contrast a given set of ends or objectives or targets with a set of available means or instruments. The ends may be consistent or competing, they may be intermediate and thus means to further, more ultimate, ends or they may represent ends that are valued for their own sake, and they may be partly or wholly determined by the preferences of the electorate or by the ideals of the planning elite.

Such a set of ends would contain the flow of aggregate consumption over time, a comparative valuation of future and present consumption, a specification of a desirable distribution of this flow between households, possibly also employment levels, the rate of price rises, conditions of work, freedom of choice and the quality of life.

If we can gain knowledge of the structural relations of the economy and of the whole society, we are able to construct a system of inter-dependent relationships. The causes discovered by economic analysis are turned into means and the effects into ends.

If competing ends can be rendered commensurable, so that we can say how much less of one objective we are ready to accept for a given increase in the achievement of a competing objective, we can reduce the problem to that of the maximization of an index. In order to separate successfully the sphere of values which determine the ends from the sphere of facts, we should have to assume: (a) that people attach to means no independent value but only 'instrumental' value, i.e. they value them only in terms of their effects; (b) that people attach to ends independent value only and never consider them as means to other ends; (c) that no other effects of means than the 'given' ends have independent value.

Yet, commonsensical though it seems, the separation of given ends from alternative neutral means is not always appropriate. More ultimate ends often emerge or disappear in the process of the attempt to achieve intermediate ends; means acquire and lose the characteristics of ends. The task is not simply to promote given ends, even those of the small elite of the planners, but to create the incentive and desire, not only in others, for new ends, e.g. to transform a society governed by tradition into one susceptible to experiment and innovation; to remove end characteristics from certain activities (ignominy or dignity attached to certain jobs and professions) and to make others into ends (business success, experimentation, novelty, enrichment).

The whole process of economic development from a tradition-bound to a modern society can be described as: let there be means where there were ends! The introduction of the contractual cash nexus where previously incommensurable duties and rights prevailed, the substitution of business obligations for those of tribal and kinship relations widen the area of instrumental values at the expense of independent values. In many underdeveloped societies the payment and receipt of interest on loans above a certain limit is immoral and illegal. The removal of the moral stigma and the legal restriction may pave the way to a rational use of scarce capital. The notion of the 'just price' endows with moral value prices which, in a more advanced society, have a purely instrumental value.*

Similarly, the choice of a profession by Hindus will lose end-characteristics as development occurs and acquire means-characteristics. For a Brahman's son in India to cultivate land is as scandalous as for a canon's son in our society to become a pimp. But the change in valuations, which deprives certain activities of their stigma, increases the flexibility of resources. As workers can be switched from tending machines to sweeping floors because caste attitudes have been shed, 'labour' acquires a signifi-

---

*At a later stage, however, independent (political) value may again be attached to certain prices (e.g. wage rates, house rents, interest rates and, above all, foreign exchange rates).

cance which it does not have if trades are reserved for specific castes. In this way changes in valuations reduce obstacles to economic development. This in turn strengthens the positive values attached to development and eases the way for further measures to reduce these obstacles.

Similarly, 'underemployment' and 'unemployment' acquire significance only in relation to a standard working week, discipline and punctuality, which do not exist in rural peasant societies. Leisure and work are not substitutes and the question of a comparative evaluation does not arise. Only the introduction of wage–labour and organized production changes the valuations, clears an area of 'means' (viz. working hours supplied) and can then be fitted into the plan. To begin planning with the notion of 'unemployment' in such a society is doubly misleading: it begs the policy issue as to what specific measures are necessary to mobilize human resources and it tacitly assumes the valuation of an urban industrial society with respect to the standard working week and attitudes to work. Yet, in the process of successful planning, as independent valuations of each trade are shed and as work and cooperation are organized, 'underemployment' and 'unemployment' and their underlying value judgements acquire significance and become meaningful and measurable.

The means-ends model lies behind much of the theory of planning and, in particular, the notion of the *Ideal Plan*. A set of objectives or targets is contrasted with a set of means or instruments. There are two major difficulties here. First, there is the problem of distinguishing ends and means. Many objectives will have not only independent value but will also be of instrumental value; on the other hand, nearly all instruments will have independent value as well. Secondly, there is the difficulty of quantifying the variables in the model. Assuming that we have complete knowledge of all relevant conditions and their causal connexions, we must then estimate their initial magnitudes and their coefficients of change; these coefficients would normally vary according to the direction, size and speed of the change, according to whether the instruments are applied autonomously or in response to other changes, and according to whether the instruments are applied in isolation or in several possible combinations.*

Quite apart from the practical impossibility of acquiring even a fraction of the required knowledge and apart from the difficulty of selecting the relevant objectives and clarifying their independent and instrumental values, there are logical difficulties in formulating such a plan. The picture presented by the model not only fails to correspond to any conceivable practical plan, but is also seriously misleading as an abstract guide for planners, though it may have useful limited applications.

First, the plan itself and its execution will alter the material and the causal relations which it assumes to be given. Obstacles to development put up by inertia, resistance and hostility, which present initial limitations, will normally be weakened or removed, though some may be strengthened.

Secondly, inhibitions of the planners themselves, when it comes to executing reforms which weaken the power and prestige of the classes to which they belong, constitute another form of initial limitation, which will change in the development process.

Thirdly, there is a basic problem over objectives. Unless these express actual valuations, relevant to the developing economy, the plan remains an academic exercise. But a plan attempts to alter the society in which these valuations are rooted.

The (workable) plan is not a complete blueprint. It is an unfolding vision with a built-in tendency for change. It neither accepts all political obstacles as ultimate constraints, nor ignores them as 'non-economic' factors. Its function is to turn means into ends and ends into means where the development process requires this, and to improve on itself by so doing. To postulate a sharp means-ends or targets-instruments dichotomy is to ignore this process of transformation, and thus the political reality of a development plan.

Albert Hirschman interprets the publications and activities of the Economic Commission for Latin America not as the blue-

*The independent value attached to the means will also normally vary with the direction, size and speed of the change and according to what accompanying measures are taken.

print of planners, but as protests against 'certain inveterate traits such as the propensity to improvise, the lack of foresight, the failure ever to see the handwriting on the wall'. ECLA's attitude springs from the 'desire to stamp out those traditional traits which are felt to be hindrances and handicaps on the road to economic progress'.[1] From this point of view the function of the planners is to reform the national framework of planning itself: the point of the programme is to change the dismal prognosis which the acceptance of existing obstacles, including institutions, valuations and attitudes, would involve.[2]

Similarly, a plan for the acceptance of certain minimum living standards after fifteen years for the poorest 20 per cent of the people was proposed by the Perspective Planning Division of the Indian Planning Commission in 1962 not only as an obviously desirable objective, but also as a rallying point of divergent political interests and as a means of achieving agreement on certain consequential policies.*

One of the tasks of planning is thus to create and improve the process of planning itself. There is no confrontation of a sphere of social ends with a sphere of available neutral means, but a continual interaction of necessarily incomplete programmes and prognoses, both containing political and social, as well as physical, limitations.

We therefore conclude that the notion of an ideal or optimum plan is misleading if it assumes: (a) that objectives are given from outside; (b) that we can draw upon a full causal analysis taking account of differences according to whether the instruments are applied singly or in various combinations, whether once-for-all

*'Another function of the perspective plan is to educate public opinion on issues of development and to promote the kind of open discussion that is likely to secure a common consensus of political parties. This is perhaps easier in a poor society in which all can agree without controversy on at least one objective: the abolition of poverty. When the purpose is nothing less than to transform society, planning ceases to be an esoteric subject or a mathematical exercise. It must be imbued with deep social purpose and revolutionary zeal.' PANT, P., 'The Development of India', *Technology and Economic Development*, Penguin, 1965.

or sustained, and that we know coefficients which will differ according to the direction, size and speed of the change; (c) that there is no interdependence between given targets and known instruments.

A realistic plan should rather be regarded as a steadily forward-moving pattern of policies, which have to be modified continually in the light of newly emerging events, changing causal connexions and revised valuations. The programmes of the planners and the prognoses of social researchers are not two independent areas, but the programmes affect and alter the prognoses, and the prognoses in turn alter and modify the programmes. A plan is not a static two-tier structure but an evolving process. Planning aims not at an *optimum* but at *improvements*. It is guided by a vision, but the vision is open-ended and flexible, not closed and rigid. It contains a rough perception of the connexions between conditions prevailing over a period of time and the possibilities of moving, through rationally co-ordinated policies, towards changing objectives.

Resource Allocation and Resource Mobilization

Another reason why the conventional model of the process of planning is not very useful is because it treats the central policy issue as the reallocation of given resources for more efficient production and as the increased supply of traditional factor inputs like labour and capital. But recent work has shown that the gains in increased production from a more efficient allocation through, say, reducing monopoly or trade restrictions or through promoting regional integration are very small compared with the gains to be achieved through improved incentives, improved motivation and better organization.[3] The crucial questions of economic policy must therefore be concerned with how the returns from expenditures and from inputs can be raised. It is now generally known that labour productivity can vary within wide limits according to the quality and motivation of the labour force. Better nutrition, health and education, as well as better organization and motivation of a given number of workers can raise output by much more than the reallocation of workers of given productivity from low- to high-productivity activities.

The same is true of capital. The variations in the capital/output ratio resulting from different forms of organization and motivation are substantial and recent work has shown that, historically, self-sustained growth has been reached with much lower investment/income ratios than those postulated by those who have followed Rostow and believed a high ratio was needed for the 'take-off'. It has resulted from an improved utilization of existing capital.[4] While these historical lessons are of limited value for the reasons given in chapter five (the technology available today to underdeveloped countries is capital-intensive, unlike that used a hundred years ago), together with supporting theoretical and empirical evidence, they point to the error of assuming rigid coefficients between capital and output.

Among economists the main controversies on policy have been concerned with the following types of question: Should the emphasis be on consumption now, or on investment to yield high levels of future consumption? Should techniques be labour- or capital-intensive? Should growth be balanced or unbalanced? Should investment be raised in agriculture or in industry? Should the emphasis be on the promotion of exports or on domestic production which replaces imports? Should planners use price incentives and market forces or control directly economic activity? Should they enlarge the public sector or leave more scope to the private? Should they improve agricultural production by one major strategic act – a dam or a road – or should they apply a package consisting of rural extension services, transport and communication, irrigation and drainage, improved seeds, fertilizers and pesticides, improved storage, credit and marketing facilities, more reliable prices, land reform, education, health and many more? Should they disperse industry widely to placate political claims and to stimulate local development, or should they concentrate it to exploit economies of scale and create growth poles?

These questions are much more complex than they appear to be. An illustration is provided by the debate about the correct strategy with regard to the time path of consumption. The choice is usually pictured as in Fig. 7.1. C_1 and C_2 illustrate two alternative time flows of consumption, which are technically possible, according to whether investment is allocated to the sector making machines to make machines for more consumption goods later (C_1), or to the sector making consumption goods now (C_2). A similar difference is presented by the choice between capital-using and capital-saving techniques.

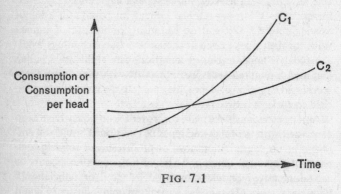

FIG. 7.1

One reason why the answers to such problems are not simple is that apparently quite distinct strategic choices are in fact inter-related. Thus, it has been argued that that technique should be chosen by planners which yields the highest surplus of production over consumption, so that accumulation can proceed at the fastest possible rate, consistent with a minimum level of living of workers and political acceptability. But this surplus depends itself upon the distribution of production between wages and (private and public) profits. For the income distribution determines the proportion of savings out of income which can profitably be allocated to investment. The choice between more consumption now and more consumption (than would otherwise have been possible) later, the choice of techniques and the choice of the allocation of investment between sectors are interdependent. The choice of techniques determines the income distribution between profits and wages, which determines the proportion of savings generated, which again determines the best techniques to be employed.

Secondly, strategy involves non-economic factors too. The choice between different time flows of consumption or consumption per head is said to depend upon the time preference of the community or the social rate of time discount. Within one generation, the lower utility of £1 to a rich man than to a poor man provides a guide, but between generations such comparisons are not meaningful. The real long-term choice is a moral and political one, depending on the weight given to the improvement of living standards of future generations and on the political process by which joint decisions can be enforced. A dictatorship would be able to give nearly the same weight to increases in future consumption as to these in current consumption and would, within the limits of avoiding a revolt, be able to impose draconian measures of saving, whereas a democracy might have to allow for the shorter time horizon of the electorate and discount more heavily future increases if they benefited future generations, however favourable the technical opportunities.

But the weakness of this type of reasoning is that – once more – fixed ratios are presupposed. Thus, the trend of consumption per head depends not only on the total ratio of income set aside as saving and the capital intensity of the investments carried out with these savings. It also depends on the success or failure of a programme of birth control, but this is only tenuously related to the amount of expenditure devoted to building clinics, training doctors and producing contraceptives.

Finally, we come to the controversy over how selective the development strategy should be, bearing in mind the need to attack on all fronts at once. The lessons to be learned from history – in developing the United States or Australia – are of limited value. Human attitudes, skills, motivations and social institutions then were already adapted to economic progress, or were easily and quickly adaptable, plentiful capital was available on cheap terms, land and resources were abundant and trade opportunities were favourable. In such circumstances, a simple strategic measure, like a canal or a railway, can spark off development. But a different strategy may well be needed in a different context. The single 'strategic' action may simply result in waste, unless

149

complementary and supplementary actions are taken in other areas to ensure that it will be effective. There is no universal or simple answer to the dilemma between trying to do everything – which is impossible – and picking out a few things – which may be futile; between waste resulting from lack of complementary, supporting measures and waste resulting from trying to do too much. Yet, it is this dilemma which a development strategy has to face. The choice of the correct policy package, selecting from all useful actions the strategic ones, but combining those that are necessary for each other, will have to be made in the light of the particular resources and institutions of each country or region. There is not much that can be said at a very general level and the correct combination of policies for each country or region is unique and has to be based on close study of the particular circumstances.

8 THE EXTERNAL ECONOMIC STRATEGY: OUTWARD-OR INWARD-LOOKING?*

We shall discuss in this chapter what is the role of foreign trade and, more generally, international transactions of various kinds, in a process of development. One of our major concerns will be to ask what can be done to prevent foreign exchange shortage imposing a severe constraint on development.

One of the reasons why trade is necessary for growth is that an increasing flow of imports is normally essential to sustain a growing industrial sector. But imports have to be paid for, and limited earnings of foreign exchange have induced many poor countries to pursue a protectionist or 'inward-looking' policy, to conserve foreign exchange and close their economies to foreign influences. This in turn has aggravated some of their balance-of-payments problems, leading many economists to suggest – and some countries to revert to – a more open policy based on export expansion, what could be called an 'outward-looking' policy.

The essentials of an outward-looking policy are the removal of, at least, many import restrictions, a more cautious use by the government of direct controls, greater reliance on exchange policy (including devaluation), and adoption of an orthodox monetary and fiscal policy. Such measures are expected to maintain price stability, increase the value of exports, restrict import substitution to industries that can produce at reasonably low costs, increase competition, and encourage the acquisition of skills and the adoption of modern technology. Most of this chapter is devoted to examining the merits of these policy approaches.

The chapter concludes with a brief mention of some of the

*The author wishes to thank the Shell Grants Committee, Shell Centre, for providing a Research Fellowship for research in economics at the Institute of Development Studies.

wider issues raised by the choice of more or less outward-looking strategies; the political, social and economic impact in the poor countries of international transactions with the rich ones.

The Role of Trade in Development

As has been shown in the previous chapter, there is no simple formula for economic development. However, economists have always recognized the crucial role that international trade can play. To begin with, resources that are valueless given the limitations of the internal market acquire value through international trade and can be brought into production; examples are metals and oil which have growing markets in developed countries, land previously unused which can be cultivated in order to export food or agricultural raw materials to the industrialized areas, or unemployed labour which can find profitable employment in labour-intensive production geared to external markets. What is more, a potential for savings usually exists, even in very poor countries, which is not tapped because of the lack of profitable opportunities for investment; so the opening of trade, by making it profitable to invest in the production of exportable goods and in the production of goods and services that supply the export sector, can increase substantially the supply of savings. Re-invested profits reinforce this process, which can lead to big increases in productivity. And the new opportunities opened by profitable trade can attract resources from abroad, capital and some types of labour flowing from the most developed countries.

Secondly, trade, according to classical theory, enables a country to specialize in the production of those commodities in which it enjoys a comparative advantage, that is to say those goods it can produce relatively more cheaply than other countries. By exporting these goods and importing those of which it is a relatively inefficient producer, the total volume of goods available for consumption and investment is increased.

Thirdly, the relations that a country establishes through trade with the outside world affect its whole economic, social and political environment. Growth depends not only on an increased supply of capital but also on the ability of entrepreneurs and workers to combine and use more efficiently the various factors of production. The learning process that is required to acquire those skills can be furthered through competition. (This point is developed below.) Moreover, by importing capital goods a country obtains the advanced technology of the rich countries embodied in their machinery. The development of new exports usually requires the creation of new techniques of production or the adaptation of old ones.* Social changes which are part of the development process can also be affected; the prestige of entrepreneurial activities is enhanced; workers become accustomed and willing to work in a more regular and disciplined way; rational economic calculation and the introduction of technological change come to be accepted as prestigious activities. All these changes have, of course, their political repercussions too, and there is one additional political effect – the government will be able to increase substantially its financial resources through the taxation of both exports and imports.

Yet the classical theory of comparative advantage cannot be taken over uncritically. Poor countries require a substantial and increasing flow of imports if they are to grow at a rapid rate. These imports consist of capital goods, raw materials and semi-manufactures, which are mainly to be used in the industrial sector, and which cannot for various reasons be produced at home. It is, of course, a great advantage to be able to import these goods, but the inability of poor countries to earn sufficient foreign exchange to pay for their total required imports, including the attractive consumer goods available abroad, has led them in many cases to adopt an 'import substituting' strategy, or what is also called an 'inward-looking policy'.

This involves forgoing some of the gains that can be obtained from trade. Moreover, an inward-looking policy can be self-defeating. It is characterized by an effort to reduce the volume of imports of goods that could be produced at home or the consumption of which could be limited (such as luxury goods), in order to

*As we have seen, this can mean that imported techniques may be inappropriate in the economic circumstances of a poor country.

153

use all the foreign exchange available to purchase essential goods. But to produce at home goods previously imported, one needs to import capital goods and a constant stream of raw materials and spare parts. Consequently while the industrial sector grows, the volume of these imports must necessarily increase for some time, and many poor countries are now suffering from particularly intractable difficulties in dealing with their balance-of-payments deficits.

The 'Trade Gap' of Poor Countries

The UNCTAD conferences of 1964 and 1968* highlighted this problem through their elaboration and measurement of the concept of the 'trade gap'. Let us look at this concept.

For the 1968 UNCTAD conference, the secretariat repeated an exercise already carried out for the previous (1964) conference, and also attempted by the GATT secretariat and Bela Balassa shortly afterwards.[1] This involves the projection of the exports and imports of poor countries at a future date, and also their payments of interest and profits, and their inflows of private capital and aid, on certain assumptions. The assumptions refer mainly to the rate of growth of poor and rich countries, and the rate of investment in the poor countries. Given the rate of growth of the rich countries, one can estimate how their requirements of raw materials and primary commodities will grow, and hence the exports of poor countries. Given the rate of growth of the poor

*See chapter one. In 1962 the Economic and Social Council of the United Nations decided to convene a conference to discuss the problems of international trade and development. The conference was organized by a preparatory committee, where the influence of Dr Raul Prebisch, secretary general of the conference, was paramount. The first United Nations Conference on Trade and Development was held in Geneva from March to June 1964 and it was decided there that UNCTAD should become a permanent body and further conferences be called. The second conference took place in New Delhi in February and March 1968.

countries, one can calculate how their imports will grow, in particular their imports of capital goods. Exports of manufactures from the poor countries, their outflows of interest and profit, the inflow of capital and aid are also estimated using more or less sophisticated techniques. The results of these calculations, as prepared for the 1968 UNCTAD conference, are shown in table 8.1.

TABLE 8.1

International transactions of all poor countries* in 1963 (actual) and 1975 (projected).[2]

		billions of U.S. dollars	
	1963	1975† Low	High
1. Exports of goods and services (at 1960 prices)	37·6	67·5	73·5
2. Imports of goods and services (at 1960 prices)	37·5	70·9	83·5
3. Factor income (interest and profits)	4·9	12·0	14·2
4. Technical assistance‡	1·0	1·5	1·5
5. Trade gap: 1 − (2+3+4)		16·9	25·7
6. Official aid, net	6·6	8·5	12·9
7. Private capital, net	2·8	4·4	5·4
8. Unfilled gap: 5 − (6+7)		4·0	7·4

It is important to understand what these projections mean. They are clearly not a prognosis of the future; they are the best estimate of what the UNCTAD secretariat believes *would* happen to various variables if the poor countries managed to sustain a certain rate of overall growth, if imports grow in a given relation

*'Poor' countries are all countries except the socialist bloc, Western Europe, the U.S., Canada, Japan, Australia, New Zealand and South Africa.

†The low and high projections correspond to rates of growth of 5·2 per cent for poor countries and 4·2 per cent for rich countries, and 6·1 per cent for poor countries and 4·7 per cent for rich countries respectively.

‡Expenditures, salaries of experts, consultants, etc. usually financed by aid.

with total production and investment in the poor countries, if exports grow in a given relation with the increase in production in rich countries, and so on. All these assumptions should be looked at critically, since changes in tastes, technology, tariff policies, exchange rates, income distribution, etc., would change the relations specified in the U N CT A D calculations.

However, if one accepts the validity of the assumptions, the results are an 'unfilled gap' of between U.S. $4·0 billions and U.S. $7·4 billions, even assuming a substantially increased flow of aid and private investment. This means that either the poor countries' rate of growth will be slowed down or new policies will have to be devised to increase their foreign exchange earnings. This is the main value of the calculations, to highlight the need and the urgency for a new and imaginative approach to the trading problems of these countries.

However, it might legitimately be asked, why should the poor countries have specially serious balance-of-payments problems? Cannot a country when in balance-of-payments deficit redress the situation through appropriate policies such as devaluation? Devaluation makes exports cheaper for foreigners, increasing therefore the volume of sales; likewise imports are made more expensive and purchases from abroad are reduced. Some income will be lost through a deterioration of the terms of trade, since exports must be sold at lower prices if the volume of exports is to be increased (reckoning prices in foreign currency) and it is very unlikely that imports will be obtained at reduced prices (since imports of the devaluing country are probably a small proportion of world demand); but this loss of income would be smaller than that suffered if imports were to be restricted through tariffs, quotas or other barriers to trade. If imports are restricted, according to traditional international trade theory, there is a loss of income due to misallocation of resources; factors of production that could be producing valuable exports are employed in the manufacture of import substitutes where their productivity is lower.*

*We are leaving out of account the rather sophisticated case in favour of optimum tariffs or restrictions. The argument is in brief that the income of a country can be increased, assuming no retaliation,

But if devaluation is to succeed, a country must be able to expand rapidly the production of its exportable goods, or develop new products for the international market, or start producing at home goods previously imported.* This requires a certain adaptability of the economic system; the ability to move resources – capital, labour, land, etc. – from one line of production to another in response to changes in the relative prices of final products or factors, and the organizational capacity to combine these factors efficiently so as to produce those goods where the country concerned enjoys a comparative advantage. And the process of adaptation should be relatively quick; if it takes five years to adapt the economy to changing patterns of world demand and supply, by the time this process – and it can be painful – is completed, a new set of circumstances will be confronting the country and a new process of adaptation will have to be set in motion.

Typically, poor countries are not adaptable. What is more, precisely those commodities they can produce relatively easily have poor prospects in world markets. As we have seen before,† their exports consist mainly of primary commodities. The world demand for primary commodities is usually price-inelastic, that is to say an increase in the volume supplied by say 5 per cent would reduce prices by more than 5 per cent. Clearly in that case it does not pay to increase the volume of exports; the total amount of foreign exchange received by exporting a larger volume of exports would be less than would be received by exporting a smaller volume. Of course, if demand is inelastic, why then not *reduce* the volume of exports? Prices would rise by a higher percentage than the fall in volume and the total inflow of foreign exchange be increased. This in fact has and is being done; the

---

by imposing tariffs at such a level as to make the best of the possibility of inducing changes in the prices of the goods it sells or buys, just as a monopolist can restrict his sales or purchases, in order to be able to charge higher prices or obtain goods or services at lower prices.

*For logical completeness, one should add that less of both exportable and importable goods could be consumed at home, by increasing the consumption of non-traded goods, and thus reducing the volume of imports and releasing more goods for export.

†Chapter one.

example of Brazil burning her surplus coffee is well known, and Canada often prefers to stock great quantities of wheat rather than spoil the market. However when there are many countries exporting the same commodity, coordination among them to raise the price is difficult. Moreover to exploit the advantage an inelastic demand curve offers to the exporters can be a very risky business; higher prices can and do stimulate the development of synthetic or other substitutes.

Even if demand for the total exports of any particular product is inelastic, demand for the exports of any one producing country can be elastic, provided it accounts for only a small share of the total market. By slightly reducing its price, such a country can greatly increase its exports at the expense of its competitors. In the limiting case, a very small country would be confronted with an infinitely elastic demand curve – at the ruling price it could sell as much as it could produce – just as the individual farmer can sell all his wheat without affecting the market price, since his output is such a minute proportion of total supply. This introduces a real element of conflict between poor countries, but, one could argue, would allow the more able among them to grow rapidly, even if at the expense of the others.

In practice things are not so simple. Many poor countries are not small, in the sense of supplying only a small fraction of the world market demand. Oil is exported mainly by four middle east countries, and Libya and Venezuela; copper by Zambia and Chile; tin by Malaysia; cocoa by Ghana and Nigeria and so on. In other cases international agreements limit the possibility of expanding exports through the imposition of export quotas. Finally, it would be very likely that if any one country started to increase its exports through an aggressive pricing policy, others would retaliate, leaving everybody worse off eventually.

The fact that demand is usually price-inelastic – in other words that devaluation might not be a very effective way of expanding exports of primary commodities – would not be much of a problem if there was a strong upward trend in demand – if, to use another technical word, demand was 'income-elastic' i.e. if it increased year by year in proportion, or more than in proportion, to the growth in the national incomes of the rich countries. In that case, poor countries would still be able to expand their exports, without suffering a fall in prices. But, as has been pointed out in chapter one, this simply is not the case nowadays, except for a few primary commodities such as oil.

Confronted with this situation, the governments of many underdeveloped countries believed that they faced a choice between a slower rate of growth or an 'inward-looking policy' of reducing imports through artificial restrictions to trade and through rapid industrialization. Some of them, especially in Latin America, chose an inward-looking policy. In more than one sense it can be claimed this policy was successful; however, after a certain time, their balance-of-payments problems have been intensified, and in some cases the net result may be a slower rate of growth, anyway.

Import Substitution Policies

As we said in the first section, certain imports are essential to sustain a rapid rate of growth, especially in the industrial sector. Rather than reduce these and harm its rate of growth, a country can attempt to cut down on non-essential imports – typically consumer goods – and manufacture them at home. However, there are some serious snags in a policy of import substitution carried out behind a high protective wall of tariffs and other trade restrictions. When a country is at a very low level of development, with very little if any manufacturing, the principal limitation to a policy of import substitution might be the size of the market. A certain minimum level of production of shoes, textiles or cement is required if costs are to be kept reasonably low and this minimum could not be absorbed in a country where either the population is small or income levels are low. A private entrepreneur would simply not find it profitable to put up a factory unless there were special export prospects. This problem has suggested to Nurkse the theory of 'balanced growth';[3] What is required, he argues, is a simultaneous increase in various lines of production. Higher incomes earned in the production of

159

shoes can then be spent in textiles and cement and other goods, and likewise in every line of production, thereby markets are expanded and an efficient scale of production can be achieved justifying each investment. Leaving aside the difficulties of implementing simultaneously a substantial production increase on a broad industrial front, one drawback is that poor people tend to spend much of their increased incomes on food. Therefore, an increased surplus of food would have somehow to be extracted from the agricultural sector. This can be done, and it does not necessarily imply an increased volume of production in the agricultural sector. But the difficulties of either expanding agricultural production or reducing the consumption of food of the peasants can hardly be exaggerated. And if an increased surplus of food could not be obtained from the agricultural sector, one would have to increase imports of food, thereby bringing back the balance-of-payments problem in another form.

There is a stage of so-called 'easy' import substitution – the production of shirts, beer and soft drinks, confectionery, etc., which can be produced for even small markets.* But most countries have already passed this stage a long time ago, and many of the larger economies have gone on (often quite justifiably) to produce textiles, cement, steel, newsprint, etc. But it takes a very large and advanced economy to go further than this and to produce (economically) engineering products, especially capital equipment. A capital goods industry requires not merely a big market, but also the ability to concentrate savings and entrepreneurship in a few big firms, and it assumes the availability of managers, technicians and skilled labour. Furthermore, this type of import substitution also induces imports; first because capital goods have to be imported to make capital goods and these are generally speaking of a high value relatively to their output, second because replacements and spare parts will still have to be imported. Moreover, as at any stage of import substitution, higher incomes can result in higher imports of food or other consumer goods.

Then the drawbacks of an inward-looking policy are felt. Protection means in general a high-cost type of industry that

*This is often 'easy' because it has been neglected previously.

hinders the growth of others; for instance, a shipbuilding industry is hard to establish wherever it has to buy its steel from the local steel mills at prices much higher than those quoted in the international market. More fundamental is the possible damage to the spirit of enterprise. Entrepreneurs who are secure from competition are not likely to be very cost conscious or to be ready to introduce modern technology. Nor are they likely to take on the long-term planning and risk-taking involved in setting up a large capital-intensive factory. The creation of such units of production is discouraging in other ways too. Since imports are kept out artificially, governments can engage in inflationary policies and keep their rate of exchange overvalued, without feeling the impact immediately on the country's reserves of foreign exchange; inflation increases the risks (relative to other types of investments) of capital-intensive projects that take long to mature, increases the difficulties of forward planning and reduces the likelihood of finding markets abroad for part of the output.

Some of these drawbacks are of course not necessarily the consequence of a protectionist inward-looking policy. Certainly, when protection is introduced, prices and costs are distorted relatively to international prices and costs; this affects the growth of new industries and especially the possibilities of developing exports of manufactures, and competition is eliminated or at least reduced. Inflationary policies, overvaluation of the exchange rate, corruption in for instance the granting of import licences, could in theory be avoided, however, if poor countries enjoyed administrations able to (and politicians willing to) operate a complex system of controls objectively.

It could be argued that the difficulties of import substitution arise from the fact that poor countries have been by and large imitating the industrial activities of advanced countries. They could try instead to concentrate on activities that depended less on imports from the industrialized countries, such as intensified food production for the home market, small scale manufacturing, housing and road building, education and health, and so on. This would have the added advantage that it would not be necessary to have a very unequal income distribution to absorb the products of these types of activities. However, in the long run a more conventional pattern of industrialization will be required, assuming tastes are more or less similar throughout the world, and the problems created by import substitution behind protection – if such a policy is followed – will have to be faced, sooner or later.

The need to increase the scope of import substitution is the main reason why poor countries form common markets. Import substitution can then be carried on *vis-à-vis* the rest of the world, the countries concerned eliminating tariffs among themselves and maintaining a tariff wall around the whole region. Each country can specialize in the production of those goods for which it is relatively most efficient, and, being able to sell in an expanded market, its industries are able to reap the benefits of economies of scale.

These are real advantages, but some snags should be mentioned. In the first place, political conflicts between neighbouring governments are not always easy to overcome. Secondly, transportation between the countries concerned is often expensive and slow, and the development of better facilities, if physically possible, takes time and money. Thirdly, when markets are joined, competition is going to kill certain existing industries straight away, while the new factories now made possible will only be built in the future. Those likely to be hurt immediately will raise a vigorous protest, whereas those who are to benefit in the future perhaps may not even realize the possibilities. Thus there is not much political muscle behind the creation of a common market; what there is comes often (rather oddly at first sight) from the governments of rich countries, since the big corporations are quick to grasp the potential advantages.

Perhaps the most serious problem arises where (as is usually the case) the member countries are at different stages of development. It is inherently probable that the advantages to be obtained from a common market will accrue to the more highly developed countries of the region; those countries can provide new industry with the required 'environment' – transport, electricity supplies, skilled personnel, etc. This tends to generate a vicious circle whereby the already richer areas attract resources from the poor areas, therefore becoming richer, and so on. This risk can however be avoided if special measures are taken. For instance, the Latin

American Free Trade Association (LAFTA) has divided its member countries in three categories according to their degree of development, and the poorer ones are allowed special privileges, such as retaining protection longer, to compensate them for their relatively low ability to attract capital and other resources. The Central American Common Market (CACM) has a scheme for sharing out new industries by agreement.

Up till now the experience with common markets among poor countries has not been very encouraging. As was to be expected, Latin America – which has carried further the process of import substitution – has made the biggest efforts at economic integration. Trade within the Central American Common Market has grown substantially, though even its combined size is so small that its experience must be of limited general relevance. The more important LAFTA* created in 1960 has to some extent increased the intra-trade of its members. However, their inability to provide for each other the goods they most require, such as transport equipment, and machinery, together with the slow growth of their economies, has limited the possibilities; in 1966 trade among the members of LAFTA was still only 8·8 per cent of their total trade. What is more, this trade still consists mainly of the interchange of goods which these countries have traditionally exported, and although the exports of manufactured goods have increased rapidly they are as yet at a very low absolute level.

Export Expansion Policies

The drawbacks of import substitution under protection have shifted the attention of policymakers and economists back to the possibilities of increasing the volume of primary exports.

*Almost all Latin American countries are now members of LAFTA, except of course members of the CACM. The difference between a free trade area and a common market is that, in the former, countries keep their own tariffs *vis-à-vis* non-members; in the latter, all tariffs are unified at a single level. In both cases tariff walls against other members in principle eventually disappear.

Although, as indicated at the end of Part Two, the demand for primary commodities is in general inelastic, there are still possibilities of developing new markets. Moreover, it is of course in principle possible for the value of exports of primary commodities to be increased, raw materials being processed further before they are shipped, or by measures to raise their prices. The final possibility is exporting manufactures.

The industrialized countries, however, put many obstacles in the way of these lines of development. They provide heavy protection for their own production of agricultural goods, using among other techniques guaranteed high prices for their own producers, variable levies against imports (in the European Common Market) or subsidies (in Britain). The United States uses a combination of high prices, government purchases and subsidized exports. Processing of raw materials in the underdeveloped countries is discouraged by the escalating tariffs imposed by the developed countries. Customs duties are usually very low or zero on the unprocessed raw material, but increase with the degree of processing. This provides a very high effective degree of protection on the stage of processing. Suppose, for instance, that to produce a volume of processed raw materials valued at 100 dollars in the international market takes 80 dollars' worth of raw materials which are imported duty free, then a tariff of only 20 per cent on the processed product would allow an industry in the developed country to charge 120 dollars, giving it 40 dollars to cover the stage of processing instead of 20. It could pay its workers twice as much as in the poor country and still be competitive (assuming productivity is the same). Of course the actual calculation of effective rates of protection is not easy, since the industries concerned will use various other inputs. Some studies have been carried out however, showing that the effective rate of protection was substantially higher in rich countries than the apparent rate for various products which could be exported by primary-producing countries.

It is only fair to point out that some poor countries have deliberately discouraged their production of agricultural and other primary goods, by fixing lower domestic prices for these commodities, discriminating in their credit policies, pumping most of public investment to the industrial sector and so on. Argentina during most of the past forty years is a classic example. If such a country finds its share of the world trade of its exports constantly diminishing, it can hardly put the whole blame on the discriminatory policies of importers.

Higher prices for exported raw materials could be obtained in some cases through commodity agreements designed to regulate the flow of supplies. The rich countries have been lukewarm towards proposals designed to alter the prices of commodities in favour of the poor countries, and little has been achieved to date; in any case there would be dangers of stimulating substitutes, especially for industrial materials, dangers already mentioned.

Another possibility would be for rich countries to eliminate their excise taxes on primary commodities, thus allowing exporters to obtain higher prices, or to increase the volume of their sales without reducing prices. These taxes are not however usually very high, and their elimination would have favourable but rather limited effects, except for the beverages (coffee and cocoa) which are heavily taxed in continental Europe and also in the Soviet Union.

If it is difficult to expand sales of primary commodities, and if the comparative advantage the poor countries have in the production of raw materials has been fully exploited, will they not be relatively more efficient than the rich countries in the production of certain manufactures? Recent work done by the UNCTAD secretariat confirms one's expectation that the poor countries (or at least some of them) do have a comparative advantage in the production of labour-intensive goods – textiles being a typical example – and 'resource based' goods, such as processed foods, leather articles, etc.[4]

In fact, their exports of manufactured goods *have* expanded substantially in recent years, as can be seen from table 8.2. This table shows a striking acceleration, in the second half of the period 1953/65, in exports of manufactures both to 'developed' countries and to other 'developing' countries. Indeed intra-trade of the latter only really started to grow after 1959. However, only four countries, Hong Kong, India, Israel and Taiwan, supplied

TABLE 8.2

Exports of manufactured goods from 'Developing Areas'[5]

	billions of dollars f.o.b.*		
	1953	1959	1965
Exports of manufactures:			
to 'developed' countries	0·80	1·42	2·80
to other 'developing countries'	0·65	0·65	1·35
Total	1·50	2·10	4·25
Of which, from			
Hong Kong	0·19	0·37	0·84
India	0·54	0·55	0·79
Israel	0·04	0·11	0·30
Taiwan	0·01	0·04	0·23

half of the total exports of the 'developing' countries in 1965 – and it is doubtful if one of these, Israel, with its high per capita income, should still be called a 'developing' country. Moreover, although expansion in the trade in manufactures has been rapid, it started from a very low level and a much more substantial growth in these exports would be required in order to solve the foreign exchange problems of poor countries.

Yet several barriers stand in the way of more poor countries joining the 'exporters of manufactures' club, or of big increases in total exports; some are a consequence of the very nature of poorness and richness coexisting, but some are the result of misguided policies in poor and rich countries alike.

To begin with, although a country may have a comparative advantage in the *costs* of production of (say) textiles, the key question is whether it has a *price* advantage *vis-à-vis* foreign producers – including, of course, transport, insurance and the other expenses of shipping the goods. An absolute price advantage depends on the exchange rate. The economic structures of rich countries are fairly similar, and changes in the exchange rate of one will, apart from making existing exports more (or less) competitive, open (or close) overseas markets for many other

*Exports do not include re-exports. 'Developing areas' as in table 8.1.

products. In poor countries where perhaps only one or two manufactures would possibly qualify for export in the foreseeable future, the situation is very different. In order to develop these exports, a very low exchange rate might be needed. This might not be appreciated by the authorities, or they might find it politically difficult because of its implications for other sectors of the economy and for the distribution of income. If a low exchange rate implied devaluation, it could also affect the prices of traditional exports, at a cost in foreign exchange. Moreover, this could well set in motion price rises which would eliminate the price advantages required to export manufactures.*

These problems can in theory be dealt with by adopting sophisticated policies, such as dual exchange rates or export subsidies, coupled with adequate monetary and fiscal policies, which can be so arranged to prevent increasing inequality in income distribution. A dual exchange rate would mean a higher price in local currency for exporters of manufactured goods and a lower one for exporters of primary commodities, encouraging the export of the former without unduly expanding the volume of primary goods exported. Even a devaluation restricted to manufactured exports could lead to inflation if either the initial rise in prices is followed by rises in wages and other incomes generating a price–cost spiral, or via a rapid increase in overall demand due to increased exports. In principle, the appropriate counter measures would be – respectively – an incomes policy, an increase in taxation and a restrictive monetary policy. The implementation, however, of such policies can be both technically and politically very difficult. Moreover, as has been mentioned in chapter one, systems of multiple exchange rates are contrary to the rules – and the wishes – of the International Monetary Fund.

It is true that multiple exchange rates, or equivalent systems of taxes and subsidies, have been used by several countries. Since they are often combined with other measures which discourage exports of manufactures, such as overvaluation of the currency, or expansive financial policies, it is by no means easy to evaluate this experience.

*Price rises could well be beneficial, however, if excessive sales of traditional exports have turned the terms of trade against the country.

In the second place, even if a country succeeds, by devaluation or other means, in making potentially profitable a new line of exports, it has further problems to solve. Firms in poor countries rarely have institutional links with wholesalers or retailers in rich countries. Therefore much time and money have to be spent prospecting potential markets, designing products according to the requirements of these markets (usually very different from the domestic markets), establishing sales organizations, investing in new plant to produce the required goods, achieving adequate control of quality, and so on. And none of these steps will be taken unless there is a reasonable expectation that domestic policies encouraging such exports will continue in the future. Often the risks are considerable, because production for export cannot be supported by production for the home market – goods sold at home being of a type and quality not accepted in international markets.

Thirdly, the potential of this type of production for export is often not realized because of artificially high wages. Strictly a country's comparative advantage depends on the 'opportunity cost' of labour – the value labour would have if employed in some alternative occupation – and in countries where labour is plentiful, this could be very near nil. But, for obvious reasons, wages cover at least a minimum subsistence level plus a certain differential to induce people to move from villages to towns; indeed usually urban wages are much higher because of law or trade union pressure or convention (see chapter seven); hence many types of manufactures remain uncompetitive in the world market.

Apart from these obstacles to increased exports of manufactures, the inward-looking policies of many poor countries have effects which reduce their competitive strength in world markets, for reasons explained above – high costs which percolate through the economy, overvalued exchange rates, discouragement to enterprise, etc. Moreover, such policies often hit the export sector with special severity. The detailed controls imposed in foreign trade on the one hand complicate the business of exporting; on the other, they make it difficult, expensive and sometimes impossible, to buy certain imported material, or equipment, that is needed to produce an article designed specifically for selling in foreign markets.

Finally the industrialized countries, apart from the various discouragements imposed on imports of primary commodities and partly processed raw materials, also follow a more protectionist policy in regard to manufactures from poor countries than towards goods imported from other rich countries. This takes various forms – the application of tariffs[6] and a variety of restrictive devices such as quotas, licensing, government monopolies and 'voluntary' arrangements with exporters. The non-tariff barriers are usually the most effective, a good example being the Long Term Arrangement in Cotton Textiles by which the main exporters among the poor countries agreed to limit their sales in order to avoid quotas being imposed. Such restrictions obviously limit the export potential of poor countries, and their mere possibility adds to the risks of manufacturers in these countries already mentioned. They are thus a serious obstacle to developing new markets, and furthermore even harmful to the industrialized countries themselves, at least according to orthodox theory, because they could employ more productively the resources used in producing those goods that could be imported at a lower cost.* The rich countries usually impose these restrictions to protect industries which are relatively labour-intensive and already in difficulties due to the slow growth of demand for their products. However, short-term gains made by such countries in terms of avoiding unemployment hardly compensate for the long-term losses through keeping resources locked up in relatively unproductive activities.†

*After this chapter was written, further thought on this problem led me to the conclusion that the discriminatory protective policies of the industrialized countries could be a source of long-term gains for them, and was indeed one of their main means for maintaining domination over vast areas of the world. See O. Braun, 'Hacia una teoría de la explotacíon' imperialista', *Comercio e Inversion Internacionales*, Instituto Torcuato di Tella, Buenos Aires, mimeo, 1968.

†In some cases restrictive policies are designed to avoid possible balance-of-payments deficits due to increased imports from poor countries. Here it is the failure of present monetary arrangements to

Trade with socialist countries (most of which belong to COMECON) is often mentioned as a means of export expansion for poor countries. Indeed exports from poor to COMECON countries have increased rapidly since the fifties; from U.S. $0·34 billion in 1953 to U.S. $1·00 billion in 1959 and U.S. $2·11 billion in 1965. These exports have been mainly primary commodities, and if the nineteenth-century experience with the industrialized countries were to be repeated with the rapidly growing COMECON markets, the prospects for commodities would be most promising.* This, however, is unlikely; the technological advances mentioned in chapter two make it possible for the members of COMECON to increase their relatively low incomes without increasing their consumption of primary commodities as fast as the industrialized countries did in the nineteenth century, and in any case they have – especially the Soviet Union itself – natural advantages in the production of many of these goods. Trade possibilities are also limited by the ability of COMECON countries to provide the goods the poor countries require, by their insistence in trading on a completely or partially bilateral way, and by the difficulties they find in accommodating larger imports in their rather rigid production plans. In fact the rate of growth of exports to these countries declined in the early sixties as compared with the late fifties, and their total value being relatively small, we might conclude that although this trade is a welcome addition to the markets of the poor countries it can hardly make a very big contribution to solving the external problem.

provide for smooth adjustment mechanisms that is to blame. Some comments on monetary reform will be made in chapter thirteen.

*Some poor countries have complained about this fact since they associate underdevelopment with exports of raw materials. There is nothing wrong, however, with exporting growing volumes of raw materials, if one is able to produce them cheaply, provided that it can be done without sacrificing the level of prices obtained.

Concluding Remarks

It is important not to believe that one must choose rigidly between one strategy or the other when there are possibilities of combining both. It all depends on local circumstances. Sometimes outward-looking policies have meant stagnation; other economies have grown rapidly under the same policies. The choice depends partly on the circumstances of each individual country; a big country with abundant natural resources, or a common market shared with a number of neighbours, is less dependent on imports from abroad. And a period of relative isolation might be necessary to start building up industry until the economy is strong enough to start competing abroad. Countries which are close to the industrial centres, and have cheap transport links with them, are particularly likely to benefit from access to their markets. Some countries, for instance the oil producers, have a natural resource for which demand grows rapidly in the rich countries; they need not suffer from balance-of-payments difficulties, though they might still find it worthwhile to protect their industries if only to absorb an increased supply of manpower.

The transition from an outward- to an inward-looking policy can involve a country in a painful process of change, but so can the reverse, especially for a poor country that would in general find it difficult to adapt its economic structure by moving resources from one sector to another. Some countries would find it easier to proceed with a relatively closed economy, perhaps integrated with some other poor countries, and delay its exposure to foreign competition until the process of development has proceeded further.

It is also too simple to suggest that less government intervention is all that is implied by an outward-looking strategy. In fact, detailed planning could well be required if such a strategy is to be pursued successfully, especially if the transition from a highly protected to a more open economy is to be smooth. Unless entrepreneurs respond rapidly to changes in circumstances, government intervention might be essential.

171

As has been suggested before, the poor countries need not, indeed cannot, follow blindly the pattern of industrialization of the rich. A concentration of efforts in small industry and agriculture could in some cases bring quicker results than an effort to absorb modern technology and to break into the competitive markets of the rich. In any case, the choice is not simply between an open or a closed economy – it may be possible to combine features of both, for instance setting up a relatively modern textile industry while subsidizing the production of small textile workshops.

The choice of a development strategy raises in any case much wider issues than have been discussed so far. A country choosing a socialist path for development is thereby reducing, if not eliminating, its chances of following an open strategy. Even if a partial analysis showed it to be superior, this obviously does not mean that it should keep the economy open as a first priority; the total advantages of a socialist path for many poor countries outstrip the disadvantages of an inward-looking policy.

Similarly a country that opts for an outward-looking strategy is in general doing more than just selecting a trade policy. An outward-looking strategy is normally accompanied by a reliance on foreign private investment, capital aid, visits by technical assistance experts, and foreign education for students – in general a much closer contact with the rich countries.

These contacts will have, as already pointed out in chapter one, social, economical and political repercussions that extend far beyond the simple change in the patterns of trading. The tastes of the population will be affected, in general leaning towards the consumption of 'western' goods; and entrepreneurs and managers, both local and foreign, will tend to copy 'western' technology uncritically, making it more difficult for the country to find the right role in international trade. Other consequences such as the political effects of aid, the costs of foreign private capital and the 'brain drain' have been discussed above. And what is perhaps more important a foreign trained elite, constantly mixing with foreigners and adopting their salaries, values and standards of living, can hardly feel and communicate the 'nationalism' or 'patriotism' that has been in so many cases a driving force in a process of development.[7] In fact the whole cultural life of the country depends on the choice, and there is no set of criteria in the social sciences for evaluating the costs and benefits.

When all this has been said, it remains true that many poor countries have, clearly, not availed themselves of all the opportunities provided by foreign trade, because of an excessive concentration on import substitution. Some of them are now trying to reverse this trend, and their efforts would be greatly eased, and the opportunities of all poor countries greatly enhanced, if the rich countries themselves followed a liberal trade policy. What they can do will be discussed later in chapter thirteen.

9 STRATEGY FOR AGRICULTURAL DEVELOPMENT

In most poor countries the overwhelming majority of the people depends on farming for its livelihood. Commonly, too, farming is the source of the major contribution to the national product. (See table 4.3.) In rich countries, of course, the position is entirely different, and development is sometimes seen as a process of transferring people from the rural sector into manufacturing, commerce or service industries. Without doubt, as a country develops, jobs are necessarily created outside the rural sector and a fall in the share of the labour force employed in agriculture is one index of development. This reasoning has, however, been pursued to the false conclusion that development strategy must necessarily aim at channelling scarce capital into the manufacturing sector rather than into agriculture.

Now, however, following the experiences of a number of countries – most notably India – the error of neglecting agricultural development has been amply recognized. Where food supply fails to keep pace with the demands of growing urban populations, a country's development is hindered by the need to spend scarce foreign exchange on food imports. Moreover, food prices rise and urban wages keep pace with them, thus reducing the potential profitability of manufacturing investment. Successful agricultural development on the other hand can mean not just a saving of foreign exchange on food imports, but positive net foreign exchange earnings from agricultural exports, a rise in the standard of living in the mass of the rural population and the creation of demand for consumer goods to stimulate investment in the manufacturing sector. Also, as rural incomes grow, they provide increasingly a source of government revenues and private investment funds.

Yet the development of the rural sector is notoriously one of the most difficult development tasks. Technically, it may pose severe problems in the breeding of new improved varieties of crops and livestock suited to the country's environment and in the evolution of new farming systems which incorporate the advances of science. Administratively, too, it makes more demands than any other sector, requiring efficiency in the coordination of programmes for the supply of physical inputs – water, seeds, fertilizers, insecticides – and services – credit, marketing, transport and storage. Above all, the development of agriculture in the Third World is not just a technical and administrative problem, it means changing the behaviour of millions of individual farmers spread over the face of the earth: farmers who are commonly illiterate, impoverished and suspicious – often with good reason – of the motives of government officials and the advice that they offer. An understanding of the issues of rural development policy must start from an understanding of the tropical farmer and his 'conservatism'.

A Grass Roots View of Farming in Poor Countries

In many parts of the underdeveloped world there are farmers with a deep practical understanding of their farming environment. Much of this relates to traditional farming systems developed to suit population pressures and technologies which no longer apply. Much of it too is embodied in folklore and habitual behaviour patterns, the logic of which may be largely forgotten. But farmers also have a direct knowledge of much that is essential to the development of new farming systems – knowledge which if available to agronomists would forestall much mistaken advice. Thus farmers will frequently know, for example, in detail the crop varieties and their suitability for different soils, place in the rotation and date of planting. Thus a crop variety that is commonly grown in one region may be scarcely grown twenty miles away. With flood-grown rice, for example, changes in patterns of varieties grown may be intricate over quite short distances. A

175

number of factors may govern variety selection but most important among these is likely to be rainfall and soil moisture regimes. These factors dominate not simply the choice of varieties but also the pattern of the total farming system in all areas, save those where rainfall is both high and reliable – and this is not generally the case.

Typically, rains are highly variable and, even where *average* rainfall in a period is adequate for crop production, the maximum and minimum amounts of rainfall that are likely to be experienced may span a very wide range, the lower values of which mean drought. If the pattern of soil moisture availability does not match the pattern of the crop's demands, then the growth of the crop is retarded and yield suffers. Where high temperatures lead to heavy losses of soil moisture, the frequency of rainfall replenishment may be critical if crops are not to suffer moisture stress. Traditional varieties, though typically low yielding, are often tolerant of poor rainfall regimes, while improved high yielding varieties are commonly not tolerant. (Though, exceptionally, new varieties have been bred or introduced which outyield traditional varieties, even in poor rainfall conditions.)

Where rainfall is markedly seasonal, the time of planting can be critical. Often digging is impossible until the rains commence and, when they do, planting must proceed as rapidly as possible or the crops with longer growing seasons may not receive enough rainfall to sustain growth. Once planting occurs, the calendar of labour requirements on the planted crop is, within limits, predetermined and weeding and other attentions will be required through to harvest. Further plantings of crops – perhaps with successively shorter growing seasons – may be made, but these must not imply clashes between the labour requirements of different crops such that the total labour requirement is more than can be supplied. And, second to water, labour, too, is likely to be scarce.

The idea of labour being scarce in densely populated areas like Bengal, or in so many areas where people seem most commonly to be seen sitting around, may appear paradoxical. But at one or more seasons of the year this may indeed be the case. The trouble with labour is that effort saved at one time cannot be carried forward to another. Thus, together with rainfall, labour scarcity may dominate farming systems for, if a farming system is to be viable, it must make no more demands on labour than can be met. Thus the year's cropping calendar will be designed to keep labour peaks within bounds and perhaps to fill in the slacker periods with less critical jobs.

This joint concern for rainfall seasons and crop labour requirements may be further complicated by other factors which dictate that the cropping pattern follows more or less clearly defined sequences on the land. For example, some crops need a fine seedbed so are not grown in the first year of a rotation; others are susceptible to weed competition and may therefore be best grown in the second year of a rotation after the land has been cleaned for the opening crop. Yet other crops may be difficult to weed so that it pays to grow them at the end of the rotation, for then accumulated weeds will not cause a problem in the following year and so on. Thus farming systems may be critically adjusted to meet rainfall conditions, labour availability and rotational considerations – not to speak of food requirements, crop storage characteristics and other such concerns.

It is a mistake to think that because poor-country farming systems use primitive tools and techniques they are therefore simple. Sometimes they are most exceptionally complex; especially in the sense that they exhibit a high degree of interdependence between activities. Frequently, such systems are so critically balanced that shifting the planting date of one crop, or changing the time spent in weeding it, will have repercussions on the timing and intensity of cultivations through the year. Failure to calculate the implications of these repercussions may result in the piling up of work and substantial loss of yields.

What we have attempted to convey in the above paragraphs is the sense in which traditional farming systems are adapted to the environment and to the farmers' resources. What we have also shown is the difficulty of effecting marginal improvements in such farming systems without causing repercussions on the total farming system. Problems of adjustment may be complex and the time it takes cautiously to adapt to a new husbandry method or other innovation may be considerable. One reason why farmers might properly be regarded as conservative is because of the time it genuinely takes to learn to adapt – bearing in mind especially that each trial modification may take at least a year to prove itself.

The peasant farmer's reputation for conservatism reflects in large measure scientists' frustrations in their attempts to improve peasant farming. In many instances the peasant farmer's reputation is unwarranted; the facts show scientists to be offering correct but irrelevant information. An example is called for: trials in Tanzania over many years demonstrated that groundnut yields per acre were increased by up to 50 per cent when weeding was carried out within ten days of crop germination. This may be taken as scientifically demonstrated and 'correct' information. It is not, however, information useful to the farmer on the basis of which he may be induced to change his ways. The farmer is hard pressed at planting time. He is short of labour rather than land. At the time the agronomist would advise him to weed his groundnuts he has the choice of continuing to dig and plant more groundnuts or of weeding the growing crop. Since the return to his scarce labour from continued digging and planting is higher than it is to weeding, the cultivator will achieve the highest total output not by weeding but by continuing instead to plant more groundnuts. The scientist's findings are correct but, in this situation, unhelpful. His advice, – to weed the crop within ten days of germination – is, in fact, mistaken.

In this example, scientific knowledge is irrelevant because it does not improve the productivity of the limiting resource – labour at digging time; increased land productivity is not relevant where land is plentiful relative to labour. In other situations, research findings may be relevant but difficult to assimilate. Thus, research into the effects of time of planting on yields (especially of newly introduced crops) might show possible advantages to be gained from revision of planting times. But this might mean adjusting the timing and balance of many other farm activities. Finding the best balance may require either intricate calculations by farm economists or years of gradual adjustment by the farmers themselves. Even then, it might turn out that some of the crop should still continue to be planted at the usual time.

Thus, farming systems may need complex adjustment if new technical or market opportunities are to be exploited. Just how complex is the problem of adjustment may be appreciated when modern techniques of farming system analysis are applied. Linear programming – an application of matrix algebra – can be used to explore the range of cropping and husbandry systems feasible in any situation given the resources available to farmers and the implications of proposed innovations. This method of analysis presents the farmer's situation as a series of equations. An adequate formulation of a semi-subsistence farm situation may require, say, 200 very long equations and the attempt at such a formulation readily impresses one with the complexity of the adjustment problem facing the farmer who in essence has to solve these equations. The only practical way that the researcher has of solving them (in order, perhaps, to determine feasible farming systems) is by recourse to an electronic computer. Farmers grope their way towards solutions by a series of steps, and impoverished farmers, especially, may move very cautiously indeed.

However great the problems of translating research findings into advice useful to farmers, it is clear that farmers all over the world have in fact responded both to pressures – e.g. changes in population density – and to opportunities – new crops, high prices and new techniques. But the possibility of gradual improvement is not always present. Where rainfall is a constraint, there may be little scope for increasing output by improved seed or by more intensive husbandry. Yet, until improved seed is available, investment in irrigation and fertilizers may not be justified. Unfortunately, the breeding of improved varieties of crops or the selection of suitable existing varieties already grown elsewhere may involve a long process of trial and error in which the appropriate husbandry methods – planting date, spacing, insecticides and seed treatment, fertilizer practice, etc. – have also to be found. When these are available, progress may demand not a sequence of step-by-step adjustments but a 'package deal' revolution and a complete switch to intensive farming with irrigation and a whole range of new and costly farm inputs, new cropping patterns and new attitudes and skills. Yet farmers have often shown themselves capable of revolutionary changes. In Uganda, a good deal of effort was directed over many years to encouraging farmers to improve their dairy husbandry. It was argued that, until management standards were higher, improved dairy cattle could not be introduced: that they would starve on the rations farmers were feeding them, if they did not die first from tick-borne East Coast Fever. But, in the late 1950s, grade cattle – Ayrshires and Guernseys – were being sold very cheaply from Kenya Highland farms. These cows offered six or more gallons of milk per day instead of one or two pints from the native Nganda beast. It did not take long for enterprising farmers to learn to eradicate ticks from pastures (by double fencing, then grazing with local cattle which were deticked until there were no ticks left), or to learn that, whereas the local cow responded hardly at all to extra feeding above the maintenance ration, the grade cattle needed a very much bigger maintenance ration and then responded very well to extra feeding. There are now tens of thousands of grade cattle managed by African farmers supplying milk to the Kampala market.

But, while it was relatively easy in this case to meet the environmental demands of existing grade cattle offering very high profit prospects, it is not always so easy to provide a suitable environment for new crops or crop varieties. We have indicated that this is especially so where water is a limiting factor and where the successful introduction of high-yielding crop varieties may require irrigation, fertilizers and substantial modification of husbandry methods. This may be illustrated by the case of the improved rice varieties being introduced in India. (Although one should be careful of generalizing from one illustration about a country where conditions may vary enormously.) Existing rice varieties are typically germinated during the dry season in hand watered seedbeds. When the monsoon breaks and the rivers flood the paddies, the seedlings are transplanted. But the onset of the monsoon is not precisely reliable and traditional varieties are tolerant about the age at which they are transplanted within a range of about twenty days. When transplanting begins, the pace of work is hectic, labour is short and much transplanting takes place later than would be ideal. Where irrigation is by flood, the bunded paddy fields hold the flood water which then stagnates and evaporates. Improved varieties may not fare well in such circumstances. Their transplanting dates may be critical to within a few days. Fertilizer may be necessary to secure their yield potential and this in turn may call for closer spacing between plants. But closer spacing takes more labour, and without additional manpower the planting programme may not be completed until late in the season. Again, the improved varieties may be more sensitive to unsatisfactory water regimes and may require water levels to start low and rise as the season proceeds with a flow of oxygenated water being maintained.

But many farmers in India and the Far East have adopted new high-yielding rice varieties and the sophisticated husbandry techniques which they require. What has been shown in India is that farmer conservatism was a wrong diagnosis of agricultural stagnation – that, given genuine new opportunities to raise incomes substantially, these are accepted, even where quite radical change is involved.

Even so, many of the changes advocated are, for a variety of reasons, unattractive to the farmer. Returns to extra feeding for traditional strains of livestock are, as we have seen, likely to be small. Similarly with crops. Mellor and Herdt[1] show that the responses of traditional Indian rice varieties to nitrogenous fertilizers are very low compared to the responses of Californian rice. Where crop yields are high, the percentage increases in yields necessary to cover costs of additional inputs – insecticides, for example – may be low compared to the percentage increase needed to justify the same application in a situation where the yield is low. Thus if an increase in yield of 100 lb of seed cotton per acre were required to pay for the use of insecticide, the farmer in Carolina whose cotton yields 2,000 lb per acre needs only a 5 per cent increase to cover his cost whereas an African farmer with a yield of 400 lb per acre needs a 25 per cent increase to cover his cost. If the African farmer faces a higher price for insecticide and a lower price for his cotton, he is even more disadvantaged.

The necessary responses not only need to be feasible but also reliable. With the use of fertilizer, for example, *average* yields may rise, but in dry years fertilizer might depress crop yields and even cause failure. The farmer is then worse off than he would have been, not only by the loss in yield but also by the cost of the fertilizer. Where a large package of inputs is necessary, the returns may well be handsome, but the annual outlays implied may be many times the total of annual cash receipts previously experienced. Even where credit is available, farmers may be unwilling to expose themselves to the possibility of failure.

Risk and uncertainty appear to be a characteristic of almost all farming. They are frequently acute in the sub-humid tropics where much of poor-country agriculture is to be found. For poor farmers, risk and uncertainty may have a seriously inhibiting effect on their willingness to innovate, for they cannot afford to suffer a setback which might mean deprivation – perhaps chronic indebtedness, loss of their land or even starvation. Farmers' unwillingness to innovate can often be seen as a quite comprehensible unwillingness to take risks.

Social Factors

Traditional patterns of social rights and obligations commonly make provision against individual calamity and ensure that in bad years everybody has some share of what food there is. The forms of such social provision range through extended family systems; systems in which chiefs may have a degree of command over the allocation of food resources; the Hindu *jajmani* system and a variety of tenancy systems, including sharecropping. However, the very existence of such 'social insurance' provisions may inhibit innovation, if only because there may be little sympathy for anyone who departs from customary behaviour on his own initiative and, possibly, in his own self interest. Yet a farmer who is successfully enterprising might have his extended family expectant of a share in his improved fortunes. In such circumstances there may be little inducement to face risks as a pioneer innovator and a farmer may need to feel that he is not alone in trying out new methods.

Traditional patterns of social interdependence may inhibit technical change in other ways. Epstein[2] has shown this in the case of the *jajmani* system in South India. This system provides for the support of labourers and functionary castes who perform traditional services in return for a share of the crop. Where new systems of cultivation demand more than customary effort, incentive payments may be necessary to induce it and this might call for the revision or discarding of the *jajmani* system. (According to newspaper reports, there were riots in South India in 1968 when labourers refused to work for customary payments for farmers using new seed varieties and intensive methods of cultivation.)

Sharecrop tenancy systems may also inhibit change. They allow rent payments to vary with the state of the harvest but, where they do not allow for increases of output resulting from new investment of cash and labour to be shared *pro rata* among those providing the new inputs, investment and innovation may be totally inhibited. In West Pakistan, landlords failed to persuade tenants to adopt intensive Japanese methods of rice cultivation. On examination, the tenant's crop share return for the extra work involved was found to be worth less than could be earned by casual employment off the farm. In fact, it would have paid landlords to compensate tenants for extra work, but the landlords' view was that sharecroppers were obliged to do work required by them.

The social costs of innovation may, as in the above cases, have solid material elements, but the innovator may be influenced by non-material concerns also. Innovators may face suspicion, ridicule, ostracism, and even violence. One farmer in Northern Uganda who used a tractor to plough an area of unused land, faced all these reactions – and for understandable reasons. By tribal custom – which long pre-dated tractors – the usufruct of land belonged to the person whose hoe- or axe-marks it bore. In this light, the tractor had frightening significance. Moreover, the tractor farmer withdrew from customary reciprocal labour obligations. In fact, he threatened the breakdown of the whole traditional pattern of labour reciprocity – and, with it, the wider structure of 'social insurance' rights and obligations – by offering wage employment. Indeed, the implications of the tractors were even more profound and they were clearly sensed by the neighbour who said, 'If you work for him now, your sons will work for his sons.' But what worried the innovator – a man with a clear sense of mission endeavouring to set an example to his people – was not the suspicion, ridicule and violence, but the fear that when he died there might be nobody at his funeral.

We can sympathize, perhaps, with a man unwilling to bear such a cost. We find it less easy to sympathize when attitudes are based on what we regard as superstition and fallacy. The West African who declined to follow advice to treat maize rust because he believed it to be his grandfather's ghost is one example of such attitudes, and many might be given. On the whole, however, such attitudes are probably unimportant in inhibiting change where other factors predispose to it.

Perhaps the most significant of all the preconditions of raising farm incomes is that it should pay in material terms to invest in change and in the new inputs that change demands. However, the reward in terms of higher living standards must be seen to more than compensate the extra effort, risks and social costs that may be incurred.

Policies for Development

Government is thus faced with the rural sector: the bulk of the population; primarily cultivating families; technically backward; mostly very poor and uneducated; often in poor health; geared to a way of life which revolves around traditional farming systems, which are in turn tightly geared to the physical environment; potentially, if not actively, politically vociferous; often a society with its own marked internal conflicts. Policy demands both that the rural sector should service national development, and that development should serve the rural community; though sometimes this latter consideration especially might be nearly forgotten.

For effecting policy, government has at its disposal a very wide range of policy instruments. In this section we shall broadly review these. Later we discuss briefly the strategic choices facing governments.

The discussion of the previous section has emphasized the constraints under which a peasant farms and the skill with which he handles them. If farming is to be changed it will be because new production or exchange possibilities are opened to the farmer. This can be brought about through the introduction of new production activities; through the availability of new resources; through the removal of social and institutional inhibitions; and through the reduction of risk. These categories of change opportunities are not easily separated, but examples might be given of each. New production activities would include new crops, new varieties or new market outlets. New resources would include, especially, irrigation water and also newly available purchased inputs such as fertilizers, insecticides, tools and machinery. The removal of social or institutional inhibitions might be exemplified by the breakdown of customary labour obligations in favour of wage employment or a land reform such as the consolidation of fragmented holdings. The reduction of risk might be achieved in any one of a number of ways from the introduction of reliable irrigation to the creation of reliable market outlets, crop insurance, or a flexible credit scheme.

While opportunities need to be created, exploitation of opportunities might imply the acquisition by farmers of new skills. Thus, as well as seeking to create opportunities, policy must aim to inform farmers of opportunities created and to train them in the necessary new skills. But the value of farmer education, treated as an investment, is the value of the extra income which the farmer can earn from having it. Unless new opportunities are created, farmer training and agricultural education programmes may be irrelevant and worthless.

New Production Activities

Considering our headings in order, the first implies policies which would seek new production activities especially through new crops, new varieties or new market outlets. The significance of introduced crops and the development of international markets has been very great in the past. Tea, coffee, cocoa, palm oil, cotton, sisal, rubber and other crops transformed many areas of the world in the nineteenth and early twentieth centuries from subsistence to cash crop production. After the Second World War the spread of these crops continued. Increasingly, however, countries have been forced to consider not so much what new crops they can grow as what new market outlets crops already in production might be geared to. For example, scope may be seen for the production of groundnuts for the international edible nut market. This would require that farmers grow an appropriate variety, harvest and dry the crop by an approved method, and market it through agencies which grade and pack the nuts in the way required by overseas buyers. In a situation where groundnuts were currently grown for the local market and where the product was a sample of mixed varieties, broken, dirty and mildewed, it would require a substantial programme to create a new farming opportunity. Variety trials, seed multiplication, advice to farmers, and a marketing scheme (private or public) would be necessary. By its nature such a programme takes time, costs money and involves risks such as might daunt private enterprise, leaving government a substantial role to play in its initiation and implementation.

It should be observed that the great historical developments in the introduction of new crops into tropical countries for production for world markets were undertaken mostly without government initiatives. That this is undoubtedly so, however, does not lead to the conclusion that one can rest assured that all existing market opportunities must already have been explored or that all new opportunities will be automatically and readily exploited.

There may, of course, be scope for developing new domestic markets. But the market does not necessarily work well within a country either, and expanding demand from growing towns may not make itself fully felt to the farmer, especially where transport and communications are inefficient. (Nor, for that matter, may the availability of new techniques and inputs.) A great deal may be achieved by the simple and inexpensive provision of a market information service. Regular mimeographed newsheets showing prices paid at market centres can do much to improve the sensitivity and operation of the market and create opportunities for farmers to grow new crops.

New Resources

In recent years, some of the most striking success stories of rural development have been associated with breeding and introduction of new high-yielding crop varieties. In India and Pakistan, recently evolved Mexican wheat varieties have been introduced and farmers have experienced yield increases from 7 cwt/acre to 1 ton or more per acre. New rice varieties, notably 'IR 8' and 'Taichung Native 1', have raised yields from $\frac{1}{2}$ ton/acre to 1 ton/acre. (Figures taken from actual situations, not averages.) These and other varieties of grains have justified substantial increases in farm inputs – water, labour, fertilizers, and insecticide. Their impact on existing farming systems has been profound and new systems have not yet been fully developed to exploit them. Moreover, much work has yet to be done to spread the new varieties even within those limited areas sufficiently well-watered for them to be grown. Seed multiplication and distribution activities have to be stepped up and associated with increased supplies of, especially, balanced fertilizer. At the same time the increased yields in some areas have severely taxed the marketing system. Transport and storage provision has been inadequate, and farmers with crops heavier than they had ever dreamed of are now concerned about their disposal. These and many other problems can slow down the rate at which the new seeds are adopted. The anticipation of all these problems is more than one can ask. It is clear, however, that unless opportunities are so great that difficulties and setbacks can be survived, an extremely comprehensive preparation is necessary, both through research in a broad range of disciplines – genetics, husbandry, pathology, entomology, farm economics, and so on – and also through administrative action – to provide seeds, fertilizers, insecticides, tube-wells, credit, extension officer training, storage, transport and so forth.

Peasant farming output is limited by the resources it commands. Even without new crops, crop varieties or market outlets, it is conceivable that an increase in the resources available to peasant farmers would lead to increased production. But what resources constrain their production and would the costs of relieving these constraints be justified by the extra output?

Typically, as we have seen, the most limiting constraints are rainfall – soil moisture – and labour. Let us examine in turn the return to extra water and labour – or, alternatively, the scope for increasing the productivity of available water and labour.

Taking water first, there may in many areas be possibilities of increasing the productivity of available rainfall quite apart from dam storage. Tropical rainfall often occurs as heavy storms. Instead of percolating gently into the soil, rain water runs off carrying soil particles with it. If the land is ridged – as in England we ridge the land for potato growing – and if the ridges are 'tied' every ten yards or so (by blocking the furrow with earth), then rainwater will collect in the furrows and percolate into the soil in due course. By tie-ridging, the rainfall available to a crop can be substantially increased and the practice may in turn justify the use of fertilizers and insecticides. The net increase may be worth the cost of extra effort, especially where land is scarce and labour is not being diverted from other more productive jobs.

However, the major developments must be sought in irrigation. This covers a wide range of possible techniques, among which there is always a choice, each having different implications not only for the resulting pattern of husbandry but also for the structure of economic and social organization. (Important issues here are the degree of control an individual has over his water supply and how – if at all – he pays for it.)

Irrigation is expensive and – where dams, barrages and canals are involved – it normally implies public investment. In spite of its expense, it may be economically justified where the growing season is extended, where the reduction of uncertainty allows the use of fertilizers and other inputs, or where intensive husbandry becomes feasible in association with high yielding varieties or new crops dependent upon improved water regimes. Irrigation also frequently creates many new jobs. But, as we repeatedly stress, the exploitation of irrigation requires the development of new and sometimes radically different farming systems. These will take time to perfect after irrigation has been provided. In appraising irrigation possibilities one is often faced with a tremendous feat of imagination, calculation and judgement about the patterns of farming systems that might be developed and their implications for the design of the irrigation system and the assessment of its potential return. Nevertheless, it is clear that – in India for example – there are many areas where land is scarce and where plentifully available water is unused, where the sun shines bright and the biological potential is enormous, and yet where without more water, or without its control, agriculture cannot develop. In such areas irrigation is of paramount significance to agricultural development.

Where labour is a limiting factor, its efficiency may be increased by engaging it in more productive activities – especially by growing improved varieties – or by applying effort through improved tools and machines. For mechanization to pay, it must first make possible an increase in total production; additionally, it must increase production by a value greater than the cost of the machines. A tractor-drawn plough may increase the efficiency of scarce labour at cultivation time, but if it cannot improve labour efficiency at other times when labour is scarce – weeding or harvesting – then total farm production may not be increased. As with irrigation, the full exploitation of mechanization might require the radical redesign of farming systems. Even where the total product can be increased by machines, the increased output may not cover the cost. Where, typically, crop values are low and

189

machinery costs high and where the increase in total output is limited by labour or other constraints that the tractor cannot ease, then there is no scope for mechanization. But even though these conditions are typical there are exceptions. Irrigation and new crops and varieties, especially, change this picture. Double or triple cropping under irrigation may only be feasible with mechanical cultivation to ease the labour peaks, if the harvest of one crop overlaps with the preparation for the next. Even where animal power is used for draught, the tractor may score not only by its speed but by the quality of the work done and by the fact that it releases land from fodder production to extend the area of cash crops.

It should be said that the shortage of labour – and of draught power – are frequently severe constraints on increasing production. Further, it should be noted that the use of tractors does not necessarily reduce employment. (Though in developed countries mechanization has proceeded precisely because it replaces dear labour.) Where tractors are found to be economic, they are bound to have profound social repercussions – as indeed are almost all the technical and economic innovations that we are considering.

Of the other resources which might be made available to farmers, credit is one which must briefly be noted here. Lifting farming systems onto a new plane of intensity frequently requires financial resources that small farmers cannot command. Unfortunately, however, experience with the provision of rural credit is that it costs a great deal to distribute and supervise and that it is very difficult to avoid it going primarily to the bigger and wealthier farmers who need it least. Another lesson is that there are not always worthwhile investment possibilities in farming, and where this is so credit schemes can suffer heavy losses.

Social and Institutional Inhibitions

The removal of social and institutional inhibitions can be a matter for policy especially with regard to land reform. Very often, however, the significance of social inhibitions is simply that people do not value the expected material gain as much as they value the social activities and relationships that they would lose as a result of innovation. The question arises as to how far such attitudes can be regarded as misguided and obstacles to true development – to be changed by edict or exhortation – or how far they must be left until economic attractions or pressures are sufficient to induce change.

Land reform is seldom considered simply as a question of production efficiency. Normally – save perhaps in the case of land consolidation – issues of social justice are of major concern. However, it is clear that land tenure does affect farm production and investment and that it may limit the productivity of land and labour.

Administrators in Africa have sometimes argued in favour of land reforms which would transform customary-communal tenure systems into legalized systems conferring private usufructuary rights or ownership. This view sees initiative as dependent on individuals having secure private tenure and the assurance of the reward for their personal efforts. Where holdings have been fragmented and dispersed the creation of legal individual tenure has been associated with programmes for the consolidation of holdings. Such programmes, together with research and advisory work supported by the provision of credit and physical resources, have produced – as for example in the Kipsigis areas of Kenya – substantial impetus to farming development. But they are not without their problems. Insofar as customary tenure systems are one aspect of social interdependence, legislation may either fail because people are not prepared to deny the claims of relatives, or they succeed at the cost, perhaps, of revealing a problem of landless unemployed who become a liability on the state. In general, land reform will commonly mean the breakdown of functions associated with the previous pattern of tenure and alternative provision for such functions may be necessary.

While one view has favoured reform towards legalized individualistic tenure, another has attempted to retain what are seen to be desirable features of traditional, communal life and to stimulate rural development not by appeal to individual

191

enterprise but by the encouragement of existing or created communities to group enterprise. By this strategy, villages or groups are assisted financially and managerially to reorganize farming and to adopt modern techniques and farming inputs. Such developments not only imply the existence of known, economic, improved farming systems; they may bring very substantial social changes which ultimately may be resisted as strenuously as those implied by establishing private holdings.

Land reform can mean many different things. It may mean consolidation and registration of titles in Kenya or Ceylon, or village settlement schemes in Tanzania, but in Argentina it means tackling the problem of *latifundias* – very large farming and ranching estates inefficiently exploited by absentee owners – and in India it means 'land to the tenant' and a ceiling on the size of holdings. These are, of course, extremely crude summary representations of complex situations about which there are many views. However, our purpose here is not so much to analyse these situations as to illustrate the variety in land reform issues – albeit that they are all concerned with equity and efficiency.

The further point to be made is that there is usually a considerable range of programmes which might be considered for any one of these situations. Land use and income distribution may both be improved by land taxes, which may ultimately lead also to a redistribution of land ownership. Alternative, or complementary, to a land tax might be compulsory redistribution, with or without compensation. Titles might be purchased by new landholders or leases might be granted for regular rent payments. When the case for land reform is argued, it must be argued not in principle but in relation to specific programme proposals. It should also be argued in relation to the predicted outcomes of alternative programmes. But such prediction may be extremely demanding – especially as so much may depend on the quality of administration of complementary programmes, e.g. farm planning and credit services for newly settled farmers. Also, as we have stressed before, if land reform is to make it possible for opportunities to be grasped, such opportunities must be available.

Reducing Risks

Much was made in the earlier discussion about the risks and uncertainties of farming and their inhibiting effects on innovation by poor farmers. Poor farmers are inhibited when the possibility of improvement is small in relation to the possibility of calamity. Where innovation is all but certain to succeed and where success means raising the standard of living onto a new plane – as it might with irrigation, new seed and fertilizers applied together and demonstrated to have succeeded with a neighbour – there is hardly any problem. The lesson of this seems to be 'think big'. However, such formulae are not always available and modest improvements could be significant to many farmers. How then to reduce their uncertainty?

Natural hazards can only be ultimately reduced by successful development to more intensive farming. But fertilizers alone, for example, might imply increased risks. Where this is so, there may be scope for underwriting farmers' innovations by credit schemes designed to relate repayments to yield as this varies with weather, pests and diseases. If it does not pay in the long run for the state to bear these risks (net of administration costs) then farmers should not be expected to bear them either. Alternatively, crop insurance schemes could be devised – though the conditions for successful crop insurance are very demanding and there has been relatively little exploration of this possibility to date.

Economic hazard is only slightly easier to provide against. Marketing services may be improved and schemes to dampen price fluctuations may be employed. Both measures are commonly employed in agricultural policy.

Choice of Policy

Good policy depends on the effective diagnosis of the existing situation, effective identification of the policies relevant for consideration, sound prediction of the consequences of adopting alternative policies and a procedure for policy making which relates the predicted outcomes of policies to the objectives of policy. At this point it is worth considering the objectives of rural development.

At first sight it might seem that the object of rural development policy is to increase agricultural production and farmers' incomes. But this would be altogether too simple. For one thing it could be an object of policy to keep farm incomes down to avoid spending on consumption goods, to channel resources into investment and to keep down food prices so as to attract urban labour and manufacturing investments. Rural development policies are thus not designed simply to achieve maximum farm output. They must be concerned with the allocation of resources, incentives, jobs, and incomes between different regions of the country, between different classes of people and between the present and the future.

The question of employment may be particularly important. In many poor countries the labour force is growing very much faster than the number of jobs in the urban sector. Thus, if there is not to be a growing mass of urban unemployed, the rural sector must absorb much of the addition to the labour force. Policies will therefore be concerned not solely with agricultural production but also with finding jobs and subsistence for an increasing number of people. At the same time, the growing numbers of people who have given up producing their own food require an increase in marketed food supplies to support them. This means not only increasing agricultural production but also increasing the marketed surplus. If domestic food demands are not met by increasing food production, food imports become necessary at the cost of scarce foreign exchange.

Agriculture can contribute greatly to increasing the development capacity of a nation insofar as it can become a net foreign exchange earner. Agricultural exports earn foreign exchange. However, production for export may be at the cost of production for the domestic market. (But not necessarily, see chapter two.) Still the food that has to be imported as a result may cost less than the value of the extra exports so that there is a net increase in the foreign exchange earned.

The benefit of foreign exchange earnings is not simply the possibility of importing needed capital and incentive goods but also the generation of domestic incomes. We have seen in chapter two that investment occurs only where there is a market for the product. In poor countries, the size of the market for many goods that might be domestically produced will critically depend on the demand of the rural sector. Where rural incomes grow only as urban consumption rises and urban consumption depends in turn on the incomes to be earned by selling goods to the rural sector, the growth of incomes and investment may be slow and even stop altogether. But the injection into the economy of incomes derived from exports can be a major stimulus to the growth of manufacturing industry. This applies especially where the product exported is grown by large numbers of farmers rather than by large estates employing relatively few people. In Africa the export of peasant-grown cotton, coffee, cocoa and palm oil, for example, has been a great stimulus for development, and in East Africa, particularly, continued development largely depends on the growth of rural incomes.* Thus one objective of agricultural policy might be to contribute to general economic development by increasing foreign exchange earnings and by the growth of rural demand.

Not all development strategies cast agriculture in this role, however. Belt-tightening strategies which aim at ploughing back any increase in national output into increasing national capital would attempt to tax agricultural purchasing power and may even – as in the early Soviet plans – invoke compulsory food procurement programmes. Whatever development strategy is pursued, some taxation is likely to be called for, and the choice of

*See the previous chapter, however, for a discussion of some factors which limit the possibilities of expanding agricultural exports.

rural development policies might be influenced by the extent to which possible policies will increase government revenues or the ease of their collection.

Nutrition targets may find a place in national development objectives in a way that may be reflected in rural development policy. Many countries encourage the production of high protein foods and the growing of drought resistant or easily stored crops as a provision against famine. However, such programmes have little impact where, as is usually the case, malnutrition is chronic and is basically a matter of poverty. In this respect food supply problems may be secondary to the creation of effective demand and the improvement of nutrition may imply income distribution objectives to provide a minimum subsistence income for all.

So far we have discussed rural policy objectives in economic terms even though they are expressions of social and political objectives. However, it is as well to recognize not only that policy objectives are ultimately social and political issues, but also that their translation into economic goals cannot be at all precise. As we have seen, one important policy concern will be the maintenance of political power (though this is not always a sufficient or even a necessary condition for development). More positively, policy may be concerned for the maintenance of stability and of an atmosphere conducive to investment. In practice, such concerns will bear not only upon policy choices as they relate to who benefits and who suffers, but also to the choice of policy instruments and agencies as these may affect the possibilities of resentment or enthusiasm becoming focused.

Concern for the quality of life, the structure of society and the attitudes of individuals may also play a part in the choice of rural development policies. This is strikingly illustrated in Tanzania where for a period there was a programme of village settlement schemes which were intended to harness modern science and capital to agricultural production by applying them to whole village communities. Although many of these schemes have not been successful and the programme is now proceeding more cautiously than before, there is still concern to avoid the encouragement of individual farmers, whose success would mean substantial wage employment and, it is thought, the creation of a capitalistic, self-regarding society. This attitude is adopted consciously and in the recognition that it has a cost in slowing down economic development. Tanzania's objectives contrast sharply with those of other countries where policies are chosen in order to encourage individual enterprise and to break down traditional attitudes to, e.g., kinship obligations, because these are seen to hinder attainment of the desired new society.

Thus, policy for rural development must normally compromise between different objectives – between employment, foreign exchange, and food supply targets; between maximizing output and spreading the benefits of investment programmes or securing desired social aims. Different policies will, of course be appropriate to different aims as well as to different environments.

The Role of Science, Research and Communication

If our earlier arguments are correct, it follows that research must be the cornerstone of development whatever strategies are adopted with regard to such issues as self-sufficiency, land reform, reliance on market forces, or the adoption of large-scale farming schemes. With regard to research, governments have the prime responsibility for its encouragement, since private businesses are likely to find that research is not only risky but yields a product of which it is difficult to control the sale. The social returns to research can be very high where it is directed at relieving constraints on farmers' production. Enormous gains are to be derived from research in plant and animal genetics, and the development of new farming systems with improved seed, water, fertilizers, insecticides and tools. While there is much to be done yet on fundamental problems of e.g. crop/sun/soil/water relationships the urgent problems for poor countries require the application of existing knowledge to the modification of farming systems for farmer adoption. This implies for these countries not simply research into crop and animal husbandry but also associated work on the economics and sociology of total farming systems.

Research is valueless until it is communicated and governments have the prime responsibility also for providing an effective extension service. There are major policy choices with respect to the organization, number and quality of extension workers and with respect to their salary, their status in the village and in the administrative hierarchy. Also there are major questions of their allocation – to advanced or backward areas? advanced or backward farmers? general advisory work or specific five-point programmes? in the field or in farmer training institutes?

Extension must in turn be supported by supplies of necessary inputs – credit, seed, fertilizers and so on. Major policy decisions affect the extent to which government needs to create, control or encourage agencies to supply these inputs.

The policies discussed above will affect the choices open to farmers and the extent to which they are aware of them. The extent to which farmers respond to new opportunities will, however, depend on their attitudes and perhaps also on their basic skills of numeracy and literacy. Thus another important aspect of agricultural development strategy is policy with regard to primary and adult education.

Insofar as there are conflicts of objectives involved in the adoption of research, extension or educational programmes they arise mainly over who gets the benefits of these programmes. Is research directed primarily at export or domestic crops? At crops grown by farmers in irrigated, wealthy regions or farmers in dry, poverty-stricken regions? Is extension to be directed to progressive, wealthy, enterprising landlords or conservative, poor, inhibited tenants? Should primary education in rural areas be expanded at the cost of improved secondary education in towns?

Price Policies

Price policies also involve such conflicts, together with some very difficult compromises in the allocation of incentives between agriculture and industry. The first choice is how much and in what way, if at all, to interfere with the market. While the free market might lead to undesirable patterns of production and distribution, a managed market requires a very substantial management input backed by considerable quantities of information and analysis, and the results of a poorly-managed market can be even less desirable than those of a free market.

Price control might be adopted in order to reduce farmer uncertainties about price, or as a means of taxing or subsidizing farmers. Price control to reduce uncertainty aims to put limits to the possible range of prices. (Though even when successful, this does not necessarily stabilize farm incomes.) The minimum of government action for such a scheme is its intervention to support prices in a glut by agreeing to buy at some announced floor price. This might involve the government in storage costs or trading losses from exporting surpluses. These impose a severe limit on the ability of governments to sustain prices to farmers.

There is a limit, too, to the extent to which governments can keep food prices down, for if prices to farmers are reduced, food supply will fall and this must result in a rise in price. Governments might seek to hold down food prices where urban wages are sensitive to food prices, and where manufacturing investment is more sensitive to the costs of labour than to the strength of farmers' demands for the manufactured product. They can only do this, however, if they are prepared to subsidize (which is hardly practicable given the limited tax base and is likely to be self-defeating anyway) or ration. India is one country which has adopted rationing of low-priced food-grains while it allows supplies in excess of rations to find their own – at times (e.g. in August 1967) very high – price. This also involves a measure of compulsory procurement of grains which is, effectively, a tax on farmers. Whether it be to subsidize food prices or to finance investment, the agricultural sector may well be looked to as a source of tax revenue. In some countries, for example Ghana, agricultural exports have provided a major source of tax revenue. Purchases of imported farm inputs, too, have sometimes been taxed in order to protect infant domestic industries. Some economists have condemned such taxation as inhibiting agricultural development and clearly this could be the case. However, we have already emphasized the fact that policies must necessarily compromise the achievement of competing objectives and the important question is what level of taxes (including none at all) affords the best prospect of attaining policy objectives? For some products at some price levels, supply and investment might be relatively little affected by modest taxation (e.g. probably coffee in East Africa in the 1950s) but in others there may be marked effects on the level of investment, total supply, the pattern of crops produced and the amounts retained for consumption. Effective price policy must be based on good predictions of its consequences both on agriculture and on the rest of the economy.

Policy Coordination

The above discussion does no more than indicate some of the broad choices of policy for stimulating agricultural development. It will be clear that the total set of national policy programmes will involve a large number of agencies and that the pattern of approach may vary considerably even between regions within a country. Not only will a large number of agencies be involved but even the ministries involved will be many. Apart from those policies which are primarily the responsibility of departments usually under the ministry of agriculture – agriculture, animal industry, research and extension – there will be other departments involved which may or may not be under the ministry of agriculture – such as irrigation, marketing, land survey and settlement, cooperatives, community development, credit and agricultural training. Other ministries will also be closely involved – especially finance, labour, commerce, education and health.

Since it is quite infeasible to contain the full range of agricultural policy instrument controls within a single ministry of agriculture, coordination of agricultural and rural development policies presents quite serious difficulties. One extreme but salutary example of lack of coordination occurred in the field of price policy. In this factual example, independent and un-coordinated policies were pursued by a central marketing board, a department of cooperative development and local government authorities. The marketing board, making conservative assumptions about the price at which it could sell the crop, offered a price to cooperative unions who (after deducting their own costs and other charges) offered a price to their member cooperative societies, who in turn offered a price to growers (calculated so as to leave a trading surplus to build up cooperative society capital and to pay a cess imposed by the local government to bring in some revenue). The resultant price, written up on a board outside the cooperative society's buying post, was *negative*!

Even where ministries coordinate policy decisions, the agencies implementing them might fail to achieve coordination. Thus we may hear stories of the installation of electrically driven tube-wells impotent for lack of power lines; of tube-wells in working order but without distributory channels; of water without seed; of fertilizer without credit; of nitrogen without phosphate; of insecticide without spraying equipment. The problems of co-ordination in agricultural policy are enormous. Yet the need for coordination is critical. Unless all the required action is taken in time a scheme may be totally abortive. Seed which arrives two weeks late is useless – or worse than useless if anyone attempts to use it. And the same may be true of tractors, fertil-izer and insecticide. Much damage may be done to the reputation and morale of the advisory service in such a case and the dam-age can be compounded if farmers are granted credit and then proceeded against when the crops fail. In these respects alone, agriculture poses far more formidable policy challenges than any other sector.

Conclusion

This chapter has explored many themes. It has tried to show how tightly and critically the farmer is integrated with his ecological and social environment and how poverty and social dependence inhibit risky innovation; how science might contribute to agricultural development and the preconditions of its successful impact; how policy must relate to the concerns of the people whose behaviour it is intended to affect and to multiple, competing, objectives; finally, it has indicated the magnitude and critical role of the task of coordinating the many agencies and policies that must be brought to bear on the task of agricultural development.

It needs hardly be stressed that the nature of this task is different from anything encountered in the richer countries of the world which, for the most part, face the problems of surplus production. It is true that few countries are without communities of poor and backward farmers and that these pose problems similar to those posed by poor farmers in poor countries, but the scale and the setting of these problems are different. Of all the contrasts between rich-temperate country and poor-tropical country agricultures perhaps the most striking and, for a while to come, the most significant is related to the growth of population. If poor countries had only to increase their agricultural production their problems would be relatively simple. While increasing production they must, for some while to come, absorb a substantial increase in population within the rural sector for it is clear that in most poor countries populations are growing faster than the number of jobs outside agriculture. If people are not absorbed within agriculture, then increasing agricultural production will lead to the emergence of, on the one hand, food 'surpluses', and, on the other, large numbers of unemployed unable to afford the means of subsistence.

In poor countries the problems both of increasing incomes and of distributing them are much more acute than in the rich countries. In the decade ahead it seems likely that the problem of unemployment and income distribution will come into prominence – even, perhaps, eclipsing the problem of production. At the heart of the problem will be the strategy for agricultural development.

10 MANPOWER AND EDUCATION

In this chapter and the following one, we turn to the resources for development strategy. The human population appears in a dual capacity. Development is of course for its benefit; at the same time the human stock is the fundamental economic resource. Capital, technology, natural resources are of course important. But without the human agent they are passive. It is the initiatives and actions of people which create and develop the other factors and bring them into use. It is thus the human resources, the people of a country, on which development ultimately depends.

In most poor countries, however, the human resources are by no means fully used. Committed to large development programmes, pressed on every hand by a multitude of urgent tasks, all of which require people to carry them out, one might expect to find a hard-pressed labour force, working long hours and strained to the limit. The situation in reality is one of almost total contrast. Major sections of the adult population are underemployed, working short hours or at half-pace for much of the year. Large numbers, especially in the urban areas, are openly unemployed, living off relatives or petty theft while seeking a wage-earning job which never materializes. Thousands leave school every year – in some countries literally millions – only to spend the following months or years looking for jobs. In one form or another, this situation exists in most countries of Asia, Africa, Latin America and the Middle East and, over the last decade, has become increasingly common.

Unemployment and underemployment are only the most obvious of the inefficiencies in the use of the human resources of such countries. There are in addition gross imbalances between the skills required and the skills available, between the tasks of priority for development and the work actually undertaken, between the rural areas where agriculturalists, veterinarians, administrators, forestry experts, engineers, doctors and a whole host of other persons are urgently needed, and the urban areas where most persons with professional training are employed. Probably the greatest need of all is for educated people willing to take the lead as enterprising farmers; yet the bulk of such people are either in the towns or trying to move to them.

As serious as the imbalances in the *use* of the labour force are the (related) imbalances between the preparation people need and what they get. Education and training, far from making up for present deficiencies in skills, are often fitting out the future generation with all the failings of the present. Nor is it only a matter of formal education. Apprenticeship, industrial training and rural extension too often do little more than maintain the present position, when they need to be laying the foundations for technological change and widespread expansion.

And in more basic respects, the physical standards of the labour force are inadequate, showing many of the deficiencies of poverty: in health, diet, housing and basic amenities, conditions for a significant sector of the population may be so low that their physical strength and capacity for work are impaired.

Though difficult to measure, the attitudes and values of the population can be enormously important for development. In this respect, the old-fashioned puritan virtues of thrift, hard work and enterprise are often emphasized. No less valuable in the modern context can be the willingness to understand and support a national development strategy, in spite of higher taxes, wage freezes, and other unpleasant policies, which may be needed to force the pace of growth or distribute its benefits more equitably.

Attitudes result from a whole complex of obvious and subtle causes but they are and can be influenced particularly by education, the mass media and political leadership. One might expect therefore to find in countries needing rapid development the media used to educate the public to the realities and hard choices involved and to win commitment to it. Not only might this make development more successful, but the greater involvement and participation in the process could be benefits in themselves. Yet again the actual situation often falls short of these ambitious hopes. Where there are television transmitters, educational programmes take up only a small fraction of broadcasting time, even compared with developed countries. The situation is somewhat better with newspapers and other printed material, but even so, the potential of these for supporting national development is never fully realized.

Why is the labour force so badly prepared and misused for the priorities of national development? The answer is complex. But in part it is because man is not bred for work alone any more than he works for bread alone. Most decisions are taken and things done with only one eye on their consequences for man as an economic resource. Moreover, even when economic objectives are central, different interests are involved which lead to conflicts in desirable courses of action. Nor are these conflicting courses of action easily reconciled in the give and take of a free market for labour. For a whole host of reasons, the labour market functions very badly in most developing countries in providing incentives for persons to acquire useful skills and education and, when trained, in providing them (and potential employers) with incentives to use their skills and energies in jobs of priority for national development.

The inadequacies of the labour market make it essential to devise a strategy for human resources as an integral part of a programme for accelerated development. Since the whole argument rests on the imperfections of the labour market, it will be useful to indicate these imperfections more precisely. In the first place, this market is divided by geographic, occupational, legal, racial or educational barriers, across which it is difficult for labour to move even when correctly informed of the opportunities.

In addition, governments, unions and particular employers exert direct pressures on the level and structure of wages and salaries, putting some up and keeping some down, affecting both incentives of where to work and what to do. More important, distortions of the labour market affect the employers' decisions whether to employ a man or a machine or even whether to set up a business at all.

In the second place, the labour market works badly because a large fraction of the labour force, particularly those with skills and education, is employed in the public sector. There wages and salaries are largely fixed by a superstructure of traditions and conventions, revised only at intervals and very unresponsive to market forces. Often well over half of the graduates of a country are employed in these circumstances and deployed in government in a way that shows little concern for development priorities, let alone productivity.

Thirdly, the whole point of a development strategy is to change radically the present situation. In the field of manpower, where changes can take years to produce results (in education for instance), priorities must be judged by the needs of ten or fifteen years ahead. The present wage structure, imperfectly reflecting even the immediate supplies and demands of the present situation, is largely irrelevant as a guide to the needs of the decade to come.

The efficient working of the labour market is doubtful in the developed countries: in most developing countries its inefficiency is beyond dispute, for all these reasons. A strategy, consciously planned, is therefore needed. The right pattern will not simply emerge from the interplay of market forces. Or rather, if it is left simply to emerge, it will be a haphazard product of conflicting and diverging influences.

The rest of this chapter sketches out an approach to an integrated strategy in two areas, education and employment. These, of course, are only two of the many aspects of a comprehensive strategy for manpower. Since the whole point of an integrated strategy is to plan a concerted effort, any adequate plan would have to take full account of all the main interrelationships involved. But education and employment are especially important in themselves and will serve to illustrate the broader themes.

Education and employment will also emphasize one major feature of manpower policy. This is that almost always human resource development serves a double objective. It is a necessary condition for more rapid economic development and, at the same time, it is desirable in itself as an improvement in present living standards. Education is both a present benefit and an investment in future skills. Employment is both a means to an end and – as in our saner moments most of us admit – a necessary part of a balanced and purposeful life. And the same is true of health, housing, welfare and other expenditures on people, particularly for persons whose living standards are at the margin of subsistence. Any adequate strategy must take account of this dual function.

Education

Education has a major role in a national strategy for economic and social development. How well prepared are the educational systems of most poor countries for this important task?

The educational systems of almost all such countries have expanded rapidly in recent years. In Africa between 1950 and 1963, primary enrolments expanded nearly threefold, in Asia and Latin America they doubled, in contrast to Western Europe and North America where they increased respectively by only a quarter and a half. At secondary and higher levels in all continents of the Third World, expansion has been even more rapid, increasing between three and four times over the period, and in Africa, after independence, at an even faster rate. University enrolments in some countries have doubled or tripled within the space of a five-year plan. Naturally the rate has been slower in countries where enrolments were already sizeable in relation to population, but even in India, for example, the numbers in higher education rose threefold, from 400,000 in 1950 to 1·2 million in 1962. At all levels, these rates of expansion are significantly higher than those which the industrialized countries have attained in recent years.

In spite of this rapid expansion, especially at the higher levels, the coverage of the educational systems in most underdeveloped countries remains limited and uneven. In Africa, the 'pyramids' of enrolments still taper rapidly to near vanishing point. Though some 50 per cent of the relevant age group are in primary schools, hardly 7 per cent get any form of secondary education and under 1 per cent get to university. These percentages are very low in relation to the needs of development. In many African countries it is still true that an average primary school student has less than one chance in a thousand of continuing his education long enough to get a degree. The situation in Latin America and Asia is better than in Africa but even in them most educational systems are very much less rational than those of the developed countries.

Two particular aspects of the enrolment structure rate create such special problems that they deserve separate mention. The first is wastage, the high rates of drop-out all along the system, often beginning after the first year of primary school. In Chile, Peru and Costa Rica, for instance, over a third of the students who entered the first grade of primary school in the early fifties, dropped out before even reaching the second grade, i.e. really before being able to show any benefits at all, and under a quarter completed the full course of six years. In spite of some improvements, drop-out still is a widespread cause of educational inefficiency in countries of the Third World.

The second feature is the sharp contrasts and inequalities within the system – between urban and rural facilities, between enrolments of boys and enrolments of girls, between the good and bad schools, between the length and quality of education for the rich in contrast to the backward, incomplete schooling for those of the poor who are fortunate enough to obtain a place. Such contrasts also exist of course in the developed countries, but in the low-income countries they are more common and more extreme.

All education falls short of its ideals. But a great deal of the content, approach and methods of the education provided in low-income countries is inadequate even by the most elementary standards. There are two main reasons. The teachers themselves often have only a primary education, followed by a year or two of training, if that. This is no reflection on the individuals themselves. In many countries, particularly in Africa, they have had little or no opportunity to acquire the education they need. The educational deficiencies of the previous generation take time to eradicate. In other cases, the poor quality of the teaching force reflects low pay and morale, only the second best being attracted into a teaching career.

The second reason for inadequacy is more fundamental. It is that the very standards to which many educational institutions in less developed countries aspire, are inappropriate, irrelevant or sometimes positively harmful to the development of the country.

One very important result of this is the unfortunate social attitudes often engendered by these educational systems. Far from serving as a preparation for tackling the country's most urgent tasks, the schools often end up producing an elite which feels itself to be far above any practical involvement. Instead of providing the skills and determination needed to grasp any opportunities that exist of revolutionizing agriculture, many schools become little more than agencies to provide passports to escape to the towns. And even then, instead of providing practical skill for urban jobs, schools encourage a distaste for manual work and a preference for the academic.

Of course, it is not fair simply to blame the schools, which to a large extent simply reflect the values and rewards of society. The whole system of incentives and rewards in the society make it rational to seek a white collar job in the towns. Any practical reform must tackle these problems as well as education. But education too must be transformed.

In spite of low enrolments and inadequate quality, the costs of education in terms of local resources are enormous. As a group, the low-income countries are spending roughly the same proportion of their national resources on education as the richer countries, but getting much less for it. Over the last decade, public expenditure on education in many poor countries has risen from between 2 and 4 per cent of gross national product to between 4 and 6 per cent – but still only a fraction of their school-age populations are in school. In country after country, the share of government budgets going to education has already reached the point where the International Institute of Educational Planning, an offshoot of UNESCO, refers to a 'World Crisis in Education' and argues that the limit on educational expenditure, at least as a proportion of the government budget, has been reached.

The Cause of the Present Educational Problems

The various facts sketched above, when taken together, present most developing countries with two major problems: their educational systems cost too much and yet at the same time they seem to be failing to take a leading role in economic and social development. Before turning to policies to deal with these problems, it is necessary to discuss their causes.

As mentioned above, most developing countries are spending about the same share of their national incomes on education as the developed countries, yet the proportion of their children who get to primary school, let alone to secondary and higher education, is very much lower. At first sight this may seem surprising. The largest share of educational expenditure goes on teachers' salaries and since these, like most incomes in developing countries, are low, one might expect education to be proportionately cheaper. Yet the fact is that at primary levels, it costs most low-income countries, relative to their national income, five to ten times as much to provide primary schooling for a given proportion of the school-age population as it does the high-income countries, relative to their national income. It usually costs a poor country proportionately very much more at secondary and higher levels. Small wonder, therefore, that in most of them enrolments should be so much lower than in Western Europe or North America.

Three reasons explain most of these higher costs. In the first place the rapid rates of population growth have raised significantly the proportion of the population in the school age groups. In rich countries, about a quarter of the population is of school age, but in poor ones it is often as much as a half. This fact alone may double the burden on the adult population (or on the taxpayers or on the government) of providing education for the equivalent proportion of the nation's children. In the second place, teachers' salaries, though often low absolutely, are much higher in relation to other incomes than in the developed countries, especially at the secondary and university levels. In Uganda, for instance, a typical primary teacher earns £150 to £325 per year. This may seem little enough but it is in fact between six and thirteen times the average national income of £25. A typical secondary teacher in Uganda earns between twenty-five and forty times the average national income and a university teacher up to 125 times. African contrasts are rather extreme, but even in India the corresponding figures run from two-and-a-half to four-and-a-half times average national income for primary and secondary school teachers and from nine-and-a-half to fifteen times for university teachers, significantly higher than the pro-portions in rich countries where the primary or secondary teacher rarely earns more than three times average income and often less than twice.[1] In many areas, in Latin America especially, teacher costs are further inflated by overstaffing both in the educational administration and in the teaching force.

The third reason for the higher costs of education is less common, though important where it occurs. It is the higher costs of school buildings, particularly for secondary schools and universities. Some countries have adopted standards for school building far above the general style and quality of buildings in the country. Sometimes this results from a desire for prestige, or from ill-considered advice from architects, or from the cost-raising ploys of an interested contractor. But foreign-aid donors are also often responsible; anxious that their aid should be seen, they sponsor a showpiece, grand enough to stand out from the others. It only takes a few such examples and a leapfrogging process begins, in which the recipient country follows the standards set by the donor only to be followed, in turn by the next donor, raising standards again to create a further showpiece. Since this process tends in time to raise to some extent the costs of other schools, it is often true that such aid, far from making a net contribution, imposes long-run burdens on the recipient country.

The second problem to analyse is education's inadequate performance in preparing the population for the tasks of development. The country needs people alert to new challenges and opportunities, ready to try new approaches and with minds and hands quick and able to take up new skills. Instead the scene one often finds in tropical Africa is a primary classroom chanting the names of the kings of England or a botany class studying French flowers for French examinations.

It is easy to laugh at such absurdities and, to be fair, many of the worst have long since passed. But the real problem is far deeper and more difficult: this is the whole question of what should be taught and how. The more difficult aspects of this have not been fully solved in any country anywhere, and probably, in a changing world, never will be. But the point is that in the low-income countries, the training of teachers, the textbooks and the general approach to the whole problem lag behind even what is generally known, tried and agreed.

On both these problems, the influence of rich countries is both positive and negative. On the one hand, they can provide obvious opportunities. They are a source of trained teachers and teacher trainers, especially at university level; they provide textbooks and teaching methods, already tested and ready to be adopted. More fundamentally, the countries which have already industrialized have over the years produced many of the ideas, discoveries and technologies which are needed in development and which – ignoring the costs of communication, royalties, patents and restrictions – are now the common property of mankind.

But as has been discussed in other parts of this book, this is far from an unmixed blessing. There is a bewitching attraction in the latest ideas and latest technology which, when applied in inappropriate conditions, can be extremely harmful. Education itself is heavily influenced by the indiscriminate adoption of the standards and even curricula of the industrialized nations. Medical education emphasizes the latest surgery and techniques when the doctor–population ratio in the country, let alone the availability of hospital and surgical facilities, makes it impossible to apply them except for a tiny minority and at great cost. What is needed is a basic medical training adapted to the general needs of the rural population. This training could be shorter and cheaper, and provide more doctors more quickly. But, by the standards of the developed countries, it is not respectable. Similar examples could be given about the content and relevance of training for engineers, bricklayers, economists, lawyers, agriculturalists and teachers. The standards and syllabuses are not universally applicable, yet there are strong pressures – conscious and unconscious – to transfer to the poorer countries those used in the rich ones (and not always appropriately even there). When this happens, the results can seriously retard development.

The Elements of Educational Strategy

Even to talk about a strategy is dangerously misleading, as if to suggest that the priorities and approaches of a hundred different countries – let alone regions and districts within the countries – could be anything but very different. And a main conclusion of this and other chapters is surely that the strategy for each country has to be constructed to fit the local environment. Wholesale imports of ideas, whether from rich countries or from poor neighbours will almost always be misfits.

Yet if it is impossible to be specific, it may be possible to indicate what may be among the objectives of any strategy for education and manpower. The following five objectives are probably common to most developing countries, though the priorities and approaches to each of them will vary considerably.

First, there is the manpower objective – the need for the educational system in its widest sense, to prepare people for all the many tasks of development. Engineers and plumbers, administrators and inspectors, accountants and businessmen, doctors and veterinarians, agriculturalists and teachers, all will be needed and most require some sort of training. There is really no substitute for some form of quantitative manpower plan, linked to the country's development plan and estimating the number and types of skilled personnel needed and the education and training they will require. Manpower plans on these lines have now been prepared for perhaps half of the world's poor countries, often crude and inadequate, but at least attempting to focus attention on the manpower required for development and the education and training needed to produce it.

But manpower plans, to be useful and effective, need careful design. They must deal as much with the needs for training, informal education, apprenticeships, etc. as with formal schooling. They must focus on education for adults as well as for school children. Flexibility must be built into the manpower plans – flexibility in the whole plan to allow for the unforeseeable changes as the economy develops and flexibility in the types of training provided to enable people to adapt quickly and efficiently to the inevitable changes in technology. Finally a plan for manpower cannot stop short at making quantitative recommendations: the whole question of adjusting the approach, curriculum, and institutions of the system must be tackled too.

The second common objective concerns the social role of education. The educational system is a major influence on the whole structure of society, opening doors to some sections of the population, closing doors to others and leaving many unaware that such doors even exist. Over the long run, education is one of the most potent influences on the distribution of income and of opportunities. Quite apart from its role in these respects, it makes a contribution, direct and indirect, to the quality and richness of a nation's culture and the ability of ordinary men and women to enjoy it. The importance of education as a means to development must not detract from its importance as one of the ends of development.

A third objective of education planning is to influence attitudes. As mentioned already, the values built into the school system, and strengthened by all the communication media can have a profound effect on the commitment and involvement of the population in development. Difficult though it is to predict all the effects, educational planning should take this into account.

This is perhaps more clearly realized, and the educational systems planned accordingly, in socialist countries. (But there is no reason to think that, though unplanned, the influences on attitudes in non-communist countries are any less profound.) The mass assaults on existing attitudes and opinions, and the whole organization to change them, can at times be fearsome. But on other occasions, as in the Cuban literacy campaign in 1961, the results are impressive even judged by liberal values. In the Cuban case, the formal objective was literacy and a national campaign for eight months was launched to achieve it. By the end of the campaign, nearly a million adult illiterates – about a fifth of the adult population – had been enrolled and over 700,000, it was claimed, had acquired basic literacy. But the campaign's importance, for the present discussion, lies more in its effect on the attitudes and commitment of the hundreds of thousands of people involved. These indirect effects on attitudes were probably more significant even than the campaign's formal achievement in teaching so many persons to read and write. A virtual army of 106,000 teenagers, mostly from the towns, had been organized to live for eight months in the country. Each stayed with a peasant, helping with farm work and, for two hours a day, teaching him to read and write. In the towns, another 100,000 adults – secretaries, government workers, businessmen and dustmen – were doing the same, teaching illiterates two hours a day in the lunch-hour or after work. The effects of this intimate involvement – bridging the gulf between rural and urban areas, crossing social barriers, differences of occupation, of age and ways of life – made a profound impression on human attitudes. This, to the common man, *was* revolution.[2]

A fourth element in any adequate strategy is relating education to rural development. This has already been briefly mentioned under the heading of meeting manpower needs. But production of sufficient agronomists, field demonstrators and veterinary assistants is the easy part. More difficult is to reform the schooling system so that it becomes a useful introduction rather than a perpetual deterrent to rural life. This is easier said than done. It involves a whole range of controversial policies, from the content of what is taught to the age span of primary education. At the moment in most poor countries, 90 or 95 per cent of all primary school children will never get into a secondary school. Some will complete six years but most will drop out, even before that. Many will look for a wage-earning job, fail to find it and end up employed (productively or unproductively) on the land. These are the harsh facts. Yet in country after country primary education ignores these facts and largely concentrates on an academic course, designed mainly for the 5 or 10 per cent who will be lucky enough to find a place in secondary school.

Or consider the problem of age. Most primary school systems are designed for children to enter aged five or six or seven. In countries where the majority of children leave after four or six years of schooling, they are usually aged eleven to thirteen years by then – too young for adult work, and thus half employed or left to kick their heels until they grow older. This is hardly the fitting end to an education. But should primary school last six years or begin at age seven in a rural community? Why should it not, as some have suggested, begin later, last four years and end with two years practical training in agriculture? None of these alternatives are certain of success and there are enormous practical difficulties. But the need to relate the school system to rural development is perhaps the most important and difficult single educational reform facing developing countries.[3]

And finally there are a number of other objectives which the educational system must fulfil. Some, like research, are common to most countries, though here again there is a need to ensure that research is related to the problems of the country and not focused simply on some imported topic or on technology of international prestige but little local relevance. Other objectives may be confined to certain countries, like the teaching of a common language in schools as a step to national unity. It is impossible to list them all here, but in any particular country one of the others may be very important.

Lest the point be missed, it may be useful to enlarge on the two examples given. Take technology. A major conclusion of this book is that the tremendous technological developments of recent years have been enormously biased by the needs and circumstances of the rich countries. They after all have financed more than 90 per cent of the technological research and development. Either the technology available cannot be used, or it is too expensive, or, very often, it is used in totally different circumstances from those for which it was designed and leads to all the consequences discussed elsewhere – high imports, low employment, sophisticated skill requirements and unemployment. Education and training in low-income countries should be designed to help achieve this development of technologies to meet the specific requirements of low-income countries.

The second example is the need for a common language. Within industrialized countries, where national unity was achieved a century or more ago, the question of a common national language is usually taken for granted; Canada is in fact an exceptional case in which about a fifth of the population are French- rather than English-speaking. But in India, Bolivia and the Philippines, fewer than half the population speak the dominant language. Estimates suggest that at least twenty African countries are in the same position. Teaching a common language in this situation is a major contribution to communications as well as to political unity.

In one way or another, all these objectives have to be hammered into a strategy for educational development, and then this has to be elaborated in all the practical details of planning schools, enrolments, classes and courses. How well the eventual programme interprets national priorities and objectives will depend on the clarity with which the objectives are perceived and formulated, the skill of the planner, and the relative strengths and interests of the parties involved.

Any plan, provided it is taken seriously, must arouse some opposition, if only because the distribution of costs and benefits favours some people less than others and everyone less than they think possible. And opposition, depending on the circumstances, may be justified and helpful. But two sources of opposition to an educational strategy and plan deserve special mention.

First the social needs education is designed to meet may be different from those recognized by individuals. There may be a direct clash over objectives but the basic reason may be that the educational plan is focused on long-run development objectives while individuals are responding to the immediate situation. There is often, for example, opposition to reforms which would make the curriculum more agricultural. This opposition reflects both the objective fact that, at present, earnings in urban white-collar jobs are much higher than in most rural, agricultural occupations, and also the subjective assessment that these differentials will continue indefinitely and that every school leaver has a reasonable chance of getting a white-collar job. In many countries, neither of these latter assumptions are justified. Indeed, if rural development is to succeed, the prospects on which these assumptions are made must be changed.

The second reason for resistance to change lies in the inherent inertia of the educational system. Changing the curriculum, upgrading standards, introducing new methods, impose new burdens on the whole teaching force and threaten the reputation and status of existing teachers, particularly the older ones. Change in education policy threatens other interests also, not only those of the teachers. The same is true of course when new ideas and approaches are introduced anywhere, but in many areas important for economic efficiency there are often direct economic pressures to punish the laggards and reward those who absorb the changes. In education, this rarely happens.

In both cases, the possibility of opposition calls for a positive response – to deal with the causes of opposition rather than to suppress it. To neutralize the support for a white collar curriculum means trying to change the ratio of rural/urban earnings and enhance rural prospects. To modernize the educational system means vast programmes of retraining and upgrading, so that older teachers are able to teach efficiently and well. What this implies, in effect, is that educational change will only receive support, and will only succeed, if it is made part and parcel of other changes in society as a whole. This is true of much of development strategy and helps to explain why it is difficult and often unsuccessful.

Employment, Wages and Incentives

Educational reform will make little economic impact – and indeed may not succeed at all – unless the structure of wages and the possibilities of employment give people the incentives and opportunity to use the skills they have acquired. Yet changes in these areas are often the most difficult to achieve.

The present situation is often far from what is required to make efficient use of the skills and energies of the labour force. The number of job opportunities has in many countries risen in recent years at barely a third the rate of the rise in production. In some, notably in East and Central Africa, wage-earning employment has often fallen for as long as ten years, at a time when output expanded quite significantly. A faster growth of output than employment signifies an increase in labour productivity, and, when labour is scarce, this is of course to be welcomed. But when there is extreme unemployment and underemployment, rising labour productivity means a slow growth in the number of jobs, which is a very doubtful blessing.

The crucial comparisons, however, are between the increases in employment, that is job opportunities in the modern sector, and the increase either in population or in the number of school leavers. Generally speaking, in recent years, employment has grown more slowly than population, which in turn has grown considerably more slowly than output from the schools. In Nigeria, for instance, about 600,000 persons leave school each year, while the number of new wage-earning jobs created has averaged about 10,000 or 20,000 (ignoring the civil war). In Tanzania, 1·25 million school leavers were expected over the period of the five-year plan while wage-earning employment was expected to rise by 55,000. These figures, though startling, are not exceptional. The general result is increasing numbers without jobs and seeking work. This applies not merely to both total population and primary-school leavers, but also in many cases to secondary-school leavers and even graduates. The problem is particularly serious for those with education, since hopes and ambitions have been raised which, when frustrated, can tear apart both the individual and his society.

There is thus a growing difference between the numbers with jobs and the mounting numbers without. But in addition, the gap between the two groups – in terms of earnings, living standards and future prospects – has also been widening rapidly. Statistics on average earnings are both patchy and difficult to interpret, but the general picture is clear. There have been rapid increases in the earnings of those with jobs, both absolutely and relatively to those in the rural areas. Again African experience is particularly startling, though similar tendencies seem to have occurred in Latin America and Asia. Increases in money wages of

7 to 10 per cent per year have not been uncommon over periods when prices have risen by only 2 or 3 per cent and when agricultural prices (which largely determine rural incomes) have fallen or remained constant.[4] As the gap between urban and rural incomes widens, the rush to the towns increases, although the diminishing chance of finding jobs somewhat offsets the growing attractiveness of urban wages.

Quite apart from its changing pattern in these respects, the wages and salary structure is inappropriate in other ways. The relative earnings of different jobs, far from reflecting their importance for development, often embody all the worst priorities of the existing economy: high pay for the overcrowded white collar, clerical, urban bureaucratic jobs: low pay for the undermanned technical, manual and rural jobs. Instead of payment by results, a big proportion of jobs seem to be paid regardless of results and almost regardless of whether they contribute to development or not. The upshot is that the present labour force is attracted to the wrong places and, even worse, that the next generation is attracted to train for and enter occupations which have low priority for development.

There are two major reasons why the wage structure differs from what is needed for accelerated development. In part it is the fault of an inappropriate wage structure in the public sector. Inappropriate differentials and levels here reflect past priorities, colonial traditions, bureaucratic confusions, political obligations, the pressure of particular interest groups, confused objectives and plain irrationality. Secondly, outside the public sector, wages and incomes reflect the pattern of labour demand (in turn reflecting the distribution of incomes) and the supply of different types of labour (in turn reflecting the past structure of education, training, etc.) but also the effectiveness or ineffectiveness of market forces. Without elaborating all the details, the essential point is that the structure of wages and salaries, imperfectly reflecting even present market forces, often differs considerably from *national* priorities for *future* development.

Before too much attention is focused on the formal wage structure, it is important to stress again that in many countries of Asia and Africa the labour force working for wages are only the minority. Most people work in agriculture, gaining their livelihood from their own food production, including cash income from sales of their crops. In addition, there are other non-wage-earning categories, persons working in cooperatives or communes or partnerships or self-employed in trade or business, often on a very small scale, depending on the country concerned.

Many of the defects of the wage structure are reflected in the distribution of income as a whole. Rural, manual workers, farmers or craftsmen, whether working for wages or not, are usually worse off than those with the white-collar jobs in the towns. Their position in several crucial points is in such sharp contrast with that in the developed countries that it is useful to explain why. A major reason is that the trade unions mainly represent groups of urban workers. Far from defending the right of the underdog to a reasonable share of the national income, the unions are a pressure group for the already privileged, against the interests of both the unemployed and those in the rural areas. This is sometimes obscured by other differentials which are even more extreme. For example, the differences between the urban wage earner and the higher-paid professionals or propertied group are usually far wider than in developed countries. And in most cases these differentials are so wide as to be very striking to the eye. When the majority live in shacks without running water, eat meat once a week and have one pair of shoes or sandals to their name, even a modestly dressed man in a Volkswagen looks ostentatious. In this connection, the importation of rich-country standards into a poor-country environment can have disastrous effects. Such standards are imported in many ways. They are purveyed by films, TV programmes and newspapers, which portray as normal living what can be achieved only by the very few. They are a by-product of the constant travellings of politicians and businessmen. They are brought by the tourists, the vast majority of whom come from countries where incomes are high enough to afford such travel and who insist on what to them are the usual amenities. Particularly important in African countries are the influences of expatriates, employed by government, large companies, on technical assistance and in the universities. Whatever their other costs and benefits, each of these introduces a further chance of comparison between what is treated as normal for the rich countries (though it is in fact well above normal, even for them) and what is the very exceptional for the poor countries. The result is intense and growing dissatisfaction within the less-developed country, which leads to strong pressures to raise local wages and salaries. This, combined with slow-growing employment, intensifies within the local situation the contrasts and deep divisions similar to those which distinguish the local situation from the one abroad.

It is not easy to escape the dilemmas posed for low-income countries. If local men are paid less than expatriates, discontent and the ugly overtones of discrimination arise. If they are paid the same, differentials within the country widen. For countries which employ few expatriates, the problem is less difficult, though tourism and other reminders of rich-country tastes and standards remain. And, even in this case, the possibility of the skilled and educated joining the brain drain and emigrating is usually enough to exert some upward pressures on the salaries of the educated, particularly doctors, engineers and scientists. The result is the large differentials between the salaries of those with education and those without, enormous in Africa, but significant in other poor countries also.

Many of the factors described, in both the discussion of wages and employment and the earlier discussion on education, inter-act and reinforce each other, contributing to unemployment, underemployment and the maldistribution of the labour force.

Two examples may illustrate the interaction. Increases in wages lead directly to higher labour costs, for the government and private employer alike. Higher labour costs increase the relative advantage of machine production, leading some employers to switch to more mechanization and cut back on labour. Although production may increase, employment rises less than it might. Similar results follow a wage increase in government; with any wage increase, and a given budget, government employs fewer people.

In a developed country, many of these consequences do not follow. For instance, if wage increases are general throughout the economy, the prices of machines rise along with wages, reducing the incentive to mechanize. In any case, since there is near full employment and government has the means to maintain this, mechanization is in itself desirable as the means to greater productivity and higher production.

In countries dependent on exports and imports, there are other serious results – and these apply whether the countries are rich or poor, though often more strikingly and with more serious consequences in the latter. Exports may deteriorate if rising costs at home cut the incentive of the exporter to produce, or price him out of the foreign market. Imports may rise, partly because of the rising propensity to import as incomes increase, and partly because higher labour costs make local production less competitive with imports. In the long run, the worst consequence is that a deficit in the balance of payments may well cause slower growth, reducing even further the future prospects of employment.

Education sometimes plays an important part in the process of increasing wages, as a second example may show. Even without any changes in the wages and salary structure (i.e. with unchanged wage rates), a rapidly expanding education system can cause average earnings to rise. The majority of those with higher education (including teachers) are employed in the public sector, where it is common practice to fix salary levels by reference to educational qualifications. There is thus a big area where incomes rise simply because of the effects of education. As the educational system expands, increasing numbers with the higher educational qualifications enter employment at the higher salaries. The escalation of average salaries continues, as long as additional educated persons are taken on, either as additions to the total numbers employed or when, in the name of upgrading the service, someone with less education is replaced by someone with more. The rising salary levels increase imports and slow the growth of employment as discussed earlier. But since at first the newly educated are finding jobs, the slow growth of employment is not too noticeable, particularly in countries where expatriates are being replaced. The numbers of school leavers may continue to expand at 5 or 10 per cent a year or even faster, until some limit is reached in absorbing the educated into employment. The acute problem of the unemployed school leaver then emerges and grows with dramatic impact.

The process as described is of course only one of the possible processes, and again it is probably more relevant to the last decade in Africa than elsewhere. In other situations other factors may be more important in explaining the upward trend in wages or the slow growth of employment. One process in primary exporting economies is due to the fluctuations in the price and volume of the main exports. When export earnings are high, producer incomes and government revenue rise, causing increases in wages and salaries in the leading sectors, which spread elsewhere in the economy. This is particularly pronounced in capital intensive extractive industries, petroleum especially, which employ relatively few people and which can therefore absorb increased labour costs more easily. But it happens also in government. Wage increases conceded in the upswing of the boom are seldom reduced when export earnings decline. The result is more mechanization and less employment.

In almost all poor countries, the root cause of the unemployment of school leavers must be found in the slow growth of employment in relation to the rapid growth of population and of outputs from the school systems. As long as these continue, it is inevitable that school leavers will fail to find the jobs they have come to expect.

It would be misleading to overemphasize the importance of rising wages in explaining the slow growth in employment. In many industries, particularly in the manufacturing sector, the use of advanced technologies is the major reason why employment has risen much more slowly than output. Since these advanced technologies tend to be labour-saving, it is at first sight surprising that they would appeal to low-income countries with surplus labour. But the main explanation why labour intensive methods are not used more widely, and more mechanized methods are used instead, is almost certainly that for any given level of output the labour-intensive method is more expensive.

There are a number of reasons for this. In the first place, the latest technique, imported from the developed countries, is often much more efficient technically. It uses less labour *and* less capital per unit of output. By contrast, labour-intensive home-produced methods are often old-fashioned and absolutely inefficient. This reflects of course the technological developments of the industrialized countries who, being richer and in the lead, sponsor the vast majority of the world's applied research and innovation. The economic preoccupations of this research inevitably reflect the economic conditions in the countries where it takes place – an environment of full employment and high and rising labour costs which encourage labour-saving developments. The fact that these new innovations are economically efficient, even in conditions where capital is more expensive and unskilled labour much cheaper, is an indication of how far technological progress overseas has surpassed that in the poorer countries. Slow growth in employment is thus in large part an example of the costs to the low-income countries of being dependent on the technologies of the rich. For there is no reason to suppose that this bias in technological progress is inevitable. If even a few per cent of the sums spent on research in the rich countries was devoted to research suitable for low income countries with surplus labour, *efficient* labour-intensive techniques could no doubt be developed.

Other important but less satisfactory reasons account for the widespread adoption of developed-country technologies in low-income countries, particularly in firms linked to international corporations. In part the transfer of technology from rich countries reproduces a system which is already well known in the firm and thus minimizes some of the uncertainties of using new methods in a new environment; in part it avoids spending money developing new and adapted technologies, particularly when top management may take a pessimistic view of the length of time over which it will be able to exploit them within the country. And in part, it may be due to the individual interests of the manager but not of the firm; by sticking with what to his overseas directors is known and conventional, he may in the local market situation achieve what seem satisfactory results, thus minimizing the personal risks and worries of achieving even better results by other methods. For these and other reasons, production methods are adopted which may or may not be the most profitable for the private firm but which are seldom the most profitable let alone the most socially desirable for the country as a whole.

The Elements of a Strategy for Employment and Wages

It is obviously not possible to suggest the best strategy for all countries at all times. All one can do is to raise certain issues for strategy which in one form or another are the common concerns of a number of poor countries.

The first issue in any strategy is to decide the importance to be given to employment in comparison with other objectives. Gone is the early optimism of the 1950s in which it was mistakenly expected that if plans concentrated on increasing output, and output rose, employment would rise more or less adequately. Wage-earning jobs have risen more slowly than expected and, at the same time, population and the numbers of school leavers have risen more rapidly. Any effective employment and man-power strategy must get to grips with this major political and social problem.

The three crucial magnitudes are the growth rates of output, productivity and the labour force. The growth in output and the growth in productivity between them determine the growth in employment. The latter must be compared with the growth in the numbers seeking work as indicated by the growth in the labour force. As long as employment grows faster than the labour force, the proportion with jobs will be increasing and eventually unemployment will decrease. This can be taken therefore as a long-run minimum target.

A few figures may suggest the ambitious nature of even this minimum objective. If we assume that the labour force grows at $2\frac{1}{2}$ per cent and productivity at $3\frac{1}{2}$ per cent per year (both rates within recent experiences of many low-income countries) output must grow at about 6 per cent, simply to maintain the same proportion of the labour force in employment, let alone reduce the number without jobs. Unfortunately 6 per cent, though not impossible, is a percentage point or two above recent growth rates of the majority of poor countries. The conclusion is obvious. If unemployment is to be reduced, either output must rise faster, or labour productivity must rise more slowly or the increase in population and the labour force must be slowed.

To some extent, slowing down productivity involves a choice between raising output and raising employment. A strategy which gives great priority to employment may involve some sacrifice in the level and rate of expansion of economic output. Even when this is realized, the urgency of the employment problem may well lead governments to give greater emphasis to employment than they have in the past.

But it is probably a mistake to over-emphasize the conflict between expanding output *or* employment. In the long run, if technologies and organization can be adapted, the harmony between rising employment and output can be very close. In any case there is a limit to what can be achieved by slowing down productivity increases. The indispensable basis for expanding employment is a rapid and sustained increase in national output. A development plan to achieve this is thus the first requirement for employment creation.

The other element, nearly as important, is to control the increase in population. As long as population increases at 2 or 3 per cent per annum, output must rise at historically rapid rates in order even to gain *proportionately* on the unemployment problem, let alone reduce the numbers without jobs. The need for action in this field is particularly urgent, since it will be fifteen years and nine months at the earliest before any successful birth control programme can affect the numbers of fifteen-year-olds looking for jobs.

Nevertheless even if population growth is reduced over the years to come, increases in wage-earning employment will not be sufficient in the short run to absorb all the school leavers, let alone the other additions to the population of working age. The present imbalances in numbers are too great to be eliminated by any rates of growth of employment conceivable on present trends, except after two or three decades at least.

Given the imbalances of this situation, there are it seems only three ways to deal with the immediate unemployment problem, within the limits of the resources available to low-income countries. (If unprecedented increases in aid were possible, other solutions might be open.) The first is the most radical, namely to throw over the working of the labour market and mobilize directly the adult populations of these countries to tackle the work of development. This would be akin to the Chinese or North Vietnamese or Cuban approach. It seems to be the only solution which so far has produced full employment in a low-income country. In addition to a radical political base, it requires a high degree of organization, an adequate system of incentives or controls to support it and an efficient mechanism for distributing food and basic necessities to those involved.

The second approach is to develop greater opportunities for self-employment in the rural areas. This appears to be the implicit hope of many countries for raising employment, and clearly it has affected strategies for agricultural development. Its chances largely rest on the possibilities for transforming agriculture so that many more rural opportunities emerge.

The third approach is the development of *ad hoc* projects to absorb labour and ease the worst pressures of unemployment. A number of countries have embarked on these – the construction of a major road or dam with large amounts of hand labour, for instance – but, since these are not part of a mass mobilization of the whole labour force as in the first approach, these measures have provided only a limited solution. In addition, *ad hoc* measures must be undertaken at existing wages, so they are often extremely costly, ending up more as subsidized relief schemes than productive investments.

It will already be clear that a strategy for employment cannot be divorced from a strategy for wages and incomes – their level, structure and distribution. The level must be in line with the resources of the country and its rate of increase adjusted to the realistic prospects for the growth of both national income and employment: if employment is to grow, then increases in the earnings of persons already employed cannot be allowed to pre-empt all additions to the total wage bill. The structure of wages must reflect differentials which are compatible with the priorities of growth and encourage people to prepare for and engage in productive occupations. Finally, the distribution of income must be considered, from the viewpoint not only of equity but, just as important, of its effects on consumption, savings and imports.

This implies some sort of national policy towards wages and incomes, which, in one form or another, is the second major component of strategy in this area. There are, of course, enormous difficulties in implementing such policies. But before the difficulties are given too much emphasis the especial opportunities for action in poor countries should be mentioned. In the first place, minimum-wage legislation, usually an acknowledged part of government policy, affects the wages of a greater proportion of the labour force than in richer countries. In the second place, a high proportion of all wage earners are employed by government itself or by para-statal bodies, and the government determines their wages directly. Finally, governments in many low-income economies in the past have put their weight on the side of the workers in pressing employers, particularly large expatriate firms, to pay higher wages; they could use this weight on the side of the unemployed and rural workers.

Perhaps the most important change this implies is in the whole approach to collective bargaining. Many governments have so far followed the pattern developed in the industrialized countries, a pattern in which employer and union wrestle together, with the government only intervening in exceptional circumstances. This approach, especially in countries with the characteristics that have been described, often results in a bargain being struck between employer and employee, which to a considerable extent satisfies the interests of each of them, but at the expense of sacrificing *national* interests. Wages and profits may rise, industrial relations improve, but total employment, domestic savings and future output may rise more slowly than would otherwise have been possible. Differentials within the country may have widened. The solution is for government to be more directly involved in wage negotiations, in one form or another, in order to represent the national interest.

A policy for wages must take account of other incomes also. This includes not only profits but, particularly in less developed countries, agricultural incomes. Since in many countries government already plays an important part in fixing agricultural prices, this may not involve an extension of government powers so much as broadening of its terms of reference to take account of the national policy for wage incomes. Exactly how this can be achieved will depend on the circumstances of each individual country. But if the failings of the past are to be remedied, a policy towards wages and incomes must be a major component of national strategy towards employment and growth.

Summary

This chapter has sketched only the barest outlines of a co-ordinated strategy for developing the human resources of a country to the full. Much more is involved if the population is to be enabled to acquire the skills and abilities it needs and to have the incentives and physical strength to use them in the right place and at the right time. Even more is required if this is to be achieved humanely, with proper recognition that people are not only a productive resource but human beings whose education, health and well-being are the very objectives of development.

11 FINANCING ECONOMIC DEVELOPMENT

Does Finance Matter?

Finance is about money and credit, taxing and spending. Such things have no obvious connexion with the policymaker's efforts to improve the use of *real* resources: doctors and farmland, tractors and houses. Indeed, the planner's objectives, in trying to raise living standards in a poor country, are similar to those of the farmers who live there: more investment, better consumption, improved income distribution. The farmer usually approaches these objectives by shifting around real resources – seeds, fertilizers, family labour. But planners and governments, in trying to divert resources from present welfare to future growth, usually operate on financial indicators – tax rates, interest rates, import duties. Why?

Some reasons why governments have financial policies apply in rich countries and poor countries alike. First, cash control is simpler and more economical than the alternative controls; price incentives use up fewer scarce administrators than do physical controls, and depend less on the case-by-case allocative discretion of the individual civil servant, who is both short of time and open to temptation. Secondly, the planner must consider the effects of his actions on many other economic decision-makers; a policy involving a cash tax or a money interest-rate will cause less inescapable interference with the flow of goods and services among persons than (for instance) a tax collected in grain or in cattle, which arbitrarily provides fierce penalties and disincentives for some people and some sorts of activity.* Thirdly, there is the

*The 'impersonality' of price incentives is sometimes bogus. They *influence* only people who know about them, and *affect* only people who are willing and able to deal in the product to which the incentive has been applied.

question of convenience; a big employer like the government can scarcely pay its workers with grain, houses and clothes. In particular, foreign trade is increasingly subject to government control because of the strains that development puts on the balance of payments (pp. 153–9) – and that has to mean cash control, since foreign resources cannot be pushed about, although one's own nationals can well be encouraged to export or to substitute for imports by cash incentives.

All this applies to rich governments as well as poor. But there are at least three reasons why 'developing' governments particularly need policies for money and credit. First, the need to borrow and lend expands hugely in the early stages of development. That is why the British transition from feudalism to capitalism was marked by a revolt against religious restrictions on moneylending.[1] To expand output and buy more plant, firms usually (and governments often) need to borrow now and repay later, as the extra capital begins to yield a return. Such credit transactions would be almost impossible without cash. For one thing, if a firm borrowed rice to pay workers building a new factory, the price of rice might change between loan and repayment. The value of money can change too, but rarely as sharply or as unpredictably as the value of a single commodity, like rice. So firms and governments, which need to be able to predict and plan, prefer cash transactions. Since development means that *producers* make increasing use of money and credit, governments need to ensure that the necessary facilities are made available.

Second, development also turns *consumers and savers* away from barter, towards transactions involving money and credit. As people move to towns, they see and buy more goods and services, and they produce more specialized items. Thus barter becomes more and more inconvenient. The farmer can exchange wheat for new shoes from the village cobbler; an assembly-line worker can hardly exchange his contribution to output for a pair of shoes. People are also made aware of new saving opportunities by development – and these opportunities require the use of cash. Thus a farmer in an isolated village might know of only one profitable use for any time he can spare from growing food for his family: to improve his land, so it will later grow more food.

Such saving needs no cash; but with the arrival of roads and radios the farmer may find out that he can use his spare time more lucratively by working for money, and saving his wages through the purchase of shares.

Third, poor people with growing families find saving difficult. Hence in poor countries, however *laissez faire* their ideology, the state increasingly (*a*) finances development itself, by taxation and borrowing;* (*b*) provides incentives and institutions to raise the amount of private saving, and to channel it into a wider range of investments;† (*c*) tries to make investment more efficient, i.e. to make it yield more output. Without such help, private saving – scarce in any case – runs to waste, in three distinct senses:

1. Potential saving goes unrealized; people indulge in conspicuous consumption on elaborate feasts, weddings and funerals, partly to gain *status* for want of incentives and institutions for saving spare cash to gain *income*.
2. Saving is embodied in the wrong investments (typically, as in Kenya, in low-yielding shops run by the saver) for want of knowledge about higher-yielding investments, such as

---

*Total savings (net of depreciation provisions) certainly form a larger share of national income in rich countries than in poor countries. Kuznets divides countries into five groups, in decreasing order of income per person in 1951–7; the richest group achieved net saving of 13·8 per cent of national income, the poorest only 9·5 per cent. This difference is almost entirely due to the upsurge of saving by *business* firms – corporate saving. In the early stages of development, *government* saving – the surplus of tax revenue over current public spending – rises sharply, but at higher income levels it falls again. *Private* saving, as a share of personal income after tax, is not much higher in rich countries – but this is probably in part a statistical illusion, since a lot of private saving in poor countries (e.g. in family farms) gets reclassified as corporate saving in developed economies. KRISHNAMURTY, K., *International Comparisons of Domestic Savings Rates – a Review*, International Bank for Reconstruction and Development, Washington, 1968.

†'Saving' is the difference between income and consumption. 'Investment' is the physical equipment – buildings, machines, roads, etc. – which is produced in a country, with the resources *not* used for making consumer-goods.

233

minor irrigation canals; or because high risks and the lack of insurance deter savers from going for a better return; or because there are no banks and stock exchanges, through which savings can be used to pay for industrial investment.*

3. Investments eat up scarce saving by being inefficient, i.e. by yielding less than they ought, among other things because there is no proper financial control.

Thus more poor states see their role as including the provision of intermediary facilities, by which *potential* saving can be realized, channelled into support of the *right* investment, and then managed in an *efficient* manner.

There seem to be plenty of good reasons why governments intervene in the money and credit systems of an underdeveloped economy. But what are the ultimate objectives of such financial intervention? Here a comparison with a firm is useful. A big firm sells output and buys input, borrows and lends, pays out wages and salaries, retains dividends or distributes them to shareholders, and engages in many other strictly financial activities. A state has more sources of finance, in particular taxation; more types of spending; and therefore a portfolio of assets (and a pattern of liabilities) generating a system of cash flows that needs to be carefully timed. Above all the state has a more complex structure of *aims*. A firm aims chiefly at profit, though also at security; even this sets up a tug-of-war for finance between risky undertakings with a high expectation of profit and safe but low-yielding activities. But the state usually aims at growth; high employment levels; reasonable price stability; better distribution of income among persons; better composition of output, e.g. fewer casinos and more hospitals; a tolerable balance of pay-

*This does not imply support for the doctrine that development in Kenya or India now implies lending from farmers to industrialists, as it did in nineteenth-century Britain or France. On the contrary, the yield from agricultural investment is frequently higher, in the short run, than the yield from industrial investment. And the institutions, by which farmers with spare cash can lend it to farmers in other villages with better investment opportunities, are at least as important (and scarce) in underdeveloped countries as are institutions to channel such spare cash into urban uses.

ments; and more personal choice. Thus a firm looking for profit will almost always buy in the cheapest market; a government looking for growth must consider whether this really economizes on scarce resources. For instance, the firm may be the sole employer of a particular type of labour, and hence able to pay it less than it is 'worth' and to price its products accordingly. A government also has to consider how its choice of supplies affects employment, inflation, choice, and so on. It may be 'cheaper' to construct a big new dam with the best modern machinery – but how will it affect employment and imports?

In trying to achieve its various aims, which may conflict, money is the state's main weapon: taken in taxes or given in subsidies, spent on nationalized factories or collected as tariffs to protect private factories, loaned to firms or borrowed from individuals, paid to teachers or collected from parents or ratepayers. Most poor countries, with their shortage of administrators, have found that direct physical controls – moving people and resources around, issuing licences to buy specific scarce imports – are usually cumbersome, vulnerable to corruption, expensive, and hard to reconcile with fairness or personal freedom. A gesture towards the price mechanism makes many unpopular policies politically tolerable. When there is hunger in Indian towns, government purchase of surplus food often works where compulsory acquisition would bring massive evasion – or rural revolt.

We have looked at several reasons why money and credit, and policies affecting their distribution among persons and firms, are critical for a government seeking to develop a very poor country:
1. Private saving must be supplemented by public saving.
2. Private saving must be increased, and channelled into the right investment appropriately managed; this usually requires new institutions, so that the appropriate forms of saving become better-known, safer, and more profitable both to the saver and to the community.
3. Cash incentives to producers, such as low tax and interest rates for preferred borrowers, are easier to manage and less politically provocative than are direct physical controls. Similarly for incentives to savers and consumers.
4. Money and credit get more and more important, both for

private firms and for individuals, as development proceeds; relevant institutions must be encouraged in an orderly way.

5. In order to improve resource allocation, increase total investment, and equalize income distribution, the government usually finds cash transfers and incentives (a) fairer, (b) more conducive to private efficiency, and (c) more economical of scarce administrative resources, than direct transfers of goods or resources.

We have not discussed the management of demand – the main aim of financial policy ('freeze and squeeze') in rich countries. The central problem of poor countries is to increase *supply* – of skills, machines, businessmen, administrators – and to improve resource allocation. In any case, tax systems in poor countries rarely affect even 25 per cent of the population directly, and fewer than 5 per cent deal with banks; so fiscal and monetary policy are even less rapid and reliable as policemen for the level of total demand in poor countries than in rich ones. In poor countries, however, financial policy has a critical role: to increase, channel and apply the resources for development.

The Difficulties of Development Finance

Financial controls are especially important in new and poor nations, because the alternatives – direct physical controls – require a sense of national unity, a qualified and experienced administration, and a sophisticated system of transport and communications. Poor countries have special financial problems (tax collection, lack of banks, etc.), some of which will be touched on later. But the main obstacle to increasing and allocating a poor country's development finances is its lack of development. To make fair tax collection cheaper, banks and state ventures more profitable to start, monetary policy more effective, one must finance the developmental use of resources. There is a virtuous circle here: more and better development finance, more development, easier finance. We are thus concerned with the national 'financing of development'. But what does this mean?

Even consumption *can* be relevant to development in a poor country. In Los Angeles, where most people are overweight, consumption of extra food is likelier to reduce labour efficiency than to increase it. But this was plainly false in the villages of Bihar during the food shortage of 1967, where weeding was carelessly done because the workers were too hungry to do it properly. If the tax system can cope – and it is a big 'if' – the best cure is to use budgetary policies to redistribute income, which includes purchasing power over food, towards the productive and hungry. Development through food consumption is a special case, and even here it means cutting down the incomes of the rich; they are the main source of private saving, and any decline in saving that results must be made good somehow, normally by extra government saving. In any event the main way to achieve development is usually by diverting as much extra income away from *current* consumption as is politically practicable, thus releasing *current* resources to produce things to make *future* income.

The farmer may divert labour from growing this year's food towards building a watercourse to raise food production later. The state adjusts cash incentives, thus diverting workers and machines from producing food towards a variety of activities such as building dams, building factories to make bulldozers, teaching people to use dams and bulldozers, and building schools (and training teachers) so that more people can be taught in future. These are classified in the national accounts respectively as agricultural investment, industrial investment, current educational spending and educational investment. But they all have one thing in common: sacrificial diversion of resources from making current consumer goods to development of the nation's capacity to make more output later.* The diversion can take place by a shift or an increase in state employment, by instruction to private firms, or by incentives; but the effect is the same in each case.

A poor country has special difficulties in obtaining such

* Just as some consumption assists future production, so some investment is irrelevant to it. In the Burmese Plan for 1958–61, new carpets for the Burmese Embassy in Washington were included in 'investment'.

sacrificial diversion of resources from current consumption to future development. In Britain or the U.S.A., workers make substantial contributions to savings, mainly through life insurance and building societies. In India or Kenya, such institutions are for the rich only. The mass of workers have to spend (or remit for spending by jobless relatives) all they earn. Nor is this fully compensated by high savings among the rich. Inequality of income is worst in poor countries (p. 15), which seems to imply a class of rich people able to save. But rich people in poor countries often embody savings in unproductive investments like luxury houses, or spend on extravagant weddings and similar forms of conspicuous consumption. Partly because of the poverty around them, this raises their social status (mainly by tying to their apron-strings otherwise unemployable persons, e.g. as domestic servants) and thus yields them a lot of 'psychic income'.

Moreover, much potential saving gets diverted into consumption (by a rich man, or by distant relatives to whom he feels a sense of traditional obligation) largely because the savings institutions for a businesslike transfer of funds from savers to borrowers are absent. Banks seldom lend in rural areas, owing to high risks, poor communications and imperfect knowledge. Few African countries have stock exchanges. In India the most profitable use of spare cash is often to lend it, at 35 per cent yearly interest, for consumer spending by poor and hungry villagers. Capital is seldom repaid, and interest repayments merely finance profitable (and growing) re-lending to the increasing population of borrowers. Thus, precisely because of inequality, much saving by the rich finances 'dis-saving' (consumption in excess of income) by the poor, instead of being embodied in productive investment.

All this is a familiar vicious circle. Private individuals find saving difficult because they are poor; and, because there is no saving to finance investment, poverty is reinforced. But how much saving is needed for adequate rates of development? This depends on (a) whether the saving is embodied in new capital of the right type, (b) whether the capital created is promptly used to make output, (c) whether there is sufficient unskilled labour, and (more doubtfully) technical and managerial skills, to work the new equipment.

Suppose these three conditions are reasonably, though not perfectly, met. Then a typical poor country needs to divert from current private consumption part of its yearly output just to replace worn-out capital stock,* part to maintain the same standard of living despite a population growth rate of 2 to 3 per cent yearly, and part to maintain minimum tolerable levels of law, health, education, defence and public administration, before it starts to raise levels of living.

Taking all these together, a poor country may have to divert as much as one-fifth of its output away from private consumption – even to *maintain* levels of living. And a stagnant level of living is unlikely to be politically tolerable – once the poor can get to a radio or a political meeting.† But at least 80 per cent of the people consume all they earn. The other 20 per cent embody much of their saving in unproductive, over-cautious or socially undesirable investment. Company saving (out of profits not distributed to shareholders) is usually too small to be of much help in the first stages of development. In countries like Venezuela or Zambia, such saving is concentrated in foreign-owned mineral companies who send much of it back home.

The Role of the State

The private sector has great difficulties in saving enough. Can the public sector – government, local authorities, nationalized industries – do better ? The belief that it can and must, that central planning centrally financed is the only alternative to continued

---

*Fortunately less than in advanced countries, because a smaller proportion of a poor nation's capital consists of moving parts – machines and vehicles – and a bigger proportion of relatively durable houses and draught animals. In the United Kingdom 9 per cent of yearly income goes to replace worn-out capital. In a poor country it is around 4 per cent.

†What minimum improvement the people will accept depends on (a) what they expect, (b) how fairly the extra income is distributed, (c) how firmly, harshly or popularly they are governed.

secular stagnation, lies at the heart of current concern with development finance. There is nothing specifically socialist or radical about this. In a Third World dominated by age-old ritual structures of tribe, caste and religious allegiance, the distinction between 'capitalism' and 'socialism' seldom means much. The public sector has to be called in to galvanize the economy, for centuries stuck in the rut of low-level equilibrium and stagnant income, and now threatened by population increase. Ideology helps decide whether politicians seek to confine financial intervention to incentives (such as subsidized fertilizers) and 'infrastructures' (such as transport or education) for the private sector, or to undertake state production. But however free-enterprise the ideology, the state assumes responsibility for increasing and allocating the nation's total sacrificial resources. Pakistan, for example, has seemed as ideologically 'capitalist' as almost any country in the Third World; but public investment rose from 28 per cent of total investment in 1949–55, to 49 per cent with the serious development effort of 1959–64.[2]

Yet the underdeveloped state, like its citizens, is caught up in the vicious circles of poverty. Just as the individual's poverty reduces his saving, so the nation's poverty reduces its taxable capacity.* Just as the farmer does not immediately get the full benefit from his first tube-well, so inexperience in running necessary basic services in health and education means that the state wastes money at first. Because the government finds it hard to raise taxes, it cannot pay high salaries, and thus loses its best civil servants to private industry; the underpaid ones who remain, because poor, are greatly tempted to collect not taxes but bribes. Hence the state's share of national resources in the poor world is much less than in the rich world.

This low involvement in the economy does not help the state

*About 1961, total tax revenue (as a share of total national product) in some typical *developed* countries was: France, 24 per cent; United States, 33 per cent; United Kingdom, 34 per cent; W. Germany, 39 per cent. In typical *underdeveloped* countries, the ratios were: Mexico, 11 per cent; Turkey, 13 per cent; Brazil, 20 per cent. KRISHNASWAMY, K., in PEACOCK, A., and HAUSER, G., eds., *Government Finance and Economic Development*, OECD, Paris, 1963.

to shunt resources from consumption towards development; but there are two comforts. Development increases the involvement, and it makes the resources easier to shift. But how, in the early stages, is the state to approach its financial task? It has to oversee the financing of total development (useful investment public and private, plus most current spending on education, health, and the necessary base of administration and law) in three ways: (*a*) by increasing and improving the allocation of public resources for development, (*b*) by persuading individuals and companies to use a larger share of resources to finance productive investment, education, etc., and (*c*) by getting foreign help to supplement internal resources.

Why not Print the Money?

But isn't there a short cut? Since Keynes's *General Theory of Employment, Interest and Money* (1936) we have laboriously unlearned our conventional distaste for deficit finance – government spending in excess of tax and borrowing, the difference being made up by printing money. If there is unemployment, these procedures are quite respectable in rich countries, as we explain below. Poor countries have plenty of unemployment. While they were colonies, the currency board system limited their note issue to the amount that could be fully backed by the currency – sterling or francs; but, outside the franc zone of 'independent' Africa, that limitation has gone almost everywhere. True, colonial officials, seldom well-versed in Keynesian economics, impressed on their 'native' successors the moral turpitude of 'recourse to the printing press' to pay for government activity. But at least this would get purchasing-power over resources into public hands, and these hands can push the resources from consumption towards development. So *why* not print the money?

There is a quite sophisticated theory justifying the printing of money to generate growth. Following it through will show us the scope and limits of such a policy in a poor country. It will also explain something of the structural difference between rich and poor countries, and the dangers of transferring theories between them.

In almost any underdeveloped country, many adults are without jobs. Extra cash is spent to create extra demand – and perhaps extra jobs for the people who satisfy it. If we followed Keynesian remedies for unemployment in rich countries, we should argue that demand should be expanded, for example by printing money which the government would use to pay unemployed workers to build roads. The newly employed workers would spend their incomes on food, clothing, etc., thus drawing more jobless people into employment to make these things; these workers would spend *their* new incomes and create more employment, and so on. Income and employment would increase by a *multiple* of the amount initially injected into the economy as a result of 'recourse to the printing press'. Yet, when Indonesia and other countries have tried to create jobs and finance development by printing money, the result has been a great strain on home demand (zooming prices) or on import demand (balance-of-payments crises) or both, with disappointingly slow growth. Why?

In the pre-war British situation analysed by Keynes, not only potential workers were idle; land, machines and managers were under-used as well, in almost all lines of production. Print cash to build a post office in such a situation, and whatever the building workers buy – food, clothes, radios – there will be spare workers, machines and managers willing to produce it. Supply responds readily to growing demand. But in poor countries these conditions do not hold. Men are idle, but other resources are scarce – land sometimes, machines and managers almost always. If the government prints money to pay a few thousand dam-builders, they will use their new incomes to buy goods which cannot be increased in supply, because resources *other than labour* are scarce.

Now two things can happen. The dam-builders' extra demand can pull in more imports or eat up potential exports, causing a balance-of-payments crisis and ultimately forcing the successive devaluations typical of inflationary finance in Latin America and Indonesia. Or it can pull up domestic prices directly, because of the inflexibility of supply. In either case, the newly employed workers enjoy their extra incomes at the cost of other people – buyers of home products, imports or both, who face higher prices. Since governmental control of price inflation is even weaker in poor countries than in rich ones, the whole process severely discourages personal savings; people feel they had better spend before prices rise even further. On the other hand, high profits during inflation may mean more company saving, which will be swiftly turned into new plant before *that* gets dearer too!

Let's look more closely at the structure of this sort of inflation. In India or Tanzania, a typical migrant farmworker, newly employed in the city at a higher wage, will spend about half his extra pay on food for himself and his relatives. (In Britain it is less than a quarter.) The extra food may not easily be produced at home. In India, Pakistan or Indonesia* there is hardly any spare cultivable land. In much of Latin America, land is split into tiny holdings (*minifundia*) already farmed up to the limit, and enormous *latifundia* where the wealthy owners feel little incentive to produce more. In the whole underdeveloped world, workers and businessmen are hampered by poor transport, ignorance, illiteracy, debt and lack of general skills, from switching jobs in response to specific increases in demand; in particular, such movement as does take place is out of agriculture. So the boost to food demand (from a bigger urban wage bill) seldom produces a swift response in domestic food supply – even if resources were present and mobile, it would take several months to plough up new land, and years to change crop rotations. Therefore extra food demand boosts food prices and food imports, not food output – at least in the short run. Inflation rather than growth, as a response to 'printing the money', is part of the essence of underdevelopment, and the immobility of labour and capital that goes with it.

The effect of 'printing the money' to finance government activity in less developed countries, then, is generally to produce little real growth, but huge rises in prices or imports (especially since the underdeveloped state can divert much less new income from consumer spending to taxation than is possible in rich

*Approximate total population of these three at the end of 1970: 810 million (China, 756 m.; Africa, 353 m.; Latin America, 284 m.).

countries) – and some redistribution of income. This might seem desirable, since people with jobs – who are presumably better off to begin with – are made to 'pay', via price increases, to employ previously idle workers. However, these do not gain as much as one might expect; in Asia and Africa, systems of extended family or caste or tribe provide a rudimentary security of income for many of the unemployed. Usually, inflation hits the poor hardest. Small farm families – over 100 million people in India alone – eke out the income from their land by working for others, and are often net *buyers* of food; they have no trade unions to bargain for higher wages. In general, the poor, unlike the rich, spend much of their income on food, where higher demand leads (in the short run) to higher prices rather than more output. The just-employed urban poor, finding their living standards eroded by price rises, can pose a serious threat to political stability in new states.

Further, when domestic prices zoom ahead of world prices, home buyers turn towards imports, and home producers find the 'soft' home market more attractive than exporting at relatively stable world prices. Poor countries are especially prone to this 'English disease'. Indeed it is implicit in the *structure* of underdevelopment, in particular the relatively slow response, to new demands, of traditional technology in the rural sector. Thus in an underdeveloped country it is even harder than in Britain to ease a foreign exchange crisis by blood-letting, i.e. by reducing domestic demand. The skills – managerial, technical, marketing – for a rapid switch to export markets are either absent or immobile.

All this does not mean that an underdeveloped government can *never* finance development by printing money, and spending it to pay workers building dams and factories – even if they do use their incomes to pull up food prices, the process does shift real resources out of private consumption into public investment. But this usually has much higher costs, in inflation and a worsening foreign balance, in a poor country with scarce and immobile resources than in a country that has already reached a higher level of development. 'Printing the money' is tolerable up to a point, if there is a growing demand for cash, as peasants emerge from a barter economy to a cash economy; if there are ample reserves of foreign exchange (as in Kuwait or Libya), so that extra demand can safely be allowed to suck in imports; if the government investment, financed by the new money, quickly produces enough new output to meet the extra demand; if commodity aid, such as food-grains from the United States to India, raises the supply of goods relative to cash; or if the same effect is produced by a good harvest, or an increase in private thrift. Thus development finance by printing money is safer as a source of real growth (rather than inflation and balance-of-payments crisis) if the government *knows* that extra demands can be quickly met from higher production, tolerable rises in imports, or running down of stocks. Such information is seldom available in poor countries, which are also statistically underdeveloped.

Basically, deficit finance is much likelier to succeed in rich countries than in poor ones. In the latter, most extra income (wages and even profits), once paid to the people making extra output, is spent on goods and services rather than saved, so that most extra *supply* creates almost equivalent monetary *demand*, though not necessarily for the goods supplied. But extra *demand* (from new cash in the pocket) seldom calls forth the relevant *supply*, at least seldom quickly and without painful adaptation, especially in agriculture. In the Keynesian world of the rich capitalist countries, more investment – extra demand by firms or governments for buildings or machinery – pulls up incomes and real output, as the workers making the machinery buy extra goods and services, and 'employ' men to produce them; and this, in turn, pulls up savings plans, because more people can now afford to save. But in a poor country this process does not succeed in increasing savings to finance investment, because (as we have seen) it is money incomes and prices – and imports – that rise rather than real incomes and output. In a rich country with significant unemployment, the effective limitation on investment is the businessman's expectations of *demand* for the products of his investment rather than his ability to borrow money; greater thrift merely cuts down this demand, and reduces real income and employment. In a poor country, investment plans are frustrated by shortage of finance rather than of demand, and greater thrift transfers resources from consumption to investment.

Crudely, in rich countries investment (because it means paying workers to make investment goods, raising demand and thus income) 'causes' the saving that finances it; in poor countries saving (by transferring productive resources away from making consumer goods) 'causes' the investment it finances. That is why in rich countries budget deficits ease unemployment and raise real income, but worsen inflation and do not raise income in poor countries. That is why governments in rich countries see the main role of finance, in the growth process, as the management and smoothing of demand; while in poor countries the main task of development finance is to increase, mobilize and allocate the supply of savings, and, if possible, of other scarce developmental resources too.

Strategies for Development Finance

We can now turn to look at the possibilities of raising development finance by non-inflationary means. The cash value of the total output of a country (Y) consists of consumer goods and services made and bought at home (C), investment goods made and bought at home (I) and exports (X). In symbols

$$Y \equiv C + I + X \tag{1}$$

Now the value of output, Y, is paid out (as wages and distributed profits) to all the producers, or left as undistributed profits with companies or nationalized industries. All this cash, Y, has to be spent on home-produced consumer goods and services (C) or on imports (M), or else saved by the government (Sg) as a surplus of tax over government current spending, or by private persons or firms (Sp) as a surplus of income over spending and income tax. In symbols

$$Y \equiv C + (Sg + Sp) + M \tag{2}$$

If we combine these two identities, we see that

$$I \equiv (Sg + Sp) + (M - X) \tag{3}$$

Equation (3) adds nothing to our knowledge, but arranges it in a way that helps us to use it. The equation* says that the value of a country's investment is equal to the sum of two types of financial resources: home savings (governmental and private), and foreign savings (the extent to which a country can run an import surplus, whether by running down reserves of foreign exchange, by attracting aid, or by loans from private overseas businessmen, usually embodied in direct investment). These excess imports may be of investment goods – or of consumer goods, freeing home resources to make investment goods while consumer goods still suffice to meet home demand.

Equation (3) tells us that an increase in any one of the components of investment finance will increase total investment only to the extent that it does not decrease other components. For example if the government increases public saving (Sg) by a bigger profits tax, there is bound to be some fall in private saving (Sp) since firms (and receivers of profit distributed as dividends) must use more of their revenue to pay tax, and thus have less left to save. They are likely to meet some of the tax by cutting spending, so that the fall in Sp is not likely to be as big as the rise in Sg, and total investment should go up; even if it does not, the rise in Sg may improve the *composition* of investment, which can increase total investment later (for example, if private businessmen spent the yield of their investments, while governments use it to finance further investments).

The point is not that public saving is self-defeating – it is not – but that planners must estimate the effects of fiscal decisions on the sources of *total* investment finance, not just on the public budget. The lack of statistics (and often the planners' remoteness from the mass of savers and investors – the villagers) reduce the prospects of this sort of analysis. Ideally, planners should ask, of each sort of tax: Who pays? Would they have spent or saved the cash, if untaxed? If 'spent' would the *receivers* have spent or saved? If 'spent'... etc. And similarly, for each form of public outlay, will the receivers spend or save the extra income? If 'spend'... and so on. This seldom happens even in developed

*Strictly an 'identity', since it follows from the definitions used. Hence the $\equiv$, instead of $=$.

countries; instead we speak of overall budget surpluses or deficits, and governments of poor countries are misled into imitating this gross over-simplification. Indeed, it is more serious in poor countries, where the proportion of extra income saved varies more according to whether the income is in town or country, wages or profits, etc., than in rich ones. Here as elsewhere, too much fiscal (and other) analysis in poor countries is in terms of enormous aggregates – total income, saving and so on.

At least we can look at interactions among *main* sources of finance. One such link is between home saving and 'foreign saving' (aid plus private foreign investment). Poor countries wish to attract aid – grants especially, but also loans below the market rate of interest. Aid flows for political and commercial reasons as well as economic ones; but insofar as donors genuinely wish to assist development, they put the recipient government in a curious dilemma. If it raises hardly any domestic savings, the donors will suspect that the recipient is not really trying to finance its own development; but successful domestic saving suggests that the recipient can help itself without foreign aid.

The volume of private investment by foreign companies, too, is linked to the government's fiscal decisions regarding home finance. Foreign businessmen want the governments of under-developed countries to finance investments that cut their own production costs – railways, power, education. They are unhappy about government subsidies to domestic competitors, tariffs on raw materials, or export taxes on their products. But the most serious conflict generated by private foreign investment concerns the repatriation of profits. If, in any year, foreign firms repatriate more money from a country (in profits) than enters the country (as new investment) then foreign capital actually *reduces* the foreign exchange for development investment.* If the government tries to take the sting out of profit repatriation by high taxes on profits and on managerial salaries – however disguised – it creates a climate in which foreign businessmen are unwilling to reinvest

*Except insofar as the foreign firms produce more in exports (or genuine import-substitutes), than they and their employees suck in as imports, and thereby free foreign exchange for developmental imports.

profits in the underdeveloped country, and reluctant to send in new investment funds.

But in many poor countries (e.g. Malaysia, Venezuela, Zambia) foreigners are responsible for very large proportions of total capital, profits and the bigger salary payments. So the governments are almost compelled to tax these, if they are to have any say in the size and make-up of future investment. But the process of taxing foreign investment incomes, the better to increase and allocate home investment finance, has the effect of frightening away new foreign investment finance. In this situation, the choice is to kill the goose that lays the golden eggs, or to be ruled by geese.

From one year to the next, investment finance can be increased by the following methods:

	Government investment	Private investment
HOME SAVINGS	1 Higher taxes 2 Lower current spending 3 Bigger profits on public enterprises 4 More borrowing 5 Deficit finance	9 More personal saving 10 More business saving 11 More cooperative finance
FOREIGN SAVINGS	6 Commercial loans 7 Aid 8 Running down reserves	12 Private foreign investment 13 Export credits

These methods will be briefly dealt with in turn.

1. *Higher taxes.* Of the wide range of taxes theoretically at the disposal of a government, many are unpractical in an underdeveloped country. Especially if the country is new or small, its civil service will contain few graduates, very few economists; and many of the graduates will be expatriates, who may leave before successors are properly trained. The visit of a 'technical assistance' expert from an international organization can help; but too often the local counterpart, whom he is supposed to train, promptly flies off to a highly theoretical course of instruction in a rich country. Furthermore the institutional framework

makes some taxes difficult to collect. In 1956, Indian income tax produced only 40 to 50 per cent of its theoretical yield, the remainder being evaded.[3] Most poor countries do much less well.

In general, subtle taxes, requiring detailed statistics or numerous administrators, or open to corruption, seldom succeed in poor countries. This means that the share of 'indirect' taxes (on goods and services) tends to be bigger in poor countries, and that of 'direct' taxes (on wages, profits and capital) smaller.* The tax base for income taxes is small, as few people can afford to pay. Even for these people, rates are low, because of political pressure. And actual yields fall far short of theoretical yields, because public tax collectors, accountants and lawyers are worse paid (and hence worse) than their opposite numbers in the private sector. Usually, only government employees – and a tiny part of organized industry – is on pay-as-you-earn. Hence direct taxes do not produce much.

Conventional wisdom suggests that this is good for incentives, but bad for equality. The argument runs: 'Income tax hits the rich harder than the poor. Usually the tax rate goes up as your income rises. Further, the application of income tax to millions of tiny impoverished agriculturists, many of them landless labourers receiving incomes in kind, is impracticable. Since poor countries feature a more unequal income distribution than rich ones, this equalizing bias of direct taxes makes the difficulty of collecting them in poor countries seem particularly unfortunate. But at least it avoids disincentives to effort and to saving; to effort, because extra work (especially by scarce managers and technicians) is not discouraged by a rising rate of income tax; to saving, because it is the very rich and the big companies which save, and these are left with salaries and profits almost intact.'

All this is theoretically correct, but almost irrelevant to the

---

*About 1961, direct taxes in some typical *developed* countries made up the following proportions of total taxes: United States 76 per cent, W. Germany 59 per cent, United Kingdom 55 per cent. For *underdeveloped* countries, typical figures were: India 30 per cent, Pakistan 25 per cent, Brazil 24 per cent. KRISHNASWAMY, K., in PEACOCK and HAUSER, *op. cit.*, p. 77.

fiscal problems of poor countries. Direct taxes are *in general* costly and hard to administer, but are neither systematically bad for incentives nor necessarily good for equality. Businessmen in poor countries fail to exploit their potential, not because their incomes are taxed, but because of real shortages: power breakdowns, poor transport, few or costly skilled workers. Taxes on profits allow governments to improve such services, which can seldom be undertaken by the businessmen themselves. Such taxes, in conjunction with the public spending they permit, are likelier to encourage than to discourage new private initiatives. Nor do indirect taxes necessarily hit the poor. In a rich country, an indirect tax either raises very little (e.g. a tax on yachts) or else hits almost everyone – even working-class families buy refrigerators and radios. In a poor country the great inequality of income and the extreme poverty of the poor means that the poor buy very few goods – and the rich spend a lot on many other goods. This can be turned to advantage by the tax authorities; indirect taxes on everything *except* simple food, coarse cloth and kerosene will hit the poor very little, yet will produce substantial revenue. Of course such policies meet heavy opposition from small, powerful and much-mulcted groups of well-off taxpayers. But so does income tax. Apart from this, inequality does not always help saving in poor countries; in South America especially, rich men often put their income into luxury spending or transfer it abroad.

The political opposition to other forms of taxation is the main reason why governments of underdeveloped countries rely so heavily upon taxation of goods entering into foreign trade.* It looks as if the foreigner pays the tax, but an export tax will make exporting less profitable, and sooner or later this must lead

---

*In *developed* countries, the following ratios of import *and* export duty to total tax revenue were typical of the early 1960s: United States 1 per cent; Belgium and Sweden, each 6 per cent; Canada and Netherlands each 11 per cent. For *underdeveloped* countries, typical ratios were: Pakistan 24 per cent, Kenya 34 per cent, Panama 44 per cent. DOSSER, D., in PEACOCK and HAUSER, *op. cit.*, pp. 140–1. Of course the ratio is also likely to be high in small countries, which must rely more heavily on foreign trade.

businessmen to direct their energies elsewhere. Even if an exporting nation has considerable market power, greedy tax policies by its government will speed up the development of synthetic substitutes, as for Malaya's rubber and Pakistan's jute. Moreover, the supply of exports rarely grows as fast as output, so that governments which rely on export taxes find themselves getting smaller and smaller shares of G.N.P. The reverse may be true for tariffs on imports; but their role in protecting infant industries is distorted (and can underwrite inefficiency at home and stimulate specific retaliation abroad) if tariffs are used chiefly as a source of revenue. Import and export taxes alike tie government revenue to foreign supply and demand, which are less amenable to policy (and perhaps less predictable and more volatile) than domestic supply and demand. But at least such taxes fall on the 'organized' sector, and company accounts provide some check against evasion. Further, the *immediate* incidence of both import duties and export taxes probably improves the distribution of income; unless a country has a big food deficit, imports are consumed chiefly by the rich; workers in export sectors, such as the Zambian copperbelt and the tea estates of Ceylon, are better off than the rural masses, and employing firms are often based abroad. The long-run effects, however, are instability of government revenue, random and rather inefficient protection of substitutes for imports, damage to export earnings, and an unnecessarily small tax base. Usually, 'fiscal development' involves acquiring administrative techniques to allow a switch away from taxes on foreign trade.

2. *Lower current spending.* One way to make resources available for public investment is to release them from other governmental uses. Most plans distinguish outlay on public investment from government recurrent spending, and they further separate developmental from administrative and other outlays such as defence. While the borderline is somewhat arbitrary, the planner does need to look at the future administrative and running costs when choosing among *present* investments. In choosing between types of secondary-school building, for instance, planners must examine not only the value of extra output contributed per pound of building costs by each type of school, but also the running

costs (in teachers, teachers' training, school maintenance and repair, children's transport to alternative locations, etc.).

This may seem obvious, but it is regularly overlooked by governments, especially in the early stages of planning when they are obsessed with the immediate shortage of finance for investment. Of course, the more rapidly the economy is expected to grow – and with it taxable capacity and the government's ability to finance activities of all sorts – the less important are future running costs, compared to present capital costs. New nationalist governments have usually overestimated the contribution of independence to economic growth, and so they have tended to assume higher future wealth than was realistic – and hence to underplay the subsequent running costs of investment. Since rapid population growth and inadequate private saving have rendered big public investment necessary to assuage the clamour (however elitist and limited) for higher living standards, 'developing' governments are sorely tempted to incur big future costs by skimping on present building standards, in order to raise the absolute amount of public investment.

But lack of forethought is not the only reason why recurrent public spending invariably grows as a result of development planning. Capital growth implies future growth in recurrent spending; and, while capital alone is not much use without new skills and new technologies, hardly any poor country can develop (because skills cannot be applied, or new technologies embodied) unless there is a big rise in the *share* of total output devoted to increasing the stock of buildings and machines. The swinging new economics, in its reaction against the view that only capital matters, has swung to the other extreme. Yet, in the 1950s, Indonesia was investing only 5 per cent of her product – barely enough to replace worn-out equipment – while the population was rising by over 2 per cent yearly. This is an extreme case, but plainly anything like this spells disaster. Extra capital, while seldom sufficient for development, is almost always necessary. But private savers respond to a sudden population spurt by saving less – they have more mouths to feed. So government *saving*, at least initially, has to go up. Some can be used to subsidize private investment, but all serious developing governments, even avowedly free-enterprise ones like Pakistan and the Philippines, have also substantially raised the ratio of public *investment* to gross national product in the early years of planning. And this implies booming recurrent outlays later: wages for teachers to staff the new schools, for maintenance workers on the new dams, and so forth. Often this is made worse because the new skills are in short supply; for example, extra hospital investment is likely to drive up not only the number of doctors the government must employ, but the salaries it must pay to keep them out of private practice (or stop them going to Britain or the United States).

Nor is the expansion of recurrent public spending limited to support of past investment. The control of billharzia and tsetse fly or the training of agricultural extension officers may yield much more extra output, if regularly repeated, than similar spending on new dams or steel mills. Development means, among other things, growing public awareness of the prospects for current outlays. Undoubtedly this gives immense scope for the pseudo-employment of relatives, empire-building and other forms of waste. But this is part of the traditional system of political insurance against poverty, and is not easy to avoid, though its excesses can be limited.* 'More investment finance through economies in current public expenditure', except in countries with swollen defence budgets, is almost always claptrap.

3. *Profits on public enterprises.* A luxury bus runs from Poona, a big Indian city, to a nearby hill station and holiday resort, Mahabaleshwar. Most of the year there is a big frustrated demand for seats on this bus – long queues, and dozens of people disappointed each day. The people who use the bus are mostly well off, and could easily pay a higher fare; and a 'market' fare, cutting down demand to the number of seats the State Transport Corporation could supply, seems an obvious solution. Yet only by tortoise-like steps does the fare rise towards this market level. The very wealth that makes the users of such buses suitable targets, even in an egalitarian society, for full market pricing

*President Nyerere of Tanzania has attempted to limit them, by stringent restrictions on the wealth and entourage of ministers. At the other extreme stands Nkrumah's Ghana, in which a minister's wife, Mrs Krobo Edusei, contrived to buy a golden bed.

gives these users the political muscle to fight against such policies.

The example is trivial, but the phenomenon is almost universal where governments are new, administrators scarce and underpaid, and users of public services rich and articulate. The supply of rail freight and electric power to Indian industry is an area of chronic and severe undercharging. After all, even in Britain governments tremble when gas prices, railway fares or council-house rents are raised towards market levels; how much more political courage is needed in Tanzania or Thailand, where the average user of public services is (relative to the rest of the community) richer and more articulate, the average administrator poorer and hence more corruptible, and the average government (see chapter six) much more hard-pressed to maintain even a minimum tolerable degree of national consensus.

So realistic charges by public enterprises, like higher and subtler taxes, like lower governmental running costs, turn out to be *effects* of development, as much as potential *causes* of more buoyant development finance. Almost every development plan includes optimistic projections of these things. Most achieve something, but hardly ever as much as they expected.

As for the running costs of public enterprises, much of what we said about governmental running costs applies here too. There is a special factor, though, that gives grounds for optimism. Two of the many arguments advanced for public ownership of an industry are (*a*) that its production costs, per unit of output, are too high in the early stages of development for it to be commercially viable, but that this will improve as managerial experience is gained and as ancillary industries grow, and (*b*) that the industry has economies of scale, encouraging the government to look for an alternative to either exploitative private monopoly or wasteful private competition. Both these arguments for nationalization suggest that, in an underdeveloped country with initially small but fast-growing markets for public services like power and transport, average costs *can* be brought down as development proceeds and experience is gained.

4. *More borrowing.* To some extent, most governments finance their outlay by borrowing from individuals. In Britain, the most familiar methods are National Savings; the weekly issue of

Treasury Bills, which the Government auctions to the highest bidder (in the 1960s at around £98 10s.) and which can be cashed at par (£100) in three months' time; and bonds, which are promises by the government (or a local authority) to pay £8 or £9 yearly interest on each £100 loaned, for periods ranging upwards from two years. All these borrowing systems, and many more, exist in underdeveloped countries; the organizational details still depend more on the colonial background – British or French – than on local needs.

Our concern here is not with such details, but with two basic issues. Does the government, by borrowing, increase *total* saving (investible resources), or merely transfer savings from the finance of private investment to the finance of public investment? And can the government help to create a more efficient 'capital market', enabling the particular requirements of many different sorts of borrower and lender to be met? Small private loans to governments, through such means as national savings or premium bonds, might divert cash from consumers to a saving government. But such loans are seldom important in poor countries. The impoverished masses cannot afford to save in this way; and the dominance of risky consumer loans at high interest rates, to tide poor villagers over between harvests, means that peasants with a little cash to spare can usually do much better as small money-lenders than through national savings. In any case, the appalling difficulty of raising finance for development often drives govern-ments to inflationary methods,* so that people are reluctant to save at fixed rates of interest.

*There is no general rule, but most poor countries have suffered from faster inflation than most rich countries since 1945; some of the poor countries have fared especially badly, and the really runaway inflations – the ones that frighten savers right away – are confined to poor coun-tries. In typical *developed* countries, cost-of-living rises in the seven years from 1963 to 1970 were: W. Germany 20 per cent, U.K. 32 per cent, Japan 41 per cent. Typical for *underdeveloped* countries: Turkey 51 per cent, Colombia 94 per cent. Horror stories: Chile, a rise of 385 per cent; Brazil, of 886 per cent; and Indonesia, of at least 70,000 per cent. *Monthly Bulletin of Statistics*, United Nations, New York June 1970, Table 60.

Major bond issues have nevertheless been a substantial source of finance for the public spending of some countries, notably India. However, these bonds are almost all taken up by rich men or companies, who have all the consumption resources they need. Thus their cash, if it did not buy public bonds to finance public investment, would almost invariably flow into private savings to finance private investments; the addition to total investible resources is tiny. Perhaps the composition of investment will improve (though, if private investment includes luxury houses, public investment includes sports stadia, jet airlines and television studios). But any improvement has to be set against the administrative costs of bond issues and national debt management.

The wish to organize government borrowing from persons who would otherwise have spent the money on consumption, rather than from traditional big savers, explains the emphasis placed on national savings schemes in some poor countries; but as we have seen the difficulties are enormous, particularly since the interest rates offered are usually very ungenerous. The Indian rate, for example, was recently raised from 2 per cent to $4\frac{1}{2}$ per cent; but even this rate reflects a colonial era of relative price stability, with few private investment opportunities. It is unlikely to attract much saving today.

Most government borrowing, then, transfers savings from the finance of private investment to the finance of public investment; it does not significantly increase total savings and total investment. However, governments of poor countries, in organizing borrowing from private persons, are sometimes driven to improve the investment situation indirectly. They create or improve stock exchanges, and thus help produce a more perfectly informed capital market. How imperfect it is can be seen from the fact that the rates of interest paid to the village moneylender (usually a local monopolist) range from 25 to 40 per cent yearly, while 'official' rates on government loans hardly ever exceed 10 per cent, and reasonably safe industrial borrowing is at 10 to 15 per cent. Local knowledge of the man you are lending to is crucial, insurance against commercial risks is underdeveloped, communications are poor; so cash does not flow from the urban lender to the poor borrower, despite the attractive interest rates available. In fact, an Indian or Sudanese* villager will seldom borrow or lend in the next village – let alone in the town.

Apart from tying down millions of peasants to their home villages (to work for creditors and pay off needlessly heavy interest charges), this imperfect capital market ties down scarce savings to unprofitable uses. The 'old boy nets' of caste, tribe and family infest the industrial capital market. A bank may lend to firms, not because they offer high or safe rates of interest, but through 'interlocking directorates' in which the same people run both the firms and the bank. Permission to float a new issue can depend on the right words (or the right bribe) to a petty official. Such abuses exist everywhere, but in the Third World the pervasive risk, and fear, of a return to rural near-destitution make everyone – banker, businessman and official – particularly prone to them. The 'institutions of exposure', taken for granted in an advanced mixed economy – a Stock Exchange Council, independent business lawyers in parliament, competent financial journalists – seldom exist in poor countries, which have often just violently rejected colonial financial institutions, or are peacefully but painfully struggling towards more appropriate arrangements.

There are many ways in which the government, as lender or borrower or creator of institutions, can improve the working of the capital market. The object of the exercise is to mobilize more savings, and to see they are used in more 'socially profitable' ways. As a lender, the government can support firms shut out of restricted or imperfect capital markets; this is done through new institutions raising money jointly with the private sector, as in the case of the Pakistan or Mexican Industrial Development Corporation. Again as a lender, the government can set up banks

---

*Moslem countries, like the Sudan, invariably find that the realities of rural need triumph over the religious laws against usury. Under 'sheil system', the hungry farmer sells his crop for cash, months before it is harvested. The farmer must sell or starve, the 'buyer' can almost name his price, and the process amounts to extracting an interest rate of 40 per cent or more.

to underwrite cooperative rural credit societies and bring down rural interest rates by destroying the monopoly of the village moneylender. As a borrower, the government's savings campaigns can, in a small way, bring in new groups of people as sources of industrial finance. Above all, the government can create or underwrite new institutions: stock exchanges, sometimes with the help of foreign firms eager to raise local equity capital, as in the case of John Holt in Nigeria; guarantors of credits for groups of businessmen who are to be encouraged, such as exporters; and so on. None of this is peculiar to underdeveloped countries. What *is* special is the newness of these activities, and hence at once their high risks (and costs) and their great promise.

5. *Deficit finance.* This has as many precise, technical definitions as there are systems of central banking. In effect it means printing money – financing public spending by means other than tax, borrowing or foreign sources. We have considered the possibilities and limits of such methods of finance on pp. 241–6 and need only add that some governments disguise the facts of deficit finance from themselves in two ways. First, they invent such titles as 'borrowing from the central bank', which means forcing it to accept government paper in return for releasing money, which then finances extra public spending. Second, many governments plan for quite impossible tax yields, current economies, etc. and thus understate the gap between public spending (current and capital) and public receipts – a gap that must be met, in the event, by uncovenanted deficits. Such windowdressing is largely due to a holy terror of a deficit (sometimes the legal prohibition of one), as against a realization that it is one of many tools of development finance, seldom a desirable one, but sometimes the only alternative to no development at all.

6. *Commercial loans.* So far we have considered only the *domestic* sources of finance for public development spending: the top left-hand section of the chart on p. 249. We now turn briefly to *overseas* sources of public finance. There are three such sources: commercial loans, aid, and the reduction of reserves of foreign exchange. Each of these methods allows a country's imports to exceed its exports, and gets the excess into government hands. So,

in terms of equation (3) on p. 246, each increases the government component of I by enlarging $(M - S)$.

Commercial loans from individuals to governments are very expensive for poor countries, owing to lack of confidence in two things: in the future exchange rate (and purchasing power) of the poor country's currency, and in the extent to which repayment is assured by economic growth and political stability. A few governments of poor countries have, in the past, borrowed on London markets; the cost of confidence can be estimated by comparing typical rates of interest obtainable on 'safe' and 'poor' countries' bonds. Both Zambia and Australia have bonds due for repayment by 1981. In 1967–8 Australian bonds typically yielded 7·2 per cent; Zambian bonds yielded 8·1 per cent.[4] Yet Zambia is more stable than many underdeveloped countries; this bond issue has some implicit support from the U.K. government;* and Zambia's reserves of foreign exchange (and copper export prospects) are relatively healthy. If a country like India or Brazil tried to borrow money through a London bond issue, the interest rate would be prohibitive – at least 15 per cent.

Commercial loans from companies to governments consist almost wholly of export credits, which are discussed below.

Commercial loans to governments of poor countries from rich governments (and international organizations supported by them such as the World Bank) are often misleadingly classified as 'aid'. The World Bank in the 1950s loaned most of its money at around 6 per cent interest – not much less than the commercial rate of interest in the rich countries. In 1964–6, about one fifth of all the 'aid' received by poor countries consisted, in effect, of commercial loans from rich governments (or the World Bank); the remainder consisted of grants, and the 'grant equivalent' value of loans at less-than-market rates of interest.[5]

7. *Aid*. This is duscussed in chapter fourteen. In the context of development finance, aid looms large. In Pakistan's Second Plan (1960–5), foreign aid financed over 40 per cent of total investment – and therefore well over three quarters of public investment[6] – though over one tenth of all aid flowed straight back to the donor

*It was originally issued when Zambia was nominally the Crown Colony of Northern Rhodesia.

to repay capital and interest on former 'aid' loans, and this share is rising sharply. The role of aid varies greatly between countries. In India's Third Plan (1961–6) aid financed 'only' 24 per cent of total investment, and 39 per cent of public investment. And almost one third of India's optimistic aid target for her Fourth Plan (1969–74) is already committed to pay off old 'aid' debts.[7] For some countries, such as Malawi, all public investment is financed by aid, and a large fraction of recurrent expenditure too.

8. *Running Down Reserves*. There are four ways to finance imports: now, by exports; later, by borrowing; not at all, by receiving gifts; and 'in the past'. The way to finance current imports 'in the past' is to have built up an earlier export surplus. This creates reserves of foreign exchange that can now be run down to pay for imports. This is the classical method of development finance, used by most European countries before and during their periods of rapid progress in the nineteenth century. A big export surplus was built up by increased output of a traditional commodity (e.g. Swedish timber, British wool). The accumulated reserves were then run down, to pay for huge excesses of imports over current exports. These imports, supplemented by private capital, helped to finance a wide range of new and more modern industries (e.g. steel, in both Sweden and Britain).[8] Can this process be repeated today?

Chapter eight indicates some of the barriers to expansion of traditional exports by poor countries. Still, some few countries (notably India, Pakistan, and the oil producers) came out of the Second World War with big 'sterling balances' – reserves accumulated by sales of scarce war commodities, hire of bases, etc. India and Pakistan spent almost all these balances in the late 1950s, to meet the enormous import requirements of development – and to help feed the growing population. The oil producers, and some other mineral-producing countries in Africa, still have reserves ample to pay for even five successive balance-of-payments deficits as bad as the worst ever experienced. Some of these countries support sterling by keeping enormous reserves in British government bonds: from their own viewpoint, the money could be much better used to finance an import surplus for development. But this possibility exists only for a tiny proportion of the people of the poor world.*

9. *Personal saving.* We have discussed the prospects and limits of personal saving as a source of development finance, and suggested some institutional encouragements that governments can provide. In each case the government has to consider the key question: is it tapping genuinely new savings, or merely transferring savings to different (and not always higher-yielding) uses? To some extent it is true that where enterprise, public or private, leads, finance follows. But it does not swell the volume of developmental resources unless it is extra saving rather than merely transferred savings.

There is no space to do more than suggest some other factors affecting the level and effectiveness of personal saving:

(a) The choice of tax measures plainly affects savings potential, which is why 'soaking the rich' implies more government saving, if growth is to continue.

(b) Success in cutting the birth-rate, by increasing the family's 'hand/mouth ratio', is almost certain to increase the proportion of personal income saved.

(c) As people move to the towns, they come into contact with new savings institutions and opportunities, and thus save more.

(d) The breakdown of the traditional 'joint family' – many brothers with their wives and children, living under the same roof – reduces the extent to which feckless people can rely on their relatives, and forces them to save for emergencies instead. But more income must be spent on furnishing!

(e) Mass rural poverty compels urban migrants to remit earnings to their families in the village; if that poverty is eased, the money can be saved instead.

10. *Business saving.* In most poor countries, most businesses are small family farms. Their motives for saving are almost the same as if they were private persons, with one crucial addition: better opportunities for farming will automatically induce them to transfer some of their incomes towards saving, embodied at

*Gold hoarding is common in Asia and Africa, and such private reserves may be run down to pay for luxury imports. This is not development finance.

once (without transfer costs or intermediary charges) into productive investment.

But while most businesses are small farms, most business saving comes from a handful of big enterprises – textile mills, sugar and cocoa refiners, owners of plantations and mines. These enterprises, like their counterparts in rich countries, rely increasingly on profits for investment finance, rather than on banks or the stock market. Because fair taxation requires good accounting, and because the biggest firms (often with foreign links) are unpopular, such profits are an important source of tax revenue – at the cost of business saving. There is a conflict between efficiency and equity; to some extent, it can be resolved by raising the profits tax on low-priority products, and cutting or abolishing it on others. But this is a fertile field for evasion by classification.

11. *Cooperative finance*. On p. 259 we mentioned the role of cooperative rural credit in destroying the monopoly of the village moneylender, and thus allowing rural capital to finance well building and fertilizer purchase at less prohibitive rates of interest than before. A cooperative credit society is a self-administering group; its main purpose is to allow small, poor farms to borrow at reasonable rates of interest, use the loan to buy fertilizers or a new well, and pay back as the goods they have bought produce a return. Eventually such societies should stand on their own feet, i.e., new loans should come entirely out of interest paid on old loans. Initially, help from the state (or, much more rarely, from a bank) is needed.

Cooperative credit, like most of the development field, has yielded a crop of horror stories and a large number of quiet and unrecorded successes. What can go wrong, and how can the mistakes be prevented?

Loans are sometimes advanced for capital projects that do not yield enough to finance repayments of interest – dry wells, inappropriate fertilizers and so forth. Proper liaison between cooperative secretaries and *efficient* agricultural extension is essential; otherwise cooperative credit is pure waste.

Loans are often diverted towards consumption. This need not be all loss; indeed, if the borrower switches from a consumption loan at 35 per cent interest at the moneylender's to a 7 per cent cooperative loan, he can well afford to repay the cooperative out of the 'yield' – the moneylender's interest that he no longer needs to pay. The real danger is that cooperative credit is obtained by moneylenders, and re-loaned for consumption at high rates to poor credit risks. Detailed local knowledge by the cooperative secretary is the only safeguard.

Some borrowers refuse to pay back loans. In particular, the traditional moneylender–borrower relation makes people expect to repay substantial interest for ever – but never to repay capital. To ensure repayment of capital, many societies restrict loans to people who can offer the security of land; if they do not repay, they forfeit the land. But the sanction is too severe to be credible, especially as it is unclear what the society would do with such land; moreover, in many African tribal tenure systems there is no true individual landowner, and in non-communist Asia those most in need of capital – the tenants – do not own land at all, while the smallholders, who work both land and capital harder than 'largeholders', cannot obtain enough credit to buy more of them, because they have less land to offer as security for loans. For all these reasons, cooperative credit societies are increasingly accepting 'future crop' as security, instead of land.

Above all, cooperative credit societies need to be run honestly, impartially and really cooperatively; and these three aims conflict. Tiny single-village societies can create a close bond among farmers, who help keep each other in line when it comes to repayment; but the secretary tends to steer funds towards his own caste, tribe or faction.[9] And there are few countries, rich or poor, where each village contains a man at once able enough to run the cooperative, and honest enough to work for low pay, with minimal supervision, and without running off with the funds. These problems can be alleviated only with time, experience and development.

12. *Private foreign investment*. This method of development finance lies at the opposite extreme to the indigenous, localized, democratic (but slow and unsure) procedures of cooperative credit. There are two varieties: portfolio investment, in which *individuals* in Britain or America finance companies in India or Kenya by share purchase; and direct investment, in which *com-*

panies like Unilever (in West Africa) or I C I and Swedish Match (in India) build and run plants themselves.

The outstanding examples of investment in poor countries, by companies in rich ones, lie in such things as oil, copper, bauxite, rubber, tea and financial institutions: all modern sectors of the economy, or sectors linked to exports or to economic control; none involving much direct stimulus to the bulk of the population, who live by growing cereals. Naturally poor countries are ambivalent towards such investment. They welcome the extra finances, and the demonstration of new techniques. They resent the big profits sent home, and the isolated communities of unimaginably wealthy managerial expatriates. But if they squeeze the profits or over-tax the expatriates, future private foreign investment is frightened off. Joint ventures by foreign investors and 'guest' government, and general 'codes of conduct' to reduce uncertainty for both parties (especially concerning remittance of profit), are among possible remedies.

13. *Export credits*. These are loans, by firms or governments, to enable private or public concerns to buy a particular export. The dividing line between aid and export credits is fuzzy, but export credits are generally short-term and tied to a particular purchase. Interest rates on export credits are either fully commercial or, if lower, used to persuade buyers to buy goods that are otherwise insufficiently attractive. Export credits are not a true resource transfer from rich countries to poor, but they may provide a useful carry-over of funds, from a time when the poor country is short of foreign exchange to a time when it is not. For countries with 'seasonal' exports like tea or rubber, this can be a major contribution to stable financing. Unfortunately the coordination of private export credits with other forms of development finance is minimal. Indeed the control of private savings, home and foreign, and its integration into development planning, is usually weak, and often based on scanty information and hopeful projection.

Policy towards overseas companies has implications for the whole tax system, especially for poor countries where overseas capital looms large. In some small countries, especially in the Caribbean, a single overseas company normally accounts for over half the investment in the entire country, and taxation of its profits, wages and salaries produces the bulk of government revenues. The right way to tax such a company is clearly *the* crucial development decision in these cases. The right balance must be struck between naïvely accepting the company's assurances that profit is small, and taxing it so heavily that it puts its business elsewhere. Often the company's accountants and lawyers are paid many times more than the host government's.

Nor can tax policy towards the investing company be treated in isolation. The prices which the company claims it pays for purchases from its foreign branches (e.g. oil for refining) are often quite arbitrary – selected to locate profits in countries where they are taxed least heavily. The balance of incentives to overseas companies ('tax holidays', import duty remissions, accelerated depreciation, etc.) must be carefully selected to attract the right investment at least cost in public revenues forgone. The problem is complex and politically explosive, and an independent organization (perhaps at the U.N.) might usefully help poor countries with the economic and legal complexities.[10]

The Uses of Development Finance

This book deals with the ways in which the resources for development have been, and could be, used. At the level of national strategies, the discussion in chapter seven covers such matters as the place of the public sector and the choice between autarky and integration into the world economy. Other chapters, like those on agriculture and education, deal with the choices open in particular sectors. But between the great national choices and the narrower sectoral decisions lies an intermediate level of planning: that of 'investment criteria'. This involves a search for principles to guide the allocation of investible resources, domestic and foreign, among major sectors, and for the best techniques to produce the factories and schools and roads. This topic is both huge and highly technical, and we can only skim the surface here.

The private firm just puts its spare cash (allowing for risk) where it expects the highest profit. The planner, by adjusting the prices of inputs and outputs faced by the firm, hopes to ensure that profit-seeking investment will be of high social value as well. But the planner would be unwise to use profitability as the criterion for deciding what sort of public investment to undertake, and that for several reasons. First, profitability depends on the price one can charge – and hence on how rich the buyer is, and how powerful the state monopoly is, as well as on the usefulness of one's product. Second, planners must look to the future more than is customary for private individuals. Third, a big part of the case for putting any investment decision in the public sector is that its 'external yield' is understated by the private profit it can produce; the great dams of the Indus Basin or Aswan would never have been built by private businessmen, who know how difficult it is to collect levies from farmers who use the water; but such schemes are amply justified economically in terms of the extra food and electric power that the water can produce.

The shortest step from the direct profitability criterion, and the first to be suggested by economists, was to measure the addition of alternative investment projects to national output as a whole: not easy, since one must assess the *lost* output involved in diverting managers, engineers, and so forth to the new project, possibly from other projects. But in any case this attempt is not enough. The real issue is between investment that produces consumer goods, investment that produces more machines to make consumer goods, investment to make machines to make machines... and so forth. The planner's decision depends on his preferences between jam today, tomorrow, and in 1984 – and on the electoral pressures applied. Excessive puritanism can be self-defeating. India's Second Five-year Plan (1956–61) concentrated bravely, and fairly successfully, on basic heavy industry – machines to make machines to make machines. The consequent neglect of agriculture helped to produce the food shortages of the 1960s; and in 1967 these forced the government to reduce industrial output, lest the urban workers spend their wages on bidding up even further the soaring price of food.

Cutting across the 'jam today – jam tomorrow' debate are two other questions: how important is saving relative to efficiency, and how important is employment relative to efficiency? In so far as growth can be explained by extra capital investment, it is the outcome of two things: the proportion of income saved (or permitted as an import surplus) to finance investment, and the productive efficiency of the investment thus financed. Three successive Indian Plans have featured great concentration on steel investment, which has so far shown persistently disappointing returns: but at least the bulk of such returns are reinvested. Even if the private sector can be shown to manage some industry much more efficiently than the state, the state can save (and use for investment) such returns as it does secure, while firms distribute dividends, some of which are consumed.

The argument about 'labour-intensiveness' as a criterion for investment is closely linked to this struggle between efficiency and saving. Some activities, notably dam-building, can be undertaken with much hard work *or* with heavy machinery; and almost always a government has some choice between activities with relatively high or low capital-cost per employee (in general, between 'industry' and 'agriculture': the inverted commas warn of excessive generalization). The case for the labour-using activities, or techniques, is obvious: labour is idle and machinery is scarce, and the creation of jobs is an end in itself. But there are arguments on the other side. On p. 56 we point out that the allegedly labour-using technique turns out, much of the time, to use more capital as well. Hirschmann[11] suggests that 'machine-paced' processes are desirable if the worker in a poor country is to be trained to shift from the attitudes of agriculture, where work tomorrow is often as good as work today, to the strictly timed attendance necessary for complex modern industry. In export production, only the most up-to-date (i.e. capital-using) technique may be feasible. But above all workers spend their wages (or remit them to rural relatives who do), while the returns on capital tend to be saved for reinvestment.

The criteria for allocating development finance among sectors are complicated and often conflicting. Moreover, the amount of practical use made of such criteria has been small, and we have had to strain reality to make them relevant to the issues that concern the practical planner: agriculture or industry, poor regions or promising regions, and so on. There are two reasons for all this. First, the criteria tend to disguise the evaluative and political nature of investment decisions: to pretend they are absolute objective choices, often with a cloak of pretentious jargon. Second, even where planners and politicians state their values and mean what they say, they usually lack the statistics needed to decide exactly which of two investment alternatives has the higher rate of return, or generates more employment, or more profits which will be saved.

It is typical of a poor country's capacity to instil a horror of the practical that the construction of useless but beautiful pieces of economic theory in Delhi or Mexico City brings more prestige than the field measurement of the effects of alternative investment decisions. Hence few underdeveloped governments really know the expected results of alternative projects in terms of output produced, workers employed, imports needed or savings generated (let alone the risk that expectations will not be fulfilled). Often development finance goes to the tribe, caste, region or uncle who makes the most fuss. Of course this happens in rich countries too. Britain has its politically-sited steel mills and its new giant liners, and the United States has its pork-barrel legislation. But poor countries can less easily afford these follies. Development finance is hard enough to get; it is desperately easy to squander.

12 PLANNING AND DEVELOPMENT

Since 1952 when India adopted her first five-year plan, the word 'planning' has become virtually synonymous with the word 'development' in the less developed countries. A massive survey by the World Bank showed scarcely a single underdeveloped country without at least one plan, and in some cases, (e.g. the Philippines) almost as many plans as there were years in the post-war decades. From Malaya to Mali, from Nigeria to Nicaragua, there has been a universal consensus that plans are the best means to development. Yet the record is not very encouraging. Something has been achieved, but the gap between what has been done and what should have been done according to the plans remains very wide. The fourth Indian five-year plan, prepared by one of the most sophisticated planning systems in the less developed world, had to be drastically rewritten while the country's economy ran for over a year without a plan. In some countries, where plan has succeeded published plan without any significant attempt at implementing any of them, a general scepticism and cynicism has inevitably grown up about the whole concept. Ministries of planning, central planning offices, planning units and planning agencies are frequently treated with suspicion and even hostility or disdain by other agencies of government and by many politicians.

Yet a world-wide revulsion against planning is extremely unlikely. In spite of all the disappointments, it still represents an ideal of rational reorganization, where less is wasted through neglect and confusion, or the pursuit of incompatible ends. The frustrations arise because the collective interest is so hard to reconcile with the immediate interests of each group represented. People are not usually acting irrationally when they react against reform. On the contrary, just because they adapt so prudently to the world as they find it, they make it more difficult to change. As earlier chapters of this book have shown, the peasant farmer who sticks obstinately to his inferior seed has calculated rainfall, labour, yields and social pressures at least as rationally as the agricultural reformer – but from the standpoint of what is, not what might be. The politician who ridicules family planning to score off a rival, or who, when in power, vetoes development to punish a disloyal neighbourhood, may be playing the game of power with all the skill at his command. The schoolmaster who ignores practical vocational subjects for academic courses knows what earns promotion and what parents wish to buy for their children with their fees. The more successfully people come to terms with all the inadequacies of their society, the more they invest their own well-being in them. The irrationality of society is sustained by the rationality of its individual members.

Yet societies do change, because the cumulative influence of individual adaptations in time overwhelms the power of even the most conservative institutions to hold their ground. Pressures mount – land hunger, unemployment, inequalities, tribal rivalries. At some point – even if it is too late – everyone must come to recognize that their own survival depends upon the collective rationality of their society's response.

The problem, then, is this: poor countries use their resources and opportunities very inadequately. In principle, it is possible to work out how they could be much better used. But in practice, innovation becomes entangled in the enormous complexity of social, political and economic factors which have to be coordinated, and whose interaction is very little understood. To foresee how these factors will behave, to manipulate them to serve a common purpose, a poor country desperately needs to tackle its problems rationally. If past approaches to this ideal have been disappointing, new ones will be worked out. What can the arguments of this book contribute to a possible improvement in planning?

This problem can be looked at in broad terms of a society's needs, or more narrowly in terms of the tasks facing a government in power. In this sense, chapters five and six have a rather different perspective from those which followed. The political scientist or the sociologist studying a developing country tends to focus on processes of change that are relevant to the goals of the various groups in society, without any necessary emphasis on the problems involved in achieving the goals of the current political leadership. To take the most extreme case, it may well seem from the point of view of these disciplines that the most natural next step in a country's development – meaning here its capacity to adapt to changes so that the various groups of society can further their aspirations – is that there should be a social revolution. The study of 'development' will in this case be a study of the forces which will bring social change to the point when it has to go forward by a revolutionary step. The point of view of economists, while it can certainly be extended to embrace this approach as well, tends on the whole to be narrower. So long as the leadership currently in power is concerned with economic change, policy choices are confronted which the economist is competent to analyse. In the post-war period the public commitment by the governments of less developed countries to economic growth as a major political goal has encouraged economists to develop their skills and understanding of the process of development within the narrower, rather than the wider, interpretation of development, focusing particularly on those policy choices which regimes currently in power had to make.

This has been for the most part the latent assumption of this book, and in particular of the last five chapters. Naturally this assumption has, from time to time, had to be brought to the surface – for instance in the discussion in chapter eight – where it becomes clear that the problem of improving the trading position of less developed countries is not really a policy choice confronting the leadership of less developed countries so much as one confronting the developed countries – or in chapter ten – where it is clear that decisions about the educational system involve the personal interests of the decision-making elite so vitally, that the economic adviser will find it hard to restrict himself to advise within the narrow limits set by the decision-making elite alone.

Nonetheless we have in this book followed the narrower rather than the wider conception of development, assuming that there is a shared conception of the public interest between those in office in developing countries and those studying development and anxious to help. This is a double limitation – accepting the definition of the development goals given by current political leaderships as the most relevant definition, and concentrating on the economic choices within that formulation. But the wider problem of development is immense, and the problems isolated in this book seem urgent and realistic enough to justify this limitation. In focusing on planning in this chapter, therefore, we will try to indicate some of the ways in which, even within the more immediately practical concept of the development problem which broadly underlies the approach of this book, other social sciences can make a useful contribution.

'Beyond Economics' – a Broader Basis for the Analysis of Change

One of the themes stressed in the first half of this book is the impossibility of making more headway with development – however defined – unless narrow disciplinary approaches are abandoned.

Is there anything more to be said about this than has been said already? Is it simply a question of taking a broader view, being more aware of complexity and interdependences, using more tools drawn from sociology and political science, learning to think as manipulatively about social and political change as we automatically do about economic change?

It will do no harm to concede that it *is* partly a matter of broadened attitudes. The force of habit is far more powerful in public policy than we care to recognize, and the next generation of policy makers will look back at the almost complete domination of development thinking by economics in the 1950s as a transient historical phenomenon as bizarre, yet also decisive for its time, as the dominance of town-planning by architects in the 1940s in Britain now appears to us, or the dominance of recruitment into the higher civil service by arts faculties of ancient universities in the twenties and thirties.

The precise implications of stepping outside a purely economic approach will depend on the problem in hand. Sometimes it will indeed be a matter of engaging the skills of other disciplines. This will come about partly because economists are increasingly seeking the collaboration of other social scientists in planning large-scale projects, and partly because of the emergence of towering problems of a patently sociological character; for instance when a government identifies as a major objective the reduction of its rate of population increase, it should turn to demographers and sociologists and social psychologists for a large part of the resources of skills which it requires.

Something can be done to facilitate this process by making available suitable training in the richer countries to which many developing nations still look for their professional and post-graduate manpower requirements. They can offer scholarships earmarked for these fields. At the same time they can examine the training being given in all the 'developmental' disciplines to see whether something more than lip-service is being paid in the graduate schools to the ineluctable complexity of development. It is a fact that it is still possible, if not the rule, to reach Ph.D. level in most British universities in one social science with virtually no grounding in any others; this is even true in schools with strong interests in 'developing' countries. A new generation of social scientists, more able to read each other's literature – and more anxious to do so – could make itself felt in the pace of development in the next decade, in a pervasive fashion rather than in any single or dramatic sphere. It is not just that a more balanced mixture of specialists needs to be available to governments for employment in planning offices; much more fundamentally, the influence of the new outlook must spread to the higher levels of administration, where the conception of what the development problem is in the first place tends to be determined.

The importance of this point could be illustrated in numerous ways. One of the most familiar signs of a failure to conceptualize the problems of development at all adequately is the extent to which scarce resources are devoted to *exhorting* people to do things. There is no doubt that people do need to be encouraged to try new things, and to be informed of new opportunities; the radio and public meetings are potent instruments of change, and district officers, agricultural officers, block development officers and so on, the massive army of 'change agents' who constitute the most expensive part of the development effort in all developing countries, cannot help spending a large part of their time making speeches, to large audiences or small ones. But there is no doubt that the means often becomes an end in itself; people are urged to 'work harder' for the sake of 'national unity' or 'progress' when there seems to be no good individual motive for doing so; they are told to sink their differences when these differences concern scarce resources – say land – which the government cannot make plentiful; they are urged to change their habits or ideas because it would be valuable to someone *else* if they did so (perhaps it will indirectly benefit them, but habitual ideas are precisely ideas that result from and are maintained by our *direct* experiences). A recent propaganda poster, adopted by the fisheries department of an African state, which reads 'Forget your old traditions; Eat More Fish,' sums up the problem. At the bottom this whole cast of mind is not so much failing to get 'beyond economics', as failing to begin from an analysis of the social forces determining the behaviour which has got to be changed. It is an essentially paternalist and sometimes authoritarian approach; and it has a lot to do with the relatively low productivity of change-agents, if the gap between their ideals and the actual degree of change is taken as a measure of it. Of course the impact of extension workers and their various colleagues must not be underestimated, but it cannot be disputed that an enormous quantity of development effort by these highly motivated, highly trained and expensive cadres is of little avail.

The essence of any policy for change is to discover a pattern of motivation which it is possible to satisfy in order to induce the desired changes in behaviour. How many programmes for development have been built up from answers to the fundamental question 'what would make these people want to do the things we need them to do, and can we find the means necessary to make them?' To get answers to this question, a fresh look needs to be taken at the objectives: what precisely is the object in view – a short-term increase in output, a medium-term improvement in output per acre, a long-term change in the organization of production? The inducements needed to secure each of these may be quite different; and so may the consequential side effects. But on the whole, development programmes are built up in a less analytic spirit. The process of gestation more typically involves applying ideas that have succeeded in other contexts – various kinds of cooperative organization, freehold land tenure, government-controlled trade unions – without any systematic analysis of the context in which they succeeded before, or the new one in which they are tried again. Small wonder that projects which get into the plan in this way rarely do quite what is hoped of them.

Planning and Politics: the Tactics of Development

A more analytic, causally sensitive approach to social change is one of the positive contributions that a broad-based social scientific training can hope to make in the upper echelons of government in developing countries. It may also help to find ways round two characteristic obstacles to development planning. The first concerns the coordination of planning and politics; the second, the coordination of action and information. For planning is both political action and informed analysis, and unless it can be integrated with the other institutions of society which try to fulfil these functions, confusion and conflict must arise.

Once it is recognized that there are not only different economic costs attaching to the various alternative programmes for development from which governments must choose, but also different social and political costs, it becomes possible to avoid some of the most familiar pitfalls that have prevented economically promising schemes from succeeding. From an economic point of view alone, for instance, a project taking several years to complete but with a very high prospective rate of return may be preferable to shorter-run, but lower-yielding schemes. But from a political point of view early results may be important.

Political life proceeds by 'stages' and 'phases' which are perceived as such, each phase generating its own hopes and promises, identified with a particular set of measures and men. Unless development planners want to see their work dissipated in a spate of pre-election spending or nibbled away by concessions to one interest after another, they must take the political cost of time carefully into account.

Another way in which explicit attention to political objectives can yield economically desirable results is in the intelligent anticipation of regional demands. It very often happens that the development of services is according to a technically rational analysis of needs: roads are to be widened or tarred according to studies of traffic flows, schools and hospitals are to be designed and located according to the distribution of population and the existing pattern of provision, and so on. In the course of time, however, areas with low traffic flows or relatively abundant previous provision bring pressure to bear for a share of current new provision. What then happens is that additional provision, of a type similar to that planned for the other areas, has to be made in the areas for which it was not planned and for which it is not technically appropriate.

A programme which anticipates such eventualities looks rather different. In principle, it aims to do something everywhere, but it contains a flexible variety of types of provision, so that the technically optimal distribution of services is approximated, without this being so visible as under the 'purist' approach. It may necessitate new organizational devices. For instance, instead of having a programme of building district hospitals, each with its complement of doctors and other staff, it may require a new network of clinics and health centres served by a new hierarchy of professional staff, some of whom would circulate from a centre at the provincial level. These sorts of innovation rarely find easy acceptance from the professionals concerned, and medical service schemes along these lines have foundered more than once in face of professional opposition. The result is that a highly expensive type of service is constantly being extended, for good political reasons, beyond the economically desirable limits. A more conscious appreciation of the nature of this process would almost certainly have led to at least a partial victory for innovation in some of the countries concerned.

It may also be important to look at the different long-run political side effects of alternative economic measures. Tanzania has provided a good example by its recent reconsideration of the effects of agricultural extension policies on rural class formation. For well over two decades, agricultural officers in Tanzania, as elsewhere in Africa, have bent every effort to identify and encourage those farmers who would adopt new goals and techniques and show the way forward to their neighbours. Lists of these 'emergent' or 'progressive' farmers could be found in most district agricultural offices. As they have begun to succeed, they have acquired more land, taken on labour, purchased equipment, tractors, lorries, taken over market stalls in the towns for some of their produce, and so on. But the Tanzanian leaders are well aware that this prosperity, achieved in this way, implies a corresponding class of employees without land, and that the distribution of wealth in a rural society led by such pioneers would be extremely unequal. An approach to growth on purely cooperative lines, without the use of privately employed labour, is almost certain to be much slower, and, perhaps, is never likely to be quite as productive, but it seems to hold out more hope of an equal distribution of wealth, and might avoid the emergence of a powerful and conservative class of rich farmers whose influence on national development might well be negative at a later stage, as it has been in many other countries.

Action and Information: the Tactics of Deciding

If development planning is sensitive enough to balance economic and social purposes, and reconcile these with the immediate interests of the political system, it still has to face difficulties of another kind. The way in which the rational procedures of society are institutionalized tends to generate conflicts which inhibit their effective use. Most governments, most of the time, acknowledge the need for detached, informed analysis, and encourage – or at least tolerate – institutions to promote it; universities, planning departments, statistical bureaux, research centres, teams of consultants, commissions of inquiry. But all of these devices, imitated from the practice of rich nations, have a characteristic which threatens their effectiveness in poor ones: the intellectual integrity of analysis is protected by divorcing it from action. The gathering of information, or the sifting of evidence, comes to be a specialized function.

A man of action – politician or administrator – holds a position in a structure of power which, for his own survival, he must maintain. He cannot withdraw from the urgent pressures which this structure weighs upon him long enough to gather detailed information and subject it to critical analysis. Nor is he free to draw conclusions impartially from the evidence: his reputation is already invested in certain policies, his choices are constrained by the prejudices of his superiors, by political horse-trading, by the jealousies of rival departments. So any rational reassessment of policy seems to depend upon the advice of outsiders, who have no personal stake in the decision taken. The segregation of intellectual criticism protects it from contamination. But it also becomes alienated.

Take, for instance, university research, which accounts for a large part of the informed analysis attempted in poor countries. The traditional principles which protect universities from political interference also isolate academics from government. The topics of research may be chosen without reference to any urgent decision, and the researcher may have no means of communicating his conclusions, apart from posting his report hopefully to the appropriate ministry. Even when he is concerned to be relevant and useful, he tends to remain a marginal contributor to the making of decisions. The context of his thinking is, besides, at heart different. He wants to establish the truth, as objectively as he can, and truth is timeless. It may be no longer to the point, when its moment comes: but it remains respectable scholarship, which is what an academic is paid to achieve. He is right to leave open what his information cannot determine, because his contribution is defined in terms of a cumulative body of knowledge and speculative ideas. But an administrator must decide, today not tomorrow, on the best information to hand. Ideally, the scholar and the administrator should complement each other. In practice, their different preoccupations tend to frustrate the coordination of information and action: timing, language, assumptions are mutually incompatible.

If research is incorporated within a government department, the opposite difficulties arise. Instead of being too autonomous, it is not autonomous enough. Unless research is free to challenge the assumptions on which policy is based, it cannot redefine the issues and shed new light on them. And since the administration is responsible for the research it sponsors, it is likely to be sensitive about awkward conclusions. Departmental research is therefore only likely to have enough scope, if it is promoted to a very senior position in the administrative hierarchy. But because it is not involved in the immediate exercise of power, it is accorded, in practice if not in principle, a lower status. Governments are organized to institutionalize, not rational procedures, but levels of authority. Since the act of decision carries the greatest authority, it stands at the top, the privilege of ministers in consultation with their senior advisers. Implementation stands below it, and fact-finding is cast out of the hierarchy altogether, since the gathering of information, in itself, carries no authority whatever. The system works downwards, imperiously, each level jealously guarding its power from the intrusion of those below, and then halts. A hierarchy of power therefore cannot easily contain a rational process which, because it is circular and self-correcting, is essentially egalitarian. Hence, too, the bureaucratic nervousness of risk, since failures advertise themselves, but missed opportunities only appear from analysis. And since a hierarchy of authority does not continuously report outcomes and information to the highest level of decision, except as the top requests it, the decisions are likely to be taken more exclusively in terms of immediate political pay-offs than they need be. So research has low prestige in an administration, just as it has the higher prestige in a university, the less it is concerned with practical questions of action.

All this matters less in a rich country, where the thinkers and the doers are at least citizens of the same society, sharing the same background of knowledge and ideas. But in a poor country, the thinkers are likely to be foreigners. Planning consultants, economic experts, United Nations commissions, World Bank survey teams, university professors, research students are borrowed from America, Scandinavia, Britain, Israel, Poland. And this aggravates the inherent weakness of segregating thought and action. Even if, in time, the critical intelligence of society becomes indigenous, its alien history may have permanently handicapped its assimilation.

In rich nations, too, the sheer abundance of information and means to communicate it help to overwhelm the institutional barriers. The mediators of rational analysis are as important as the research itself – newspapers, television, journals, societies for the promotion of reforms, foundations. But poor countries are poor too in competent intellectual middlemen. Less gets across, because there are fewer people to put it across and fewer means. There is also, of course, less to communicate, because there are relatively fewer people engaged in research – especially research into questions of social or political analysis, where ignorance is perhaps greatest.

But there is another consequence of the segregation of fact-finding and analysis from action which affects rich and poor nations alike, and is even more damaging than the failure to inform decisions. The procedures for measuring the outcome of governmental action are seldom included in the plan of action itself, and at best evaluation is very imperfect. Often, only a few crude economic indicators are kept in review. It is not just a question of whether the policy worked, but whether it was carried out. Inexperienced, ill-trained field staff may misinterpret instructions, or baulk at the difficulty of carrying them out; funds are not allocated; crucial personnel diverted; institutions stolidly ignore the directives of reform. The makers of policy need to know urgently what happened, and why. There is seldom anyone appointed to tell them. Yet unless the consequences of decision are continually reported back to the decision-makers, there can be no rational progress.

The model of rational action is information, analysis, decision, implementation, feed-back, re-analysis. Its validity does not require that information be ever complete, because the process is self-correcting. In everyday life, we take its logic for granted. And since, as individuals, we revolve the whole sequence continually in our minds, it works fluently and spontaneously. But it does not work for society, because in our attempts to institutionalize the same process as a collective intelligence, crucial stages are missed altogether, and others are uncoordinated.

Is it possible, even in principle, to systematize a process for collective decisions which corresponds more closely to the rational behaviour of individuals? The difficulties are enormous. The complexity of the purposes to be satisfied, the range of information needed to determine how they might be achieved, and at what cost, the haste with which they must be analysed and synthesized, may well be unmanageable. And there is a more fundamental problem. An individual can compare the value and cost to himself of very different kinds of satisfaction, by consulting his own feelings. Intuitively, he can balance the desire for a new house against the advantages of a better pension. But society cannot balance housing against social security by intuitive introspection: only its decisions, not its desires, are collective. So it has to invent a way of measuring satisfactions which seem scarcely measurable in the same terms.

But for all the difficulties, the possibilities of more systematic procedures are worth exploring. The most ambitious experiment yet was inaugurated in America, in August 1965. In that month, all the departments and most of the agencies of the United States government were ordered by President Johnson to adopt a 'revolutionary' new form of decision-making, called a Planning–Programming–Budgeting System (PPBS), which had been pioneered under Robert Macnamara's administration of the Defence Department. The system required each department to define the principal objectives it chose to pursue, to analyse systematically the ways in which it might pursue them, and plan its spending several years ahead. The proposal does not, perhaps, sound so very revolutionary. But its methods, just because they are deliberately rational, imply a radical innovation in the whole style, structure, and even the philosophy of government.

PPBS 'attempts to do three things: (1) to display information about the functioning of actual government programs so that it is possible to see easily what portion of Federal resources is being allocated to particular purposes, what is being accomplished by the programs, and how much they cost; (2) to analyse the costs of achieving particular objectives so that it is possible to rank the alternatives in terms of their relative costs; (3) to evaluate the benefits of achieving objectives as comprehensively and quantitatively as possible in order to facilitate the setting of priorities among objectives. These three activities are inter related and build on each other.'[2] PPBS concentrates its methods upon the budget, because the allocation of resources is the most crucial decision a department of government makes – and especially the allocation of any increase in its vote. A large part of government spending is committed from year to year, in the salaries of permanent staff, the maintenance of plants and buildings, servicing of debts. The chance to innovate lies mostly in the marginal increments of its resources over routine expenditure. But PPBS does not put the question as 'what shall we do with these uncommitted funds?' but rather 'what would be gained by spending on this or that?' In this way, a department is forced to justify its appropriation of funds, not only in terms of explicit objectives, but in terms of how much progress it could make towards these objectives at how great a cost. To do this, it has to submit the choices to an analysis of their comparable costs and benefits, somehow bringing within the scope of its calculations not only monetary outlays and returns, but the consequences for the well-being of different groups of people.

The radicalism of the whole approach seems to depend, above all, on the insight with which purposes are articulated. Certainly, many departments of the United States government had never before asked themselves what they were about: a bureaucratic institution tends to take the value of its functions for granted, and concentrate on protecting and aggrandizing its jurisdiction. So by its nature the question was challenging. But the articulation of aims is a subtle process, and the analysis of alternatives can only be as penetrating as the question which defines the objective. If a department of education asks, say, how it can best increase primary school enrolment over the next five years, its analysis of costs or benefits is likely to turn on the relative advantages of building more primary schools or running double shifts, of building more teacher training colleges, recruiting more teachers overseas, raising salaries. But if it asks instead, 'how can we best increase the employment of young people?' the whole analysis is cast in a wider frame, where the relevance of education itself has to be set against all the other possibilities of fitting them to earn a livelihood. And this, too, may not be self-evidently the crucial question, but rather how can we best achieve a literate population? or a creative one? Means and ends change places as the question changes, and only by turning everything upside down and inside out can one discover how they hang together.*

If the framing of questions is the most creative art in the PPB system, it is also the most vulnerable, both because it remains an art, rather than a science, and because it seems to pre-empt decisions which belong to politics. The systems analyst who explores the logic of ends and means cannot justify the way he articulates them except by appeal to a consensus of values. Critics of PPBS would argue that if it ignores the political constraints upon choice, it becomes unrealistic: and if it does not, it is competing with political authority – opposing the legitimacy of rationality to the legitimacy of democracy as the arbiter of choice. In reality, the risk that the Rand Corporation will pull off a *coup d'état* is not yet serious. The American tradition of political horse-trading is still very much alive. But PPBS may help, at least, to bring a better breed of horses to the market. If the game of power has its own imperatives, which cut across the rational deployment of resources, there is still much to gain by setting each beside the other, and trying to reconcile them.

Cost-benefit analysis, the second crucial element in the system, is politically less suspect. Its weakness is rather that it is, for the most part, impossible to complete. The benefits, and even some of the costs, may turn out to be incalculable. Information is not available, or not quantifiable in any comparable form. How many

*The experience of United States administrative agencies in learning to apply PPBS illustrates very well the inappropriateness of the model of planning in which ends are 'given', discussed in chapter five above.

children, munching their peanut butter sandwiches in a nature reserve, are worth how many hours off a journey down a new highway? How many elephants are worth a field of corn? But these apparently unanswerable and even ludicrous questions at least stimulate a search for consequences which broadens the range of analysis, and forces the ingenuity of rational comparison to its limits. After all, however impossible it seems to calculate the sum of human happiness, a decision has still to be taken.

The trouble with cost-benefit analysis is not that it cannot be done at all, but that parts of it can be better done than others, so that the comparisons are biased towards the most readily measurable outcomes. Where knowledge is so imperfect, the rationalization of the costs and benefits best understood may even be stultifying. Albert Hirschmann, for instance, has argued that development is sometimes achieved only by a delicate balance of ignorance. If, at the outset, the difficulties that were to beset a project had been foreseen, it would never have been undertaken. But when the difficulties arose, human ingenuity solved them. Planners underestimate the capacity of society to meet problems: the benevolent hand of providence therefore conceals from them the difficulties in their way.[3] The principle is familiar in everyday life: it achieves nothing to be obsessionally rational, revolving interminably alternatives whose consequences can only be guessed at. The most successful decisions have an element of gambling, an entrepreneurial brashness that refuses to be daunted by the endless, plausible possibilities of failure. Where the outcomes are largely unpredictable, rationality alone is not productive, since it can only reinforce the anxieties of uncertainty by finding more and better reasons for scepticism. Unless it is allied with a creative imagination, which asks the right questions, and the courage to take risks, systematic procedure will not provide the most hopeful decisions, only the apparently safest.

With these reservations, PPBS is still the one attempt at a coherent system of rational decision to have been generally applied by government. Its success seems so far to be limited to rationalizing decisions within a department, where costs and benefits are easiest to determine. It could show, for instance, that if the object of health policy is to save lives, money spent on encouraging the use of motor-car seat belts was a thousand times more productive than some forms of cancer control. It has had more difficulty in making meaningful comparisons between different kinds of vocational education programmes, and even more in extending these comparisons across different departments.

But it does attempt to implement three principles which seem crucial to an effective process of planning. Firstly, it integrates planning with the budgetary decisions which in practice mostly determine the allocation of resources. Secondly, by insisting that a policy be articulated in terms of its essential purpose, it obliges departments of government to justify their spending by broader arguments than the needs of their own administration, and helps to break down the autonomy of different jurisdictions. Thirdly, by comparing the cost and contribution of a proposed policy with other possibilities, it brings the gathering and analysis of information more centrally into the process of decision. PPBS itself may be too elaborate and too difficult to work to suit countries poorer than the United States – even if it succeeds there. And neither PPBS nor any similar system can achieve much, so long as the political obstacles we discussed earlier, and the vested interests of economic planners themselves remain.* But the need to integrate planning with budgeting and short-term decisions, to coordinate one department with another, and to exploit methodically all the information that can be brought to bear are still crucially important everywhere. And these principles are also relevant to the integration of planning with politics. They incorporate rational procedures more fully within government, so that while their scope is more limited by political demands, they may also be more honoured within those limits.

*The introduction of performance budgeting in the Philippines is a notable case in point; although performance budgeting has been formally established there for some years the actual budgetary operations of the country have not noticeably improved from the point of view of protecting them against the influence of sectional interests, and making them more instrumental for the purposes and methods outlined in the succession of Philippine plans.

In the light of this analysis, how far can less developed countries reasonably hope to improve their ability to control their future through planning?

New Approaches to Planning

In the past, the adoption of development planning has generally meant the following: the recruitment of some professional economists, usually expatriate in the early stages, to a central organization either established as a unit in an existing ministry or in the office of the president or head of state, or in an independent new ministry. These personnel have seen their task as the preparation of a medium-term plan (i.e. three to six years as a rule) framed on the basis of an analysis of the general characteristics of the economy and estimates of the levels of investment which must be made in each year of the plan, in order to achieve the aggregate target for levels of income, etc. set by the political leadership for the end of the plan period.

In a sense, the reasons why these plans have not been too successful are implicit in this bald statement of the way they have been made. There have been three main reasons why this exercise has often been a failure. First of all, the economic models used for the formulation of such plans have very often not been appropriate to the conditions of underdevelopment. They have usually been derived from the experience of developed economies, and where the assumptions in the models did not fit the new conditions the planners tended to make heroic alternative assumptions instead of scrapping the model; not surprisingly, the gap between theory and reality became altogether too wide. Secondly, the data which have had to be used are notoriously imperfect. This becomes more significant when considering medium-term plans for up to five or six years ahead, although it is bad enough when only looking one or two years ahead. Very great efforts have been poured into sophisticated econometric models to handle data which are extremely crude (and in some instances simply invented). Thirdly, approaching planning in this way involves an implicit assumption that the economic planners' activities would be well related to and fully accepted by their political and administrative environment: in other words, that the politicians, having set the plan targets, would support the planners' proposals for achieving them; that the agencies of government would correspondingly adapt their operations closely to the new lines of action implied in the medium-term plan; while the private sector – in most underdeveloped countries accounting for the greater part of the gross national product – would equally follow the routes indicated in the published plan document. In other words, this approach to planning tended to assume away the entire problem of converting the historically established administrative process, and the currently operating political process, from established routines and competitive struggles for sectional benefits, to a new coherent search for the public good. The result was that planning often remained largely a paper exercise.

Any new approach to planning has got to overcome these deficiencies. The task will not be easy. It now implies not only tackling the problems neglected in the past, but also overcoming the commitment of economic planners themselves to modes of thought which underlie the old approach. They must wean themselves from the unreal, static conception of planning as the delineation of optimal means to achieve fixed and externally given ends, discussed at the outset of this section, in chapter seven. They must be willing to reconsider radically the way in which a social system as complex and politicized as a nation-state can in reality take advantage of their particular skills. What does this mean in practice?

One set of proposals to emerge from the experience of the last twenty years has been put forward by Albert Waterston, and illustrates the issues at stake.[4] His proposals are focused on

1. Improving the budgetary process in quite simple ways, to bring it more in line with economic thinking over an annual planning period. These ways may be as simple as the establishment of inter-ministerial committees for discussing proposals for inclusion in the capital budget. In other words, the degree of rationality that is emphasized in this approach is

quite elementary, not a sophisticated concept related to economic model building for a period of several years.

2. A concentration by professional economists on annual planning. This gives them a period that corresponds with the budgetary cycle, and brings their expertise to bear on a disposition of resources that is extremely real and is geared to data that are at least the best available, inasmuch as they relate to the immediate future.

3. An emphasis on the accumulation of a stock of projects in all sectors which in the opinion of those professionally responsible for those sectors are practicable and appropriate, and are then ready to be incorporated in the annual plans year by year.

In other words this approach emphasizes a shorter run, and focuses on the improvement of those fairly elementary features of the development process which *are* within the scope of the government's control and which have been so conspicuously weak in the experience of many less developed countries. In focusing on the budgetary process, it concentrates on the one device which virtually every government, in however underdeveloped a country, has had to adopt for managing and organizing its public spending. The discipline of the budgetary cycle means that political efforts to affect the pattern of government spending are focused on the pre-budget period, that parliamentary and other conventions prescribe rules of access for politicians to budget-making, that auditing systems exist to control against major mis-spending. However imperfect these disciplines may be, they are one of the few sets of disciplines that constrain the political process to some general concept of the public interest. By directing the planning effort along these pre-existing channels this approach might well achieve more than earlier ones which assumed that some much more·extensive system of political discipline would simply 'grow up' to support and protect the proposals embodied in the five-year plan document.

The approach also recognizes the rather obvious fact that the administrative systems of most states were built up historically for other purposes than the rational allocation of scarce economic resources: if this is to be made the new rationale of administration, it must first be effectively established where the action already lies – in an *annual* administrative cycle. In effect, the Waterston approach says that before looking at what would be the optimum pattern of public economic activity over five years, there should first be a serious effort to get a more rational system of determining the components of the budget for one year. Ministries of education should not be allowed to build schools for which ministries of works are not proposing to build roads, ministries of health should not be allowed to build hospitals according to standard patterns for districts with quite different population distributions or health needs.

The focus on sector programmes implies, what the experience of every development planner confirms, that priority should be given to getting a proper supply of effective projects lined up in ministries before making plans which depend on the productive investment of public funds in the sectors for which they are responsible. By working up projects before considering their incorporation in annual plans the 'orthodox' order is reversed; instead of ministries being asked to find projects which will add up to the investment totals implied by the targets of a medium-term plan, the ministries are encouraged to find projects out of which a short-term plan can then realistically be made. The ministries are given a strong incentive to develop projects which are in their opinion technically and administratively viable because if they can do this there is some likelihood that their projects will have priority in the capital budget of each succeeding plan year.

This list could be considerably extended, yet it would be silly to give the impression that these particular proposals constitute a new formula for development planning. The experiences of no two countries are identical; some have well organized budgetary processes, but are weak in the capacity to furnish properly evaluated development projects; in others the situation may be reversed and in yet others some different kind of weakness may be critical. What is really significant about Waterston's approach is that it lays emphasis on those aspects of development planning that have been neglected in the past; above all, on the administrative and political relationships which must be altered in sympathy with the new rationality which the economist brings to the assessment of what ought to be done.

In the future, this emphasis is likely to imply changes even more radical than Waterston proposes. New types of personnel must be recruited to planning offices, including other kinds of social scientist and other kinds of skill than that of the analyst – especially the skills of the tactful and ingenious administrative manipulator who can bring his other administrative colleagues in the ministries, and political leaders at all levels, to collaborate more closely with the patterns of activity suggested as economically advantageous. Or, instead of cabinet economic committees, supposed to take critical 'decisions' affecting the whole pattern of public development over a five-year period or more, the future may see study units established, to explore how the conflicting social and economic goals of various key groups can be made more compatible.

All these suggestions attempt to make the process of planning less monolithic. The notion of a sovereign political body, competent to take major decisions about society's goals, binding for long periods on all the members of the community, is clearly inept. Government must decide the immediate issues, and here planners can only assist the leadership to steer a slightly more rational course each year than the last, among the conflicting lines of interest of which the political system is composed. But over a longer term, planning can become more flexible and exploratory – examining problems from the point of view of different groups and various purposes, and in different time perspectives. Looking five or ten years ahead, a single development plan, which attempts to decide the relative claims of economic growth, social equality, regional distribution and military power all at once, needs to be supplemented by a series of plans which takes each of these claims as its defining purpose, and works out the implications. And the more government can direct some of its administrative talent to this kind of problem-solving, the more usefully applied research and systematic evaluation can be integrated with the process of decision.

PART FOUR

INTERNATIONAL DEVELOPMENT POLICIES

13 TRADE AND INVESTMENT

As we have seen poor countries face problems that differ from those of rich countries, and also from those that confronted the rich countries when they were poor. In the world economy today, most countries dependent on the export of primary commodities enjoy only slowly expanding demand, and a demand subject to violent 'short-term' changes. Coupled with growing import requirements, this leads to chronic balance-of-payments problems, which are both causes and effects of inflationary pressures. Of course these problems are not equally acute in all poor countries; some, such as the oil producers, enjoy a rapidly growing foreign demand for their exports; others, such as the producers of temperate zone agricultural products, can hope to increase their share of the world market at the expense of the industrialized countries. However, the problems are common enough to allow one to talk in general about the 'trade problems of the poor countries' and about the strategies which these countries might adopt to surmount them.

As was pointed out in chapter eight, the poor countries face a choice between an 'open' and a 'closed' economy, or – more exactly – of how open to let their economies be. The choice ought to depend on the evaluation of many relevant factors, among them, naturally enough, the opportunities offered by the international economy. Although the rich countries, as donors of aid, are prone to lecture the poorer members of the international community on the benefits of an 'open economy', they often tend to behave as if they did not believe that those benefits applied to their own relations with the Third World. Thus restrictions on imports from the latter are generally greater than on trade with other industrial countries.

In this chapter we shall examine how the prospects of poor countries could be enhanced, first through trade policies and second through policies on investment. We shall see that although certain new policies are highly desirable, political and social resistance to change makes it unlikely that they will be adopted. These rather pessimistic conclusions should be qualified. Proposals that today seem utopian might prove feasible eventually, so pressing for 'unrealistic' changes is often realistic if one has a long-term perspective. What is more, the governments of poor countries have hardly mustered their full negotiating power, nor have they tried to mobilize support within the rich countries from those groups that would benefit from changes of policy. Thus time, persuasion and more effective tactics could overcome some of the resistances to improving the present set of international economic policies.

Trade Policies

A number of ways in which rich countries could improve the trading position of the poor have been suggested in recent years. They differ in the degree to which they are moves towards freer trade or protectionism on a worldwide scale; in how far they impose a burden on the rich countries (or even benefit them); and in how acceptable they are to pressure groups within the rich countries. One should bear in mind these differences when discussing the various measures proposed to promote trade – whether in primary commodities, semi-processed goods or manufactures – since they affect both the relative advantages of different policies, and the prospects of their being implemented.

1 *Trade in primary commodities.* The difficulties experienced by the exporters of primary commodities have already been mentioned. Now we shall discuss some of the solutions proposed, asking whether they are mainly designed to stabilize prices; to stabilize export earnings; or to expand the opportunities for trade.

Price stabilization will normally require some form of commodity agreement.* Although many efforts have been made by governments thoughout this century to reach commodity agreements, and although these efforts have been multiplied since the end of the Second World War, there is not much to show for them.† This is partly because the objective is not altogether clear: are they supposed just to stabilize unit prices of exports or export earnings at their long-term average, or are they meant to push prices up above this, so as to transfer resources from consuming countries to producers?

Even where the objectives are clear, the obstacles to agreement are very great. In the first place there is the very difficult problem of forecasting accurately long-term average prices which would, over a period of years, clear the market through the equalization of quantities supplied and demanded. Secondly, assuming this could be done, this price would have to be translated into a schedule of prices for different grades or qualities of the commodity concerned – and some commodities cannot easily be graded. Moreover, this schedule would have to be revised as the passage of time enhanced or reduced the demand for different grades, or the costs of their production. And finally, if these difficulties are overcome and the bargaining process successfully concluded with the signing of an agreement, it may be highly profitable for individual countries not to abide by it, and then illegal transactions can wreck it.

These agreements can take several forms, of which only the most common can be briefly noted here.

*Price stabilization can, by reducing uncertainty, increase demand – especially when primary goods are competing against synthetics. It can also facilitate long-term planning by producers, reducing costs and wastage.

†Since the war, agreements have been concluded for wheat, tin, sugar, coffee and olive oil. These commodities constitute a small proportion of world trade in primary commodities and the agreements have not been very successful in stabilizing prices. At present the tin agreement is not in operation, and the olive oil agreement is limited towards maintaining quality rather than influencing prices. See CUTAJAR, N. Z., and FRANKS, A., *The Less Developed Countries in World Trade*, Overseas Development Institute, 1957, and ROWE, J. W. F., *Primary Commodities in International Trade*, Cambridge, 1965.

Under quota agreements all (or most) exporting countries agree to limit the volume of sales, with each generally keeping the same proportion of the market as in the past. Quotas are then expanded or contracted so as to keep prices stabilized. Not only can prices be stabilized in this way; if demand is inelastic, income can be transferred from importing to exporting countries by forcing prices up to a higher plateau. However, the danger then arises of importing countries starting to produce the commodity themselves, or buying it from countries that are not members of the agreement; or worse, they may buy instead some other natural raw material or a synthetic as a substitute.

There are other snags in this kind of agreement. First, as mentioned above, it is precisely the type which tempts countries to break its rules, especially since prices are likely to fluctuate very widely in the 'free' market. In particular, small exporters of the commodity concerned find it extremely profitable to smuggle out some of their surplus production. Secondly the system can work very uneconomically if some way is not found of reallocating quotas so as to permit the more efficient producers to increase their share of total production. Finally, one must mention the political difficulties each time the agreement comes up for renewal, and countries try to improve their relative positions. Negotiations are difficult, and the results unpredictable when the circumstances of the parties vary so much in their volumes of sales, their cost structure, and the importance they each attach to the commodity concerned – depending partly on their other sources of foreign exchange earnings. It is not surprising, after all that has been said, to find that this type of agreement has rarely proved successful in the past.*

More sophisticated quota agreements include as members the importing countries as well as producers – this makes policing the agreements much easier. The present International Coffee Agreement is a good example of this type of arrangement; another is the Commonwealth Sugar Agreement. Prices are fixed, and so are the volumes that importers undertake to buy

*Some of the inter-war agreements in sugar, rubber, copper, etc. provide illustrations of quota-type agreements. See ROWE, J. W. F., op. cit.

and exporters to sell. If the prices are inappropriate, this would mean that income was being transferred to or from exporters; such transfers can in principle be prevented through adjustments of the export or import quotas, but difficulties of renegotiation are if anything even more acute.

As an alternative to the quota system, the 'world organization of markets' was proposed by the French Government at the first UNCTAD, even though this would mean considerable interference with market forces. It was suggested that world prices of primary commodities produced in both rich and poor countries be raised to the level obtaining in the former, and in similar proportions for commodities which rich countries did not produce. This would be achieved through the imposition of taxes on commodity transactions made below the fixed prices, the proceeds of the taxes would be used to finance the disposal of surplus that would probably be created, and/or they would be returned to the poor countries.

The French plan has been widely criticized as a roundabout and inefficient way of giving aid to the poor countries, and because it would perpetuate the misallocation of resources due to rich countries producing primary goods at high costs.* Perhaps the biggest flaw in the plan is that its burden would fall very unevenly between various industrial countries. Those which have fewer natural resources and follow a more liberal import policy – Britain in particular – would suffer proportionately very heavily. This makes its adoption very unlikely.

A system which has been used involves buffer stock agreements. Under these agreements an international authority is set up and provided with some stocks of the commodity concerned, and with financial resources. The authority then buys the commodity if prices fall below an agreed minimum and sells when they exceed a given maximum.

This type of scheme, of which the tin agreement is an example, has some important advantages. No country would gain by breaking its rules, since there is only one price in the market and

*In addition, the pattern of consumption is distorted; less primary commodities would be consumed, because of their artificially high prices.

no restriction on exports; indeed it is not at all necessary that all exporting or importing countries become or remain members of the scheme. Moreover, since each country can produce and export as much as it likes, an optimal allocation of resources is easier to achieve.

However there is one inevitable weakness – limits to the financial resources and the stocks held by the authority. The tin agreement failed to stop a fall in prices in 1958, when the authority ran out of cash, and export and import controls had to be introduced. Later, in 1961, the authority used all its available stocks in an effort to avoid a rise of prices, and finally had to withdraw from the market. Since then, prices have stayed above the agreed maximum and the agreement has not been implemented.

If price trends could be accurately forecast, the upper and lower limits could be adjusted from time to time, but such accuracy is very unlikely. An additional problem is that stocking commodities is expensive, especially if they are semi-perishable goods.

A fourth possibility lies with bilateral long-term contracts. These can involve either governments, public corporations or private firms. The basic principle is an agreement to buy (and sell) the commodity concerned at given prices for a certain period. The volume can be fixed or allowed to fluctuate according to some specified circumstances. Payments can be required in convertible or inconvertible currency, or sometimes in volumes of some other commodity.

Agreements of this type were very common during and after the war. Nowadays a substantial fraction of the trade with socialist countries is covered by agreements of this type. But there are many other examples too, such as the former Cuban sales of sugar to the United States, Australian contracts to provide iron ore to Japanese firms, Algeria's sale of gas to France, and North Sea gas sold by private firms to British public corporations. Of course Cuban sales of sugar to the United States were discontinued soon after the revolution of 1959, but, as this particular arrangement showed, there can be reciprocal concessions given by the exporting country – even if not specifically linked to a trade contract – in this case, the free entry of United States goods to the Cuban market.

Arrangements of this kind help to stabilize foreign exchange earnings and can promote the growth of exports, by guaranteeing a secure market for some years to come. They are particularly suitable when heavy long-term investments have to be made. However, once again, if future prices are not correctly forecast, either buyers or sellers can suffer huge losses.

The limited success achieved through price stabilization agreements of various kinds has prompted governments to search for more direct ways of stabilizing export earnings, since, after all, stabilization of export earnings is the ultimate aim of price stabilization. Up to now two schemes, one of which is already in operation, have attracted most attention.

The International Monetary Fund introduced the compensatory finance scheme in 1963. It allows member countries to borrow from the Fund sums up to 50 per cent above their normal borrowing rights, if their total export earnings fall short of the average export proceeds of recent years. Since the conditions for borrowing under this scheme are rather strict, and in any case the sums available are not very large, the use made of this facility has been limited.

The limited success of the system just described has prompted suggestions for a supplementary finance scheme which would be more effective. One has been proposed under which the International Bank would pay the difference when actual exports fell short of what had been assumed in the country's development plan. National plans of course would have to be approved by the Bank – otherwise countries could adopt widely optimistic export targets. Some argue that this would be one of the advantages of the system; plans would have to be realistic in order to get the Bank's approval. Since reasonable programmes for increased exports would be effectively insured against failure not attributable to the exporting country, there would be a big incentive to develop traditional lines of exports and to search for new lines.

Both schemes combine a certain transfer of resources from rich to poor – aid in other words – and a system of insurance against fluctuations in export earnings. Insurance means security and security ought to help long-term planning and investment. But the success of these schemes depends in the last analysis on the provision of the financial resources which are nowadays lacking since the rich countries are anxious to limit their aid commitments. Moreover, some governments object to the supervision of their policies which these schemes (especially the second one) imply.

Perhaps the easiest steps for rich countries, if they really wanted to help the poor countries, would be dismantling the barriers they have established to trade in primary commodities, including not only commodities which they produce competitively with the poor countries in production, but others as well.

All industrial countries protect heavily their own agricultural producers, who receive prices above those ruling in world markets – this is done through subsidies, as in Britain, or by a system of tariffs, as in the European Economic Community, or some combination of the two. Naturally, the effect of these policies is to reduce the import requirements of the rich countries, and sometimes – notably in the United States – they generate surpluses that are then dumped in the international markets or sold at concessional terms. Similar policies are also followed for some non-agricultural commodities, as for instance with petroleum and copper in the United States.

The elimination or reduction of this complicated apparatus for the protection of the producers of primary commodities within the rich countries could have a tremendous impact on the growth of the Third World – especially on exporters of sugar cane and temperate-zone agricultural goods (such as wheat). Of course such a far-reaching rearrangement of world trade would cause problems of adjustment. The farmer adversely effected would raise a powerful political protest, while those likely to benefit, mainly the consumers, are an ineffective lobby. This should be qualified by saying that sectoral interests can be spared the losses suffered. Thus any liberalization of imports would need to be complemented with protective measures. This is not only to safeguard the interests of farmers in the rich countries, but also those of some poor countries (such as the Commonwealth sugar exporters).

The rich countries would benefit in the long run from a policy of free trade in agricultural commodities. Although the international prices of most commodities would no doubt rise, labour and capital could be moved away from agriculture and into industry and services where they are more productive. However, either for political, strategic or other reasons, such big changes in protectionist policies are unlikely in the foreseeable future.

Tropical agricultural commodities, which do not compete with local production in rich countries, are often also taxed with either tariffs or excise duties. The purpose of these taxes is mainly to raise revenue, since the demand for goods such as cocoa, coffee, bananas, etc., is rather inelastic. The removal of such acute distortions in prices would have some effect in increasing the value and also prices of exports of primary producers.[1] While the consumers in industrial countries would benefit by lower prices, this would presumably have to be made up by raising other taxes. Still, this would seem to be a relatively easy step for rich countries to take.

2 *Trade in semi-processed goods.* As was pointed out in chapter eight (p. 164) escalating tariffs on semi-processed goods make it almost impossible for poor countries to add much value to the commodities they export. This is not necessarily balanced by a benefit for the rich countries: if the latter reduced the extremely high protection of processes, the imports would be cheaper than the products of domestic producers. The case is the same as for the protected farmers of Europe and the United States. Here too, however, there would be a process of adjustment while resources were moved into new lines of production. Some indication of the power of the interests affected is provided by the row between the United States and Brazil, at the beginning of 1968, over the latter's exports of 'instant coffee'. Under pressure of higher-cost local processors, who were losing their markets to cheap imports from Brazil, the United States government refused to sign the International Coffee Agreement unless the Brazilian government limited the exports of instant coffee. Not surprisingly, the stronger bargaining position of the United States eventually forced Brazil to impose a tax on its own exports.

In some cases the fact that United States firms which own mines or plantations overseas also own the facilities at home for processing the primary commodity, (e.g. aluminium and steel plants) gives them little incentive to process overseas.

The elimination of discrimination of these kinds would certainly be of great help to poor countries. But the difficulties of adjustment, and political pressures, make this a rather unlikely prospect.

3 *Trade in manufactured goods.* In chapter eight (p. 165) reference was made to recent studies that seem to show that the poor countries enjoy a comparative advantage in the production of certain manufactured goods. If this is true, and given the size and rapid growth of the markets for industrial goods in the rich countries, there is a basis for greatly expanding trade between rich and poor countries. This would allow the latter to use their resources more efficiently and in many cases employ previously unemployed factors of production, improve their industrial efficiency through competition in the world markets, and ease their ever-present balance of payments disequilibria.

However, as has already been explained, the rich countries discriminate in their trade policies against the poor countries. It can be argued that this discrimination runs counter to the interests of the rich countries themselves, especially if one takes a long view and allows for the expanding markets they would enjoy for machinery and other manufactures. But the problems of adjustment, already discussed, would arise here too. Moreover, such arguments do not take into account that in the real world trade policies which promoted the industrialization of the poor countries migh cause the rich countries to lose, at least in relative terms, political and economic power.

But, if the rich countries really want to help in the development of the poor countries, a reversal of their present trade policies on manufactures might be the cheapest and most effective way of doing it. Before listing the specific measures the rich countries could take, it is important to note that a more liberal policy would not help all the underdeveloped countries in the same way; in fact, at least at the beginning, only a small number of them would benefit, and these would in general be the ones that are at present relatively more advanced. What is more, some poor countries who at present enjoy preferential treatment from one or more rich countries, as for instance some Commonwealth countries or francophilic African states (which accede to the Yaounde Convention) might be actually harmed.

The elimination or the reduction of the high tariffs that protect production in rich countries of those goods where the poor countries have proved to be internationally competitive – such as textiles, leather goods, footwear, toys – could be effected unilaterally by all or some of the rich countries and considerably expand the opportunities for profitable trading. Without going into the question of whether this would benefit the rich countries themselves or not, there are some practical complications that would arise if one tried to implement such a policy.

To begin with, especially in view of the rigidities of the present international monetary system, a country giving concessions might run into a balance-of-payments deficit. This would be most likely to happen if only one country reduced its trade barriers, because – under the GATT rule of non-discrimination – this reduction ought to be extended to all countries including other rich countries, which could then also increase their exports of the goods concerned. Secondly, the usual way of proceeding in international negotiations is to make mutual concessions, which has been sanctified as the 'principle of reciprocity'.

Having said all this, a step-by-step reduction of tariffs should be feasible, and given its potentially most beneficial effects, it would appear as one of the most feasible policies to press for.

Very similar arguments apply to non-tariff restrictions, which have proved to be one of the most effective ways of preventing an increase of exports from the poor countries. What is more, import quotas are strictly illegal, according to the GATT rules, unless used for short periods of time for safeguarding the balance of payments. The rich countries, using their superior bargaining power, have been able to avoid the application of these rules, as for instance in the Cotton Textiles Agreement mentioned earlier.[2] Although it would be unrealistic to expect the immediate elimination of all non-tariff barriers, one could realistically ask for a ban on future restrictions and a phased elimination of the existing ones.

A system of international non-reciprocal and temporary trade preferences, that is to say a discriminating reduction of tariffs by the rich countries which would apply only in favour of the poor countries for a period limited to a given number of years, was approved in principle at the second UNCTAD in 1968. The rationale behind such a system, or so it is claimed, is the infant industry argument. If some industries in the poor countries are given a certain preference over the competing industries of other rich countries, they ought to be able to raise their level of efficiency and, after a period, be able to compete without further preferences. This is in effect an extension of the 'infant industry' argument for protection (already accepted under GATT rules); what has been agreed at UNCTAD is that the rich countries would bear its cost.*

One must, however, take into account that even though a general extension of preferences would benefit the Third World as a whole, it would hurt some individual countries, in particular those that now enjoy certain more limited preferences as members of the Commonwealth or associated members of the European Common Market. Because of this and other difficulties, both political and technical, the implementation of this resolution would certainly take time.

But in many cases it is not the lack of opportunities that impedes the increase of trade, it is rather the inability of the poor countries to grasp them. This may happen for lack of information, or because personnel capable of promoting foreign trade do not exist, or because financial support is not available, or for a host of other reasons that really all boil down to lack of experience.

Until the governments and businessmen of the poor countries get used to dealing with the sophisticated techniques that are used in foreign trade, they need help, for instance in marketing arrangements, training of personnel, design and packaging, provision of export credit and insurance, publicity and so on. Some of the ways by which this help could be forthcoming were discussed at the second UNCTAD conference.[3]

*This cost is measured by the difference between the price they have to pay to import from a poor country, and the lower price at which they could import from another rich country. This difference cannot be greater than the amount of preference given.

It has to be emphasized that although the adoption of policies suggested above, which are mostly in accordance with the liberal tradition of the capitalist countries of the west, would radically alter the development prospects of the poor countries, and would in many instances be in the long-run economic interest of the rich countries themselves, their application is not an easy matter.

Not only would important economic changes be needed, within the rich countries, of types already described. Substantial reform would be needed in international institutions such as GATT and in the international monetary system. If one rich country on its own reduced its trade barriers, its balance of payments could be thrown into deficit. Yet it is difficult to achieve agreement on a multilateral liberalization of trade, especially when the countries concerned see no pressing need for it. Of course, when the rich countries are negotiating among themselves, agreement comes more easily. Prospects of the expansion of trade encourage the large corporations to press their governments to achieve agreement somehow. Moreover, as we have seen, substantial government intervention would be required to effect a smooth transfer of resources and to compensate those who would suffer in the process. And most governments in the rich countries seem to be fully occupied pursuing policies that are higher in their order of priorities.

The problem is further complicated by the malfunctioning of the world monetary system. Even if all rich countries do cooperate in taking the steps indicated above simultaneously, many may still run into foreign exchange problems. The present 'gold exchange standard' does not provide enough liquidity to stand the shocks of the adjustment, and inflexible exchange rates may make these shocks both more severe and more prolonged. At the present time, the chronic crisis of the international monetary system has raised the real possibility of moves in the opposite direction, with increased protection in the rich countries, which would make even more gloomy the trade prospects of the Third World. However, there are no insuperable technical or political obstacles to a rational system for expanding international liquidity and adjusting exchange rates more flexibly. With such a system established, the prospects of a new trade policy towards the poor countries have been greatly enhanced – apart from any benefits they might get directly from the way in which greater liquidity is fed into the world economy.

Private Investment Policies

Foreign private investment certainly has a tremendous impact on the economic development of many poor countries; the effect can, in certain circumstances, be favourable, but it would be naive to assume this is always or generally so – as has already been pointed out by Paul Streeten in chapter seven. It is not easy to analyse the effect of foreign investment; simple mathematical models with only capital and labour as factors of production are certainly too restricted to reveal what is happening in the real world, but a listing of all the possible causal links would be probably tedious and certainly inconclusive, and in the next few pages only some of the more important effects of foreign investment will be discussed.

Foreign capital can be used to raise the rate of investment over what it would have been in the absence of it. This can happen directly, when it is added to home investment, but it can have further indirect effects, by inducing local entrepreneurs to make further investments linked to the foreign concern either as suppliers of goods or services or as buyers of its products.* But if foreign investors using their superior managerial skills, technical know-how and financial resources, pre-empt the best investment opportunities, local entrepreneurs may reduce their own investment plans and their savings. In that case, instead of adding to the volume of investment, foreigners would be replacing local entrepreneurs.

It is sometimes claimed that foreign investment is needed for balance-of-payments reasons. It is certainly true that the first

*In many cases the government too might be persuaded to step up its investment efforts. The contract between Litton Industries and the Greek government is one example, both sides undertaking to complete a series of complementary projects over a period of years.

effect of an inflow of capital is to allow the country which has received it to increase the level of its imports without having to increase its exports. However, the outflow of interest and profits will eventually reverse this advantage, unless the inflow of new capital and/or the reinvestment of profits is constantly growing. In fact the rate of growth of foreign-owned capital – new capital plus reinvested profits – has to be higher than the rate of profits in order not to reverse the original help to the balance of payments; and since the rate of profits net of tax is probably not lower than 10 per cent and the rate of growth of capital in industry is almost certainly lower than this figure, this would mean in most cases that the poor country's industrial capital would gradually come to be owned by foreigners.* In the case of some very poor countries (especially in Africa), where few indigenous savings are available for industrial investment, the inflow of foreign capital must necessarily generate at some future time a reverse flow of interest and profits higher than the inflow of new capital – always assuming that the rate of profit is higher than the rate of growth of capital.

Where foreign enterprise can be most useful is in providing and teaching managerial skills and technical know-how where they are in short supply – and in poor countries this is usually the case. In practice, however it very often happens that foreign firms provide little or no training of local personnel, and that in any case the techniques they import are not suited to local conditions. Moreover the best way to learn is the hard way, even if it means making mistakes. Countries which have left the exploitation of their natural resources in the hands of foreigners find, in

*In fact what can be observed in many countries is both an increase in the total of foreign-held assets and an outflow of foreign exchange in terms of interest and profits that exceeds the fresh inflow of new capital. For instance, KIDRON, M., *Foreign Investment in India*, Oxford, 1965, p. 310, finds that for the period 1948/61 foreign investors brought in Rs. crores 247·1, taking out Rs. crores 718·4; meanwhile total foreign assets in India increased rapidly. In Latin America the outflow of profit and interest exceeds not only the inflow of capital but also that of private capital plus government aid, even without taking into account the apparently considerable outflow of private Latin American capital.

due course, that they are unable to boast of even a few experts in the only activity on which the country depends.*

Given the need of poor countries to increase exports, the big international concerns could be particularly helpful; they have the marketing channels and institutional links with the rich countries needed to generate new currents of trade. But they are not always willing to do this; in some cases the subsidiary is precluded from competing with the parent company in world markets. Subsidiaries may also buy from their parent company goods that could be produced cheaper in the host country, or buy their imports at needlessly high prices. Oil companies, for instance, have been accused of importing oil at the so-called 'posted prices' which are much higher than prices ruling in world markets. Ceylon and India have had long and bitter fights with the oil companies; and the row between Cuba and the oil companies, which refused to import cheap Russian oil, leading to their nationalization and the eventual ending of diplomatic relations with the United States, is only too well known.

Finally foreign capital brings with it a more dynamic, aggressive and competitive view of the business world. This can shake up the conservative tendencies of local entrepreneurs, by introducing more rational methods of personnel selection, and new ideas about management and control, thus stimulating more modern and original ways of doing things. But it can also divide the economy into a modern enclave and a traditional backward agricultural sector impervious to new attitudes. Sometimes, the effect is not so much that the work practices of the foreign executive are copied as that his patterns of consumption are simulated – including expensive trips abroad and high imports of luxurious consumer goods. And the foreign-owned sector almost inevitably distorts the structure of wage and salary scales, increasing income inequalities because payments to managers

---

*In Chile, a country that has been heavily dependent on copper exports, mainly produced since the second decade of the century by big American companies, it could be said in the Senate in 1965 by the Director of the Institute of Geological Research: 'A few years ago ... there were no geologists in Chile.' *Senate, Diario de Sesiones*, 1965, Santiago de Chile. Many similar examples could be quoted.

and professionals, and perhaps to a few skilled workers, are raised to levels comparable to those prevailing in the investing country itself.

All these general comments do not of course apply to all poor countries, or to all types of foreign investment. Some of the African countries, for instance, are desperately short of skills and their choice might be between foreign investment or no investment at all – or aid from a socialist country, which might well have its own drawbacks. On the other hand an advanced country such as Yugoslavia can accept foreign investment without fearing that her local concerns would save or invest less. Foreign investment designed to raise production for export could – provided it does not replace local investment – hardly be accused of damaging the balance of payments.

Whatever one's political sympathies, it is hard to give an overall appraisal of foreign investment advantages and disadvantages; it is for each government to make up its own mind whether to accept or not the inflow of foreign investment, and if yes how much and of what particular type. But the aim of this chapter is to discuss the policies of the rich countries, not those of the poor countries, and what they could do to improve the effectiveness of foreign investment if and when poor countries are willing to have it. Assuming that to invest abroad is in the interest of the investing country – actually another debatable point – the rich countries would also benefit themselves by making it more palatable to the host countries.

To achieve this, although it is stating the obvious, one should try simultaneously to maximize the advantages of private overseas investment for the recipient, and yet reduce as much as possible its various drawbacks, through collaboration between the governments of the countries concerned. Big international companies could also be brought into the discussions on policy, and to participate in international agreements such as providing insurance against expropriation or other non-commercial losses.

Poor countries must accept that to want foreign investment implies allowing foreign concerns to make profits and to repatriate them – or at least a substantial proportion. But profits on this investment may be higher than they need be, if overseas investors feel that an exceptional rate of profit is required in order to compensate for the extra risks involved in setting up an industry or other business in a foreign country. High profits generate resentment and, through profit repatriations, difficulties in the balance of payments. Thus for political and economic reasons the poor country's government may feel obliged to impose controls on profits and their repatriation, therefore increasing the risks for the foreign investor who would then feel, in turn, justified in requiring a still higher rate of return. If appropriate guarantees existed, profits could be much lower.

In fact several bilateral agreements among investing and host countries already exist, and various rich countries have institutions that provide assurance to their investors abroad. There seems to be scope for extending these efforts; for instance to have an international organization financed by poor and rich countries alike, that could provide assurance against expropriation by collecting a small premium either from the investing companies or from the host countries. Having the receiving countries as members of such an institution, and thus potential debtors if it should fail to balance its accounts, would make it politically easier to put pressure on a poor country that took advantage of guarantees to expropriate its foreign capitalists without compensation, since the pressure would be applied by its fellow poor countries.

No amount of guarantees will, however, convince foreign investors that it is risk free to invest in the poor countries, and it would still take more than a small reduction in the rate of profit earned by overseas investors to convince public opinion in the poor countries that they are not being exploited by foreign monopolies. What is really required is a new attitude and a partnership between poor and rich countries and foreign concerns, and a flexible approach to different circumstances. It ought to be possible, for instance, for a country to take over (perhaps by stages) a mining concern that has been operating for a long time in the country while their managers and technicians are being trained, paying of course adequate compensation, and at the same time to receive fresh foreign capital to build a fertilizer plant that used new techniques not available locally.* The governments of the rich countries could help encourage this type of deal, by providing aid to buy out overseas investors and by so doing eliminating or reducing the tensions that expropriation might otherwise arouse. Although to expect such an enlightened attitude from the rich governments might be a little optimistic, one could at least ask these governments not to cut aid or otherwise retaliate against a poor country that is trying to acquire control of some foreign-owned enterprise.

When what is required is the inflow into a country of managerial ability, but if for good or bad reasons the poor country is reluctant to admit direct foreign private investment, management contracts can be agreed under which a foreign company would undertake to run a business for a number of years and meanwhile train nationals to occupy the management posts. This could be combined with partial equity investment by the management contractors, loans from them or aid from the rich country.

More could be made of joint ventures, between foreign concerns and the host government or local capitalists. In general, overseas investors are reluctant to lose control, in some cases because they are afraid the local managers might not be efficient, in others because they want to preserve commercial or technical secrets. However if confidence could be established and reasonable compensation paid, there are no insurmountable objections to management and equity gradually passing into the hands of the poor country's nationals.

More ambitious programmes could be drawn up for integrating the foreign investors into the development plan of an industry or a region, combining their investments with local investment by private citizens and the government. The foreign investor would then have a stake in the success of the plan and his managerial abilities could be used to coordinate and give impulse to the whole programme. Furthermore he could take an active part in encouraging and advising local entrepreneurs to start new projects

*Recent agreements between for instance the copper companies and the Chilean government, and some deals between oil companies and Middle East governments, suggest that this approach may now be more readily accepted.

linked to his own, providing them with know-how, markets for their products, financial assistance and so on.

Balance of payments problems could be eliminated when an investment is coupled with long-term contracts to buy its production – as is the case for instance with French investment in Algerian oil and gas exploitation – or with simultaneous trading agreements which would open the markets of the investing country to other products of the host country. Similarly if some rich countries did not authorize new investment in their own territory in industries – such as textiles – where they have a comparative disadvantage, the flow of capital towards the poor countries would be stimulated and the balance of payments problem would not arise as the rich countries would be buying the product concerned.

Finally, the governments and entrepreneurs of the rich countries should recognize the right of the host country to forbid certain types of investment, to require that the foreign investor employs a growing proportion of local personnel, generally to regulate his operations, and eventually to buy him out. In so far as the host country allows foreign companies to make and repatriate profits, establishes and keeps timetables for taking control in the cases where it wants to do so, and pays reasonable compensation, the government of the investing country has no legitimate ground for complaint. However, political pride, governmental attitudes moulded when most of the poor countries were colonies, the strong desire – in some cases an obsession – of corporations to have as little interference as possible in their operations, and the undeniable fact of the relatively minor force that poor countries can bring to bear in international negotiations, makes the establishment of a more friendly relationship between the foreign investor and the poor country – and perhaps one which is more mutually profitable – something to be aimed at, rather than easily realizable in the near future.

14 AID

It will be evident from all that has gone before in this book that the poor countries are very largely on their own in their efforts to overcome their poverty. This arises, of course, because the problems involved are so deeply domestic, but it is also partly because the solutions involve efforts which the rich are not at present prepared to make and partly because a far larger measure of collaboration between countries, as much among the poor themselves as between the rich and poor, would be required than is yet attainable.

In this chapter, some account will be given of the help which rich countries do in fact provide to foster development. By far the largest part of this is direct government-to-government assistance. Against the contribution this makes to development must be set the disadvantages of the donor-recipient relationship involved. Only a small element is internationally organized – such as the funds which are administered by the World Bank and its affiliates or the technical assistance and pre-investment support provided by the Development Programme of the United Nations and by its specialized agencies.

Since much hard work, sacrifice and genuine philanthropy are involved, it is sad to have to say that the total volume of this aid is meagre in face of the manifest needs, that much aid is in fact provided for reasons of the donor's national self-interest, and that some of it is on hard commercial terms. Aid has to be seen as a very limited response to the needs of poor countries. Yet in its present form it is a relatively new phenomenon, which does mean at least that poor countries are not left wholly without help.

Twenty Years of Aid

In the twenty years or so during which official programmes of aid have operated, public opinion about them has fluctuated considerably and often been sharply divided. Hopes were at first high that financial aid would provide the necessary infrastructure of transport and communications, power and public services which would secure rapid development. Later more emphasis was put on the need of support by technical assistance, which would provide the 'catalyst' or the 'missing component' of skills and experience. Despite slow progress, mistakes and miscalculations, there have in fact been important and widespread advances, in which local resources and efforts have been reinforced by aid programmes. A belief has also developed that, even if the results are less spectacular than was once hoped, the effort to help has to to be made. A recent booklet comments: 'Giving aid seems to be largely an instinctive reaction. It is part of an observable phenomenon: the area of our concern for other people has been progressively widening. A sense of solidarity has made remarkable progress in the last hundred years within states and it is now more or less accepted that certain levels of poverty within a rich country are intolerable. It seems that this feeling is becoming extended to the world as a whole.'[1]

Whether this is a tenable view or not, it does not by any means dispose of the critics, and their views on the effects of aid must be examined.

The two gravest charges are, first, that aid helps to maintain governments that have no serious concern for the economic and social progress of their peoples, that exist only to perpetuate their own privileged classes and groups; on this view, aid enables such regimes to postpone or even entirely avoid difficult and painful decisions to reform institutions and practices. The second charge is that by transferring unsuitable institutions, practices or attitudes from rich to poor countries the dualism in the structure of poor countries is strengthened, elites of privilege and wealth are reinforced, the costs of development raised against the poor countries and the possibility of significant economic and social advance diminished.

In any case the benefits of financial aid may be significantly diminished by being made conditional upon the acceptance of proposals for change in domestic policies and administration based on an inadequate understanding of local conditions, by tying to procurement in the donor country, or by tying to specific projects which gain donor approval. Above all, the debt service built up, since little of this aid is provided as grants, absorbs an ever larger part of the foreign exchange available to the poor country, whether earned or acquired by further loans and grants.

Technical assistance, although valued by poor countries, brings its own costs of supporting facilities of various kinds which are difficult for an undermanned administration to provide. Pre-investment surveys make fairly heavy demands for professional manpower and technical services as well as personal housing, office space and transport, all of which may be very scarce, while the 'institution building' favoured by donors involves locking up these and similar essential services for little immediate gain. Compounding these difficulties are the extravagantly high administrative costs, as they seem to the poor countries, of aid missions which are counted in the cost of the assistance given, for which the poor country is expected to return grateful thanks. Finally, the high standards of living enjoyed by technical assistance experts cause dissatisfaction among their local counterparts, lead to demands by them for higher salaries and fringe benefits, and probably accelerate the brain drain.

This is a formidable indictment and since most points can be substantiated by actual cases, no simple rebuttal is possible. Yet if these were the only results of aid, few countries, rich or poor, would involve themselves in it; 'Trade not aid' was in fact an indication of such a mood, but the slogan was soon adapted to 'Trade as well as aid'. The fact is that for many countries aid is now an essential support of their development work. As a result of experience, closer and more thoughtful consultation and planning, and greater care in selecting projects by both partners, serious errors are generally rarer, operations better conducted and expectations more realistic. Nevertheless, Sir Andrew Cohen, the former Permanent Secretary for the British Ministry of Overseas Development, once said, 'Like most other aid donors we are still relatively neophytes in this new human activity,' and this could also be said by most aid receivers.

Maintaining ineffective governments in power or supporting them despite their refusal to face hard decisions to reform may well occur. In fact, aid is not an effective device to change governments nor even to precipitate radical reforms ahead of public opinion or government policy, as some aid givers have discovered. Rather it is a method of helping those governments (or those elements in a government) which are concerned with economic and social betterment. Aid can only operate with and through existing institutions and with government support. Since economic development is not the sole preoccupation of government in a poor country (see chapter six) and aid provides only a very small part of the total resources devoted to development, administrators of aid have had to recognize important limitations on its effectiveness, and therefore upon their power to induce such changes. Aid has been handicapped by excessive expectations of far-reaching change; recipients have been rightly suspicious of intervention, over-optimistic donors disappointed.

The drawbacks of some methods of giving financial aid are acknowledged by donors and efforts are made to mitigate them. Financial aid is nowadays based on feasibility studies, preinvestment surveys and the like which offer safeguards against major errors in project selection. Coordination of donors' efforts, through consortia or consultative groups, under the aegis of the international financial agencies such as the World Bank give greater assurance that sensible decisions about aid are made. There is less enthusiasm nowadays for the imposing and spectacular project to which a label can be attached; experience has shown that on a misconceived project such labels are an embarrassment.

The tying of aid to procurement from donor country suppliers or in other ways limiting a poor country's use of financial aid usually means higher prices, less suitable equipment and commercial intervention. A recognition of such drawbacks is implied in the OECD Development Assistance Committee's resolutions urging members to reduce progressively the scale of tying.

However, urgent balance of payments considerations and commercial interest have combined to frustrate any freeing of aid and tying is in fact increasing.

Short-term loans at market rates of interest present poor countries with increasingly unmanageable financial situations; as a result, there has been some easing of terms on new loans and rescheduling of payments on earlier ones. However, here also financial difficulties have halted the gradual improvement which was being made, and the most recent trend has been towards higher interest rates and shorter terms.

In the field of technical assistance, where the funds are only a fraction of those involved in financial aid, quality is being improved and better use is being made of aid. Governments which appreciate the costs involved are more selective in requesting help and realize that only by providing counterpart staff and suitable working facilities will they derive any real benefit. The selection, recruitment and briefing of experts is now done more professionally. At the same time the supply of qualified and experienced professional people in the wide range of services being requested seems to be dwindling, as does willingness to accept overseas appointments. This decline is itself partly responsible for the increased efforts being put into recruitment. Special measures have been taken in a number of countries such as offering extra inducements and making supernumerary appointments to cover the period while local staff are trained.

Yet effectiveness still varies widely; some overseas assignments can be easily handled once the transition to strange surroundings has been made. Other posts may involve substantial adaptation in working methods as well as in personal life and call for great flexibility and for an instinctive sympathy and understanding of local problems; such qualities are scarce and by no means necessarily found in those with the technical skills which are in demand. The report-writing expert who occupies the time of hard-pressed officials, and contributes little more than a summary of what he has learnt is now very much less common; and although Africa still absorbs very large numbers of operational experts in its education, health and administrative services, and in Asia non-specialized needs can increasingly be met from local resources, the need persists for specialist advisers, in the private sector as well as the public.

The training given under assistance programmes has also shifted steadily, though not yet sufficiently, away from the rich countries towards the poor country or region, where training institutes are being established in a wide range of technical subjects at middle or high levels, with provision for field work and research. For more advanced studies, students still have to go overseas and large numbers do so, but more attention is now paid to their particular needs in specialized institutes or in departments seriously concerned with the problems of poor countries.

Specialized research supported by private foundations has produced some notable results; the work of the International Rice Research Institute supported by the Ford and Rockefeller Foundations is an example. One striking success, such as the new rice variety known as IR8, does not solve the world food supply problem, but such work illustrates a new and overdue trend in the direction of research and gives agricultural extension services an additional lever to use in their efforts to raise production.

In addition, aid programmes have launched and supported a variety of new development institutions. The regional development banks – Inter-American, Asian and African – have a special interest in inter-country projects but stand ready to help governments in project surveys and project preparation as well as in their financing; United Nations institutes in the same three regions provide government officials with training in planning techniques and work closely with the regional banks. In most poor countries development finance corporations have been established, with the support of both international organizations and bilateral agencies. The World Food Programme, sponsored by the United Nations and the Food and Agriculture Organisation, and provided with supplies of food or funds by many of the rich countries, provides 'food aid for development'.

It cannot be disputed that many rich-country institutions and practices are unsuited to overseas conditions and that their introduction, whether by aid programmes or otherwise, has brought little or no benefit. We still understand little of what is and what is not advantageous for development. For example, the copying of trade unionism and cooperation (among both producers and consumers) have had bad as well as good results, both have been misused, and considerable adaptation has been – and still is – necessary to meet poor-country requirements. Instances of other well-meant but sometimes unhelpful innovations are widely reported.

At the same time much philanthropic effort has gone forward from the provision of relief to an attack on some of the causes of local misery. Volunteer organizations on the model of the Peace Corps and the British VSOs now have a place in all official technical assistance programmes and the movement has developed in the poor countries themselves, with the emergence of the Inter-American Volunteers for Development, though some of these efforts have been relatively ineffective.

This is not an exhaustive review of all assistance efforts but rather a quick survey of recent trends and changes. There have clearly been set-backs such as the hardening of loan terms and the renewed tying of aid, yet there have also been some promising new ventures and fresh starts while the machinery of aid-giving remains intact. The volume of aid remains practically unchanged; it is small relative to the efforts of the poor countries themselves and very small in relation to the need.

The Financial Transfers

Measurement of aid in simple quantitative terms – funds spent, man-months of service provided or training given in terms of student years – is insufficient; the benefits received from different experts, or different training institutions, or different capital projects, vary greatly. This is specially true of technical assistance services, where the range of work done and its effectiveness depends greatly on the circumstances of the project and the expert's adjustment to them.

The measurement of financial assistance, although easier, is far from straightforward; the degree to which aid is tied, the division between project and programme aid, or between bilateral (government to government), and multilateral aid channels (using international agencies such as the World Bank or the United Nations Development Programme), all influence the uses to which aid can be put by the recipient and the benefit it may be expected to produce. If questions of the burden of aid – the sacrifice involved – are included, the matter becomes still more difficult because it is necessary to take account of any advantages given by the recipient in policy matters, of territorial facilities provided, as well as of the use of aid to settle earlier obligations, such as pensions to former state employees.

The public debate tends to centre on the aggregate flow of funds being provided by the rich countries for all purposes and through all channels – to governments direct and through the multilateral agencies. Table 14.1 below gives these totals for the fifteen members of the Development Advisory Committee of the OECD, which apart from the Soviet Union and eastern European countries, includes all main donors of aid. It should be noted here that 'aid' in this context includes loans at various rates of interest as well as grants, the provision of technical assistance and funds for other payments from rich countries to poor, e.g. the 'topping-up' of salaries for expatriate officials, pension payments and the like. The figures are *net*, i.e. they are gross disbursements *minus* capital repayments.

The total net aid flows provided by governments rose in 1968 to US $7,250 m. and the OECD Development Advisory Committee anticipated further increases in the 1970's. However, it is clear that the recent rate of increase is very much less than in the period from 1956 to 1962 and is below the rate of increase in the gross national products of the donors. The smaller donors, such as Canada, Denmark, Netherlands and Sweden, have all maintained a more rapid rate of increase, but this has been insufficient to offset the slowing down of the response of the major contributors, which now provide a declining proportion of their national incomes.

Part of the reason for this is the rapid growth of repayments, which, together with growing interest charges, has involved a big offset to the rise in gross disbursements. The total receipts by all DAC members of amortization and interest payments are

TABLE 14.1

Flow of Net Official Financial Resources from DAC Countries to
Less-Developed Countries + Multilateral Agencies[2]

(million U.S. dollars)

	1956	1964	1965	1966	1967	1968
Australia	34	(104)	122	128	167	157
Austria	—	15	31	33	27	28
Belgium	20	81	102	81	99	93
Canada	30	128	124	212	213	214
Denmark	3	11	13	26	28	29
France	647	831	752	745	826	855
Germany	142	423	471	486	547	595
Italy	43	40	93	115	156	150
Japan	96	211	353	498	627	809
Netherlands	48	49	70	94	114	134
Norway	8	17	12	13	16	23
Portugal	3	62	21	24	47	35
Sweden	3	33	38	57	60	71
United Kingdom	205	493	481	526	498	428
United States	2,006	3,445	3,627	3,660	3,723	3,605
Total DAC Countries	3,288	5,942*	6,314	6,701	7,150	7,245

*After deduction of expenditure by multilateral agencies in DAC
member countries amounting to $1.7 million.

compared overleaf to the funds they promised to transfer; the
figures of aid flows are smaller than those just given by reason of
the exclusion of official payments to multilateral agencies.

Thus interest and loan repayments by poor countries amounted
to US $1,574 m. in 1968; in 1963 they had been US $796 m. The
hoped-for softening of loan terms and greater availability of
grant aid was of limited duration and the prospects of any
further improvements have been deferred because of the larger
donors' financial problems. Meanwhile, as grace periods run
out, capital repayments have to be increased, and some recipients
face the possibility that the outflow of funds on account of past
aid will wholly offset their current receipts.[3]

TABLE 14.2

Official Government-to-Government Transfers: Commitments and Disbursements: 1968[2]

	(US $ million)
Bilateral (i.e. Government-to-Government) Commitments	8,043
Actual Bilateral Disbursements, Gross	7,548
Less Loan Repayments: Receipts	962
Total Bilateral Disbursements, Net	6,586
Less Interest paid on loans	612
Bilateral Net Transfer i.e. funds retained by poor countries	5,974

The geographic distribution of aid provided by different DAC countries shows widely differing patterns, with British assistance devoted primarily to the Commonwealth, French assistance going mainly to the franc area and the United States' aid directed primarily to countries bordering on China and the Soviet Union. However the distribution is changing in two respects. There has been a decline in the proportion received by Africa and Asia between 1960 and 1965, and 'there is a definite trend in members' programmes towards greater geographical concentration on individual developing countries.'[4]

United States aid to Latin America rose sharply after the Alliance for Progress was formed. The regional distribution overall has changed as follows:

TABLE 14.3

Regional Distribution of Net Official Bilateral Assistance 1960 and 1965

	Per Cent of Total Aid		Per Capita
	1960	1965	1965
	%	%	$
Europe	9·0	6·2	3·9
Africa	31·0	25·8	5·2
Latin America	6·5	14·6	3·5
Asia	50·2	48·0	2·8

Source: *Development Assistance Efforts and Policies: 1969 Review*, OECD, Paris, 1970.

Although Asia has almost maintained its share of total bilateral aid during this period, and was still getting nearly half the total in 1965, its per capita receipts are considerably less than that of other regions, because it contains over 60 per cent of the population of the Third World. The tendency to concentrate on individual countries is strongest in the United States, where Congressional approval of development loans has restricted the number of countries to which loans can be made. On the other hand, the growing support for multi-national projects by the regional development banks and through such organizations as the Mekong Basin Investigation Committee will slightly offset the concentration on fewer national programmes. This development is, however, still in its early stages, and in Africa, where there would seem to be most scope for such projects, not very much progress has yet been made. A more important factor offsetting geographical concentration of bilateral aid is the disbursements of international agencies. Although the aggregate flows are very much smaller than the amount of bilateral aid, they have grown in recent years with commitments reaching nearly two billion US dollars in 1966; disbursements, which lag behind commitments, are shown below.

TABLE 14.4

Gross Disbursements of Multilateral Agencies 1962, 1966, 1967 and 1968.[2]

	(Million US Dollars)			
	1962	1966	1967	1968
IBRD	409	564	561	605
IDA	25	273	368	215
IFC	18	30	26	31
Inter American Development Bank	37	142	183	233
Asian Development Bank	—	—	—	20
EEC – European Development Bank	54	112	105	121
EEC – European Investment Bank	—	28	39	10
UN Agencies	182	272	207	300
Total	725	1,421	1,551	1,537

Source: Development Assistance Efforts and Policies: 1969 Review, OECD, Paris, 1969, p. 75, table IV – 1.

The future however will be less encouraging as commitments rise above current receipts. The delay in reaching a decision on the replenishment of IDA is typical of the difficulties likely to arise in other cases, namely a reluctance to increase contributions coupled with an urgent need to set conditions which would safeguard balance of payments positions. The 1972–74 replenishment for IDA amounts to US $2,400 million; although the Bank's present policy of full international competition for procurement of all goods and services financed by IDA has been maintained, the United States balance of payments difficulties have caused them to insist that their contribution should be used at first for procurement only in the United States.

The President of the IBRD speaking to the 1967 meeting of the Bank's Board of Governors said, 'It was but a few years ago that the principal limitation on the World Bank Group's activities was a shortage of well-prepared and economically sound projects in countries where the general economic position warranted financial assistance.' After describing the efforts made through technical assistance and related work to identify such projects, by the Bank and other agencies, he continued, 'Today things have changed greatly. We have been able to identify more projects which are, or soon will be, ready for financing than we now have the resources to finance.' The Bank Group's new President has recently stated that his policy for the next five years is to achieve a doubling of the rate of lending with a new emphasis on assistance to education and agriculture.

Technical Assistance

The contribution of the rich countries in maintaining technical assistance programmes, both bilateral and multilateral, has been of greater value than the modest financial outlay would indicate. Not only has it identified new development projects, it has also helped to launch and operate them and has supported a host of other valuable development activities. The demand outstrips the capacity of the providers of such help. Still, the scale of technical assistance is large in terms of the numbers of persons involved as experts, students, trainees or operational staffs in government departments and in establishments for research or training. Thus for Britain alone, persons recruited or financed for overseas service in 1967 numbered 5,300 and those overseas at 31 December 1967 totalled more than 20,000. These figures include volunteers and others privately sponsored; those financed from public funds numbered over 15,000 on that date.[5]

Of the estimated 56,000 students and trainees from developing countries in Britain for the academic year 1966/67 some 5,500 were publicly financed and 4,300 were financed by the British Government; of these over 3,400 were students and 850 trainees.*

The technical assistance operations of DAC members involve large and still increasing numbers; a few figures will indicate the scale in 1968. It will be seen that France provided much the biggest contribution, and that the pattern of technical aid varied greatly by country.

TABLE 14.5

Publicly provided technical assistance personnel overseas in 1968 by category and main donors[2]

| | (thousands) | | | |
	France	Britain	United States	Total†
Advisers	5	–	9	19
Operational Personnel	7	10	–	20
Teachers	26	6	–	38
Volunteers‡	–	2	17	26

The technical assistance given by the international agencies largely depends for funds on UNDP, but also on the regular

*British Aid Statistics, Ministry of Overseas Development, 1968. Students are persons on a systematic course of instruction in British institutions of higher education at both undergraduate and postgraduate level. Trainees are persons at any level receiving mainly non-academic practical and vocational training through visiting tours, or attending ad hoc non-academic courses and seminars.

†Including countries not specified.

‡The volunteer effort is about equally divided between education and other activities.

budgets of the United Nations and some specialized agencies. The actual projects of technical assistance, pre-investment surveys, resource investigation and development and the like carried out by international agencies are particularly valuable. This is due to several factors. Such aid is available to any member country of the United Nations or the specialized agencies as of right within, of course, the financial resources available; assistance is given without obligation other than the requirement that it be effectively used; it is more objectively administered than any national programme could be; and it can draw on many sources for recruitment (including the poor countries themselves) and equipment. But it cannot be claimed that international agencies are unquestionably the best providers of assistance. Their procedures tend to be complex and slow as compared with the British; their projects smaller and less well endowed than the United States; and mixed manning is sometimes a problem. So is the rather rigid demarcation of fields of interest between the several specialized agencies; it is hard to achieve coordination in areas of common interest and (for projects of a multi-purpose character) to identify the responsible agency.

Expenditures by United Nations agencies on technical assistance more than doubled between 1965 and 1968, rising to US $231 million in that year. In 1968 UNDP expenditures were US $208 million of which US $112 million was for Special Fund projects of a pre-investment character, including resources surveys and support for technical and vocational training and similar institutions.

In addition to this, recipient governments provide counterpart facilities – land, buildings, supplies and local staff. This is an essential requirement for all UNDP/Special Fund projects, providing both a guarantee of governments' intentions and an assurance of continuing support. By 1966 such facilities amounted to US $93 million (as against the UNDP/Special Fund contribution of US $79 million) on the 116 projects completed by then. Moreover, these moneys can lead to substantial investment in the projects surveyed; in 1968 it was reported that 37 projects had generated some US $1,900 million in such financing.

The other main item is technical assistance, of which 75 per cent is spent on the provision of expert services, the rest being used for fellowship awards (the equivalent of 29,000 man-months in 1966), and equipment and supplies.

When it is recalled that this US $231 million is a voluntary contribution by member governments of the UN and that they have no direct influence on its use, the size and growth of the total are remarkable. The rich countries however have set clear limits to the United Nations power to disburse capital aid. They almost unanimously boycotted the UN Capital Development Fund 'pledging' conference in 1967, because of their preference for the World Bank group's machinery where they have a much bigger say in policy (see chapter one). That boycott has continued.

However, the total United Nations effort (apart from that of the World Bank) covers a very wide range of subjects. Its agencies include the ILO, UNESCO, FAO, World Health Organization, International Civil Aviation Organization, International Telecommunications Union, World Meteorological Organization, International Atomic Energy Agency, Intergovernmental Maritime Consultative Organization and the United Nations Industrial Development Organization.

Of course most of the contributions to multilateral programmes return to donors in the form of equipment orders and service contracts, as is brought out by the following table:

TABLE 14.6

Sources of Multilateral Agencies Service Requirements: 1967[5]

	Experts Recruited (Numbers)	Project Equipment Ordered (U.S. $m.)	Fellows Studying (Numbers)
France	840	1·3	436
Germany	231	3·5	n.a.
Italy	216	·7	328
Japan	96	1·6	n.a.
USSR	195	—	588
United Kingdom	1,024	2·8	521
United States	695	6·0	443

Although multilateral operations have certain advantages and their enlargement would make fuller use of the specialized agencies, it is clear that international organizations as presently constituted could not handle the volume of work which is presently undertaken by bilateral programmes. Technical assistance activities have been added to the work of the international organizations, which were mostly established before it became important, and thus are not structurally oriented towards operational activities.

Fortunately this is not an 'either-or' question; an addition to the resources of multilateral programmes would be highly desirable, but enlargement of *all* programmes is what really matters. It is encouraging that the dividing line between multilateral and bilateral aid programmes is becoming blurred; each tends to adopt the other's practices, and an increasing number of projects is supported by both. There are various examples of this growing interdependence, ranging from the joint financing of large-scale projects to the joint staffing by national and international teams of technical assistance projects or the assignment of nationally sponsored volunteers to the projects of international agencies. Recipients would benefit if assistance through both channels were made still more flexible.

Aid Targets

Before discussing the motives which prompt rich countries to supply aid, it will be useful briefly to review the efforts, chiefly made by the poor countries, to get a target established for the volume of aid-flows – to which reference has already been made in chapter one. The poor countries have sought the acceptance of such a target for two main reasons; first, to obtain a measure of security, and second to relate aid to the growing wealth of the rich countries. Both purposes seem to them to be manifestly reasonable; planning of any kind of development operation requires a reasonable prospect that resources will be available, and – as to the second purpose – if rich countries accept some obligation to provide aid, as their current decisions imply, this obligation should bear some relationship to their growing prosperity.

This view of the poor countries led to the adoption in 1964 by UNCTAD I of the 'one per cent of national income' target which referred to a net transfer of resources from each economically advanced country. This was a weak resolution. It did not refer to the distribution of the resources; transfers included all types of long-term capital flows, including not merely loans on hard terms but also private investment; it treated bilateral aid, even tied aid, on the same basis as multilateral; the target was 'net' of repayments of government-to-government loans, but not of private capital flows towards the rich countries; and the term 'national income' was left (apparently deliberately) vague – it could refer to national income net of depreciation at factor cost (as the rich countries claimed) or (as the UNCTAD secretariat preferred) to gross national product at market prices – i.e. including both depreciation and indirect taxes. In fact a number of rich countries, including Britain, were already meeting this target; French aid, in particular, was considerably greater. Nevertheless, the rich countries claimed that it was in no way mandatory on them, although the annual reports of the Chairman of the DAC have used the target (on various definitions) as a yardstick for the performance of donors.

At the confrontation between rich and poor countries which occurred at UNCTAD II in 1968 a great effort was made by the latter to establish the target in more precise terms and on a basis which would provide poor countries with a larger flow of resources. The outcome of protracted discussion was a new definition. The Conference recommended that 'each economically advanced country should endeavour to provide annually to developing countries financial resource transfers of a minimum net amount of one per cent of its gross national product at market prices in terms of actual disbursements . . .' This should be regarded as 'an incentive to greater efforts . . . rather than as a ceiling'. The new base was estimated to increase the amount of the transfers by some 25 per cent, compared to the more restrictive interpretation of 'national income'. Reservations were made by a number of rich countries as to the date by which they might hope to reach such a figure – dates between 1972 and 1975 being offered, while some countries claimed that their financial position did not allow any firm commitment at all. A more encouraging outcome has been that some countries, not unfortunately the largest suppliers, accepted this as a national objective and others have made firm commitments for the next few years; these countries include Canada, Australia, Netherlands, West Germany and Japan.

Many observers, including some aid contributors, would favour something like a mandatory levy as a next step. This is not only for the reasons presented in justification of an aid target, but also because a major policy decision of this kind would recognize the moral obligation of rich countries to provide aid.

The Motives for Aid

At the beginning of this chapter it was suggested that, at least in some quarters, the provision of aid was regarded as being, among other things, an expression of human solidarity. The late President Kennedy put this in its simplest form when he said 'We pledge our best efforts to help them help themselves for whatever period is required, not because the Communists are doing it, not because we seek their votes, but because it is right.' The moral reason plays an important part in the justification offered for all major aid programmes, and it will perhaps be this motive which will prompt in due course an increase in its volume. However, especially in times of economic strain, other objectives are emphasized. And when choices have to be made as to aid allocations between countries, or between types of projects, other criteria are applied.

Traditional historical association and strong cultural links are obviously important in British, Belgian, Dutch and French bilateral programmes. A sense of responsibility to sustain work started previously, the long-standing relationship between institutions of many kinds, the common language, legal system and educational standards all tend to reinforce the association and assistance may also lessen feelings of guilt over past mistakes.

Many programmes, including that of the largest aid donor, the United States, are largely free of such obligations. Moreover, the moral motive is by no means the sole one; indeed debates in legislatures show very clearly that political prestige and influence, strategic and related considerations exert considerable force. The relationship between the aid given and the influence gained is not so direct and clear as is often suggested; but the fact is that donors tend to help their friends, or those whom they hope to make more friendly, and from these some other benefits may be sought.

Through all bilateral programmes runs at least some expectation of commercial advantage as well. At its best, or least selfish, this is the expectation that with the progress of the poor countries will come also a growth of the world economy; this is, for obvious reasons, particularly a British argument, but many others endorse it. In addition, however, as has already been noted, aid tying in one form or another brings an immediate accession of trade to the donor, and may well lead to a flow of subsequent (and un-aided) orders for spares and replacements. Training may be given for the best of reasons, but it is not altogether forgotten that in time trainees will one day be ordering plant and equipment. Likewise experts serving in a poor country under an aid programme may well be wholly objective in their advice, but nevertheless recommend the adoption of practices or the use of equipment with which they are familiar.

Governments of poor countries can be permitted a measure of scepticism about the motives for aid-giving and consequently some toughness when negotiating agreements, despite their real need for aid. It is, in fact, at the point of negotiation that motives become evident. Donors are confronted with many more requests than they can meet and are obliged to be selective. Historical and cultural links may help to narrow the field of applicants, but so may political, strategic or commercial advantage. 'Absorptive capacity', the ability to use the aid given effectively and well, is also certain to be tested, as will be the measure of local effort, of 'self-help' in the development effort. As the United States A I D says of its 1967 programme 'Self-help – the most important single factor in successful development programmes – will receive even greater stress. . . . The less developed countries will be required to provide the major share of the resources required for development programmes.' This will come as no surprise to the poor countries for it has, as they well know, always been the case. However for the donor some evidence of performance is understandably a prerequisite of aid. The British position is less sharply stated, but successive White Papers have defined the responsibilities more clearly, ending with the statement in 1967 that 'no function of the Ministry [of Overseas Development] is more important than aid management' and defining this in terms to ensure that any assisted project should be doing good and doing the intended (and approved) good. Other donor governments follow comparable policies, modified in some cases by special circumstances or considerations, as for example the regional interests of the Japanese.

In its simplest terms this can be seen as a very natural wish to get value for money, since parliaments need to be convinced that good use is being made of the funds they provide. Conversely, for poor countries also, selectivity is important in ensuring that aid is worth receiving. As President Nyerere said at Arusha, 'Independence cannot be real if a nation depends upon gifts and loans from another for its development. Even if there was a nation or nations prepared to give us all the money we need for our development, it would be improper for us to accept such assistance without asking ourselves how this would affect our independence and our very survival as a nation. Gifts which start off or stimulate our own efforts are useful gifts. But gifts which weaken our own efforts should not be accepted without asking ourselves a number of questions.'

Most donors would claim that it is indeed their purpose 'to start off or stimulate' the efforts of a poor country, but of necessity aid widens the reproduction of rich country installations, patterns and practices – and as has been repeatedly indicated in this book, these may well be inappropriate or even damaging.

Selectivity accordingly becomes a vital principle for poor countries too, since not everything on offer to them is relevant to their needs and circumstances. No poor country can afford to waste its scarce resources on unwanted or unfruitful projects, however tempting the offers of assistance may seem. Yet, as has been shown in earlier chapters, planners may be less than well-informed of needs, politicians face a variety of obligations and choices not all of which concern development, while sheer lack of experience on both sides about the relevance of a project can produce mistakes and failures.

Awareness of these possibilities of waste has led to emphasis on evaluation as well as to the stress on self-help. But evaluation has proved difficult.

It is a fair comment that 'Development success depends on many factors of which aid is only one. There is not the same difficulty in spotting aid failures. This asymmetry – that one cannot demonstrate success easily but can show up failures – has been important in giving aid a bad image which it does not deserve.'[6] Moreover, it is not always clear when aid has really been wasted; improved hospital services may seem a luxury (and even damaging in so far as they aggravate population problems), but apart altogether from the social benefits, these contribute to productive capacity. On the other hand, while DDT and cheap transport are plainly benefits for communities previously without them, if the first precipitates a population explosion and the second facilitates a rural exodus and produces unmanageable urban growth and 'shanty-towns', it can be understood why misgivings should be felt. Many projects that 'succeed' produce assets which make a negligible contribution to economic development – though before writing them off as 'negative assistance' other needs of the community such as national unity or political stability must also be considered.

The difficulty about evaluation, as with self-help criteria, is that the judgement is made by and large with rich countries' objectives, or performance, or benefits, in mind, and many of these may be irrelevant to the needs of the recipient. Current doubts about aid stem from a lack of confidence about the total effects it will produce and the costs involved; this has displaced some of the earlier enthusiasm felt by both parties about aid and in particular has deprived aid administrators of the certainty they once had of holding an important key to development.

The Future

Some of the leading ideas have already been indicated and only a brief résumé need be attempted here.

Firstly, self-interest may be a necessary element in aid, but if it is invoked to maintain the flow of aid, it should not be permitted to determine the use to which aid is put. Some such neutral intermediary as the World Bank is a possible solution and/or the complete untying of bilateral aid. In place of self-interest, the acceptance by the rich countries of a continuing obligation toward the poor needs to be fostered so that it becomes as accepted internationally as, in most rich countries, it is accepted nationally. It should also be seen as a long-term and firm commitment, not to be set aside whenever political or economic factors seem unfavourable, for such uncertainty plays havoc with poor countries' plans and makes aid administration almost unworkable. Such a shift in attitude may be presented as an acceptance of a 'moral' obligation; it is equally a restatement of 'self-interest' in the larger context of a world community, a recognition of the fact of interdependence.

Secondly, criteria for the provision of aid also stand in need of review as poor countries gradually take firmer control of their own affairs, gain experience and the services of their own newly-trained staffs. The paternalism that once characterized aid is now generally irrelevant and standards of performance, 'self-help' and the like are really the business of the poor country. Are we then, it will be asked, to hand over our aid to corrupt or incompetent administrations which will simply pocket the larger part? It would, of course, be reasonable to establish checks against blatant malpractice, safeguards such as those used by the World Bank and which, since corruption is not a poor-country monopoly, should not be applied in one direction only. But this danger is less serious than it seems at first sight since the bulk of aid is delivered as goods and services with specific uses agreed beforehand by both parties. Criteria are at present largely devised to reassure the home public that 'their money' is being well-used; since policing is as costly as it is ineffective, it would be better to devote the effort to informing and educating the public about the uses of aid. Aid management equally should not be seen as solely a rich-country responsibility; once it is established that the purpose of aid, which is anyway not the preponderant element, is local development, it follows that local judgement on how to achieve this has to be supported, not usurped.

Thirdly, methods of aid giving need overhaul if only to remove the obviously counter-productive elements. Tying of aid is clearly the chief of these and the case for its elimination is – even in rich countries – widely acknowledged. Secondly, short-term and high-interest loans, like payments for past services, can only be described as 'aid' by stretching the meaning of the term. Thirdly, while some aid is encumbered with an administrative overhead which is costly and slow moving, other aid is so weakly supported that it becomes a liability; both defects place a quite unnecessary burden on poor countries and divert resources from better uses. Lastly, competition between aid donors is a consequence of over-much self-interest and the elimination of this motive would help to lessen it. Aid-management by poor countries is harried by such competition, which causes wasteful and unnecessary rivalry between ministries, frustrates coordination and adds nothing to the objectives sought. Even international aid programmes are not free from this defect. A method of aid giving which promoted full and frank discussion of objectives and methods for all forms of assistance would be of the greatest benefit to all.

Finally, evaluation, or the assessment of the success of aid, itself needs critical re-evaluation. Evaluation of aid which merely emphasizes adverse local conditions, unfamiliarity with modern methods or reluctance to discard traditional patterns of responsibility and behaviour, is as unseemly as complaining of the slow progress of a cripple. Some evaluation is no doubt an inescapable consequence of accepting aid, but it would be better if donors were less exigent and more willing to have the recipients undertake it as part of a general appraisal of their own progress. Moreover, evaluation by rich country criteria introduces standards of operation, accountability and performance which they have evolved over a century or more and which are only just appearing in this form in the poor countries. Not only is their overnight adoption unlikely but, in the process of being adopted, they may well need substantial modification.

What these comments suggest is that those who wish to help development by providing aid need to be clear themselves, and to make very clear to the poor-country recipient, what it is they have in view. On the one hand the intention may be to make an unconditional gift to support a developing country while it copes with the formidable task of changing its entire structure and direction; on the other hand it may be a bargain with advantages and benefits to be set off against the support given. Too often aid is given the appearance of a gift but turns out in fact to be a deal, negotiated between partners of very unequal bargaining power.

Of course poor countries have a responsibility in both cases; they must make sure that they can afford to receive a gift, or honour the overt terms of a bargain. What is particularly hard to live with is the concealed expectation or condition, or the unsolicited advice and sometimes interference, which accompanies the nominal gift. Poor countries have been subject to endless investigation and evaluation, and been given constant advice as a consequence of accepting aid; some impatience is a natural reaction, especially when benefactors differ so among themselves as to what should be done. 'People in developing countries seek assistance, but on the basis of mutual respect; they want to have friends not masters'. This opinion, voiced by Ayub Khan of Pakistan, is shared by many recipients.

15 THE TOTAL RELATIONSHIP[1]

It is easy to exaggerate the importance of aid. It is also common: the percentage of a country's national income going on aid is often used as a measure of its virtue. This mistake is at root due to isolating one element in a complex relationship. In this chapter I want to sketch the totality of relations between rich countries and poor that affect development.

To bring out the issues, let me take as a starting point the targets which have been discussed at the UN, at UNCTAD and in the Pearson Report. The last named is specific: aid *plus* private investment should equal 1 per cent of GNP by 1975.[2]

Underlying this approach is a rather simple model. (1) Development is taken to consist essentially of economic growth, measured by changes in the national income; (2) economic growth is seen as depending mainly on capital (and, in some cases, on the supply of foreign exchange); (3) the role of foreign 'donors' is to supplement, either by private investment or by aid, the domestic supply of savings (thus incidentally relieving any foreign exchange bottleneck).

Each of the links in this argument have already been, by implication, questioned in the earlier chapters of this book.

(1) Part One gave a number of reasons for querying the use of the national income as a measure of development. This adds together activities of very different significance – rents paid to big landowners, salaries of soldiers and wages of those who are suffering from undernourishment. At best it is only a long-term indicator – a country may be making good economic progress through creating the infrastructure and the educational

capacity for growth, although its national income is stationary (or even falling) for a few years.

Nobody who has read the opening chapters will, I imagine, fall into the very tempting trap of saying that, since poverty consists of low income per head, therefore income growth means development. After all, one could hardly talk of development having taken place in any true sense, if average incomes had risen, but at the same time inequalities had grown more severe, unemployment increased, and the lowest quarter of the population became absolutely poorer.[3] In fact, one would hesitate to say that the state of a nation had improved if it had suffered *any* of these setbacks. Income growth is, in brief, a necessary but far from sufficient condition – in the long-term – for development; it is by no means identical with development, even in the economic sense. (And the second part of this book has warned us against thinking of development in purely economic terms).

(2) The less we concern ourselves with economic growth as such, the less significance does capital investment have. But this is far from the only determinant of the national income, anyway, as Part Three of this book has brought out. A shortage of high-level manpower can be as serious a constraint as lack of capital, or even more so; capital is little use if there are not enough staff to prepare and carry out projects. But economic growth also depends on the success with which resources can be mobilized and the right strategies worked out, both overall and in the key sectors.

(3) But, even supposing, for the sake of argument, that the national income were a measure of development, and that it did depend on capital investment, this would not necessarily imply that development depended at all closely on the volume of capital transfers from abroad. The two chapters which preceded this one have already thrown doubt on this. Generous aid may be offset by tariffs, excise duties, quotas, etc., imposed by 'donors' on exports from aid recipients. Other policies of 'donors' may also affect the availability of foreign exchange (or a country's saving potential) e.g. the freight rates (and passenger fares) charged by their companies.

These rates may be kept artificially high by conference agreements or by the regulations of cartels such as the airline association, I A T A. Insurance of all types is another heavy foreign exchange cost. Donor governments support 'their own' transport and insurance companies in negotiations, so this is also ultimately among the ways in which their policy affects growth.

In an important minority of countries – those dependent on exports of oil and metal ores – the capital available for economic growth depend very much on the terms of concessions to foreign companies and rates of taxation imposed on them. Here again the attitude of the metropolitan government may be crucial.

But once we allow that capital is not the only source of growth, let alone of development, we open up the analysis, and have to look critically at many other policies of rich countries. The recognition of the importance of high-level manpower has led to a realization that 'manpower aid' – technical assistance and overseas training – which were mentioned in the previous chapter, can be as important as 'financial aid'. This however depends very much on educational systems in the rich countries. Courses designed primarily for engineers or doctors or economists who are going to work in industrial countries are likely to be of only limited use for those coming from overseas – or as a preparation for those going abroad on technical assistance.

If high-level manpower is scarce, the 'brain drain' from poor countries can constitute an important loss, perhaps outweighing technical assistance (which is in any case far from an adequate substitute for the contribution of local citizens). The volume of the outflow of professional and technical personnel depends very much on the immigration laws of rich countries, in particular whether those with an education qualification find it easier to migrate than those without it. The adequacy of the educational systems in the rich countries, especially in the fields of engineering, science, and medicine, also has a big effect.

We must not forget the transfers of technologies and consumption patterns from rich to poor countries – which were discussed in the opening chapters. We can now see how inappropriate these can be, and thus how damaging to development, especially in creating modern sectors with levels of living very far removed from those of most of their countrymen, especially rural workers. This can impede the social and economic integration essential to a healthy development process.

Perhaps the most widely overlooked influence on development, however, is the foreign policy of rich countries. This had various types of impact. Sometimes an aid recipient is encouraged to arm, perhaps even to buy armaments from the 'donor'. One result is to facilitate military coups with, of course, far-reaching implications for development. Neighbours may also be provoked to arm against each other (India and Pakistan in the 1960s); this can even precipitate wars.

Military intervention by the big powers is not completely unknown. Examples are the Soviet invasion of Iran after the war; British action to suppress 'subversion' in colonies (Guyana and Aden); French military assistance to a number of West African governments in danger of being overthrown; U.S. interventions in Guatamala, Cuba, the Dominican Republic and (especially) Vietnam. I shall not go into all the ramifications of the impact of military intervention on development – my point is not that its impact is necessarily negative,* but that it is undeniably important.

Attitudes of an aid 'donor' to neighbours of recipients also have their implications. For example, Britain's failure to stop the Smith regime declaring independence for Rhodesia has had enormous consequences for the development of other Central African countries, especially Zambia, outweighing by far the value of British aid.

Some types of foreign policy are closely linked with aid. A recipient government knows that by accepting aid it foregoes certain options which the donor would abhor, such as expro-

---

*The verdict of the historian may eventually be that in this century intervention has mostly stimulated development by strengthening nationalism. This seems to have happened in the Soviet Union and China, and it may well turn out to be the case in Cuba and Vietnam. Conversely, aid can weaken the resolve to develop, by undermining nationalism.

priating American companies without heavy compensation (the Hickenlooper Amendment) or recognizing the government of East Germany (the Hallstein Doctrine). These are rarely very serious limitation, because the aid receivers may have no intention of doing what the donors prohibit, and in any case the prohibition turns out after all not to be total in all circumstances; still, some erosion of bargaining power is implicit in any such conditions. Rather more serious in their developmental implications are prohibitions on recipients trading with certain countries, such as the embargo which recipients of U.S. aid are required to uphold on exports to Cuba and North Vietnam.

'Leverage' influences not merely the policies of a government but also what sort of a government it is. The embassies of rich countries often follow the internal politics of recipients very closely and favour some political groups (even some civil servants) more than others. Governments which facilitate foreign private investment are especially popular with donors – yet often these are precisely the ones which check, or fail to foster, social change. They also tend to be governments which fail even to attempt to control the outflow of private capital. Yet aid helps to keep them in office; on the other hand, the knowledge that political parties or leaders who oppose foreign investment and favour (e.g.) genuine land reform are ineligible for aid from some sources may affect their chances of getting or keeping power.

So the effect of diplomatic intervention on development is far from random – it may well be negative in many cases, using 'development' in the sense which I have suggested above.* The fact that 'donors' often use aid for their own selfish ends does not imply that they know what is in their own interest. In the longer term, this would probably be better served by the development of the Third World. Nor does it imply that such

*A well-known finding of most analyses of the geographical pattern of aid is that small countries tend to be very heavily aided on a per capita basis. One reason may be that they have less capacity to resist such pressures. On the other hand, even big countries are also vulnerable. For example, the replacement of the Goulart government in Brazil by a military regime is widely believed to have been due primarily to foreign interference.

political strings are very effective (sooner or later people resent being pawns in other countries' political games). But to say that aid 'donors' in the end lose by such procedures is not by any means the same as saying that recipients gain from them.

The conditions imposed by the 'donor' sometimes reflect not so much its own interests (however it interprets these) as its view of how recipient governments should be run. As chapter fifteen has pointed out, aid sometimes specifies so-called 'self-help' (or 'performance') conditions, which may range from balancing the budget or devaluing the exchange rate to raising bus fares. They are spelled out in 'letters of intent' drafted by the 'donor' but signed by the recipient; IBRD loans and IMF balance of payments support are often subject to similar conditions. Typically such stipulations are justified on the grounds that they are designed to check inflation or corruption. These are in themselves unexceptionable ends. But the actual steps which recipient governments take have far-reaching political implications as well. They may lead to the cutting of public investment, or to the curtailment of expenditure on social services. In other and more fundamental ways, they affect development strategy. Broadly speaking, such criteria reflect on ideological belief in one particular route of development, namely relying on market forces and leaving the economy as 'open' as possible, i.e. with few controls on foreign exchange or imports and an open door to foreign investment (the point at which ideological conviction and the self-interest of rich countries merge). (See chapter eight.) This route may be the only one possible for some governments, especially those of very small countries (unless of course they integrate with other very small countries), but the attempt to follow it may seriously damage many others.

The whole set of relations between a rich country and a poor one, therefore, may well be to obstruct instead of to stimulate development. The most important developmental inplications of aid are not so much the resources it provides as what is in the total 'package' of which it is an integral part. This may include, to recapitulate, trade arrangements discriminating in favour of the 'donor', the spread of attitudes, technique and tastes which are inappropriate for poor countries, the establishment of military bases, a stronger position for certain ministers, or a ceiling on the expansion of social services.

This is not to say, as a generalization, that aid is 'a bad thing'. Many countries would face severe withdrawal pains if it ceased to be available; and while for some this might turn out in the long run helpful to development, in the sense I use the word, in others (including India) the challenge might well prove far too great, even in the perspective of history. Often it provides the breathing space within which necessary reforms can be carried out and it can actually strengthen national independence. This depends on many questions – how large it is, how it is managed, and the sectors to which it is directed. Perhaps most important is its source. When aid is provided by 'small donors' and international agencies, its political conditions are less likely to be damaging. One is not so sure about the bilateral programmes of one or two other 'donors', especially France and the U.S., since some of the governments receiving large quantities of aid are themselves the chief obstacles to development.

To raise such questions does, however, undermine the rationale of 'targets' such as the 1 per cent target mentioned at the beginning of this chapter. In the first place, does it make much sense to add together aid and private investment in a total figure for 'transfer' of resources, since there is so much difference between their impacts? – for one thing, private investment generates an early and big transfer of profits and interest in the reverse direction. But, more basically, is there even much point in adding together aid to governments of such different complexions, especially since there is such a range of terms and so many different conditions, explicit or implicit?

It is an interesting question why one of the elements in international relationships attracts so much attention, for example in the Pearson report, especially since it is usually inextricably bound up with others. How is it that the total package, which is what matters, is so often ignored? One explanation is that aid can at least be quantified (the defence for using the 'national income' as an indicator of development is also that it is quantifiable), whereas the other elements are more difficult for the social scientist to handle.

But this does not seem to be a sufficient explanation; the model linking aid to development is so obviously facile. Perhaps attention is concentrated on the volume of aid for the reason, possibly subconscious, that many of the other elements which have been described are both complicated and raise awkward questions, especially for any political leader in a 'donor' country. There is a certain lobby for transferring money. This receives support both from those who feel, sincerely, a bad conscience about international inequalities and also from those who hope to benefit from the trade and other opportunities opened up, in various ways, by aid. It would be very difficult to arouse the same political support for lowering tariffs, reducing shipping freight rates, limiting the immigration of doctors, stopping the sale of military equipment, or switching diplomatic support away from conservative (usually military) political groups in recipient countries. On all these questions there are powerful and know-ledgeable opponents to change, inside the bureaucracies of donor governments, supported by strong pressure groups outside.

We live in an age of archaic attitudes to international policy. Once (less than 100 years ago) the main way of relieving poverty in Britain was by charity – whether from individuals or through charitable associations or the parishes. In retrospect, we can now see that, though charity undoubtedly alleviated some of the worst social miseries (and also relieved the consciences of the affluent), it was in itself entirely inadequate to change the social structure and to achieve the development which has occurred. Indeed, in as far as it had political and social implications, charity may well have helped to consolidate the status quo – the category known as the 'deserving poor' testifies to the climate of the time. Opinions differ as to the influence of various policies in changing and developing the industrial countries – a process that is clearly still far from complete. But a big element was clearly the creation, in response to political pressures, of a fiscal system for transferring money to the poor on the basis of objective need (rather than of 'self-help criteria' applied by individual poor law officials) and for financing education. The creation of a fiscal system was in turn partly due to the growth of trade unions and political organizations; these have also had their own influence on the pattern of British development, for example through affecting wages. Charity was indeed in a way an evasion of the rich-poor issue in industrial countries.

What we have really been talking about in this book is the need for a world-wide system of co-ordinated policies, national and international, in many different fields, to tackle the problems of world poverty, which become increasingly repulsive as the rich – which now includes virtually the whole population of the industrial countries – become richer. Aid does have a function, but treating it as the *central* policy issue provides, for some people, a way of evading the realities of a divided world.

BIBLIOGRAPHY

Chapter 1: Rich Countries and Poor

1 The sources for table 1.1 are: for Africa, *World Bank Atlas*, IBRD, 1966; for other areas, and totals, UNCTAD Secretariat, based on UN statistics.

2 KUZNETS, S., 'Quantitative Aspects of the Economic Growth of Nations: Distribution of Income by Size', *Economic Development and Cultural Change*, vol. XI, no. 2, Part II, January 1963. The corresponding figure for rich countries is 20 to 25 per cent.

3 See PATEL, S. J., 'The Distance between Nations', *Economic Journal*, vol. LXXIV, no. 293, 1964, pp. 119–31. The coverage is not quite the same, but the size of the change is so great that this does not make much difference.

4 ZAFIRON, R., Unpublished paper based on Cairncross and a Chatham House study group report.

5 KUZNETS, S., 'Level and Structure of Foreign Trade: Long Term Trends', *Economic Development and Cultural Change*, vol. 15, no. 2, Part II.

6 The source for table 1.2 is: 'Partners in Development: Report on the Commission on International Development', Pall Mall Press, 1969.

7 The source for table 1.3 is: *International Trade, 1969*, GATT, Geneva, 1970.

8 *Development Assistance Efforts and Policies; 1967 Review*, OECD 1968.

9 *Annual Report*, International Bank for Reconstruction and Development, International Development Association, Washington D.C., 1968.

10 See MORGAN, T., 'Trends in Terms of Trade and their Repercussion on Primary Producers', HARROD, R., and

348

HAGUE, D., eds., *International Trade Theory in a Developing World*, Macmillan, 1963.

11 See, for example, MACBEAN, A. I., *Export Instability and Economic Development*, Allen & Unwin, 1966, which summarizes earlier studies.

12 These are combined by the author in 'A Model of Comparative Rates of Growth in the World Economy', *Economic Journal*, vol. LXXII, no. 285, March 1962, pp. 45–78.

Chapter 2: More on Development in an International Setting

1 For an illuminating account see YOUNGSON, A. J., *Possibilities of Economic Progress*, Cambridge University Press, 1959.

2 The existence of a powerful economic mechanism of diffusion, frustrated by wrong-headed policies, has been strongly argued in JOHNSON, H. G., *Economic Policies Toward Less Developed Countries*, Allen & Unwin, 1967, especially pp. 48–52. See also KEESING, D., 'Outward-looking Policies and Economic Development', *Economic Journal*, vol. LXXVII, no. 306, June 1967, pp. 303–20. But some of the differences between Professor Johnson's arguments and those put forward below depend upon what one considers established and what removable features of the current scene and also on what one wishes to call economic and political forces.

3 *The Transmission of Inequality*, unpublished paper read at the Haile Selassie I Prize Trust Conference in Addis Ababa, October 1966. See also SEERS, D., 'Graduate Migration as an Obstacle to Equality' in *Unfashionable Economics*, Essays in Honour of Lord Balogh, ed. Paul Streeten, Weidenfeld & Nicolson, 1970.

4 MYRDAL, G., *An International Economy*, Routledge & Kegan Paul, 1956.

5 STREETEN, P., 'The Use and Abuse of Models in Development Planning', in MARTIN, K., and KNAPP, J., eds., *The Teaching of Development Economics*, Frank Cass, 1967, pp. 57–83.

6 See SEERS, D., 'The Other Road', *International Development Review*, vol. IX, no. 4, December 1967, pp. 2–4.

FURTHER READING:
1 AGARWALA, A. N., and SINGH, S. P., eds. *Accelerating Investment in Developing Countries*, Oxford University Press, 1970.
2 BALOGH, T., *Unequal Partners*, Blackwell, 1963, and *The Economics of Poverty*, Weidenfeld & Nicolson, 1966.
3 GRIFFIN, KEITH, *Underdevelopment in Spanish America*, Allen & Unwin, 1969.
4 MYRDAL, GUNNAR, *Asian Drama*, Penguin 1968.
5 SINGER, H. W., *International Development*, McGraw-Hill, 1964.
6 STREETEN, PAUL, ed., *Unfashionable Economics*, Weidenfeld & Nicolson, 1970.

Chapter 3: The International Diffusion of Technology

1 For a contrary view, that demographic necessity is the mother of indigenous rural invention, see BOSERUP, E., *The Conditions of Agricultural Growth*, Allen & Unwin, 1965. Her interpretation makes sense of much of African economic history, but the opportunities for directly inventive responses from peasants are much smaller nowadays.
2 UPTON, M., 'Costs of Maize Storage 1959–60', *Annual Report of West African Stored Products Research Unit*, Nigerian Federal Ministry of Commerce and Industry, 1962, pp. 83–5; a similar return is reported by UPTON, M. 'Cost of Guinea Corn Storage in Silos', *ibid.* pp. 89–90.
3 ENKE, S., 'The Economic Aspects of Slowing Population Growth', *Economic Journal*, vol. LXXVI, no. 301, March 1966, pp. 44–56: CASSEN, R., 'Population Policy', in STREETEN, P., and LIPTON, M., eds., *The Crisis of Indian Planning*, Oxford and Chatham House, 1968. Such estimates are full of hair-raising assumptions and traps, well discussed by Cassen, but the figure of 15 is almost certainly a minimum.
4 *Fact Book on Manpower*, Institute of Applied Manpower Research, New Delhi, 1963, p. 200.
5 THOMPSON, S. W., *Population and Progress in the Far East*, The University of Chicago Press, Chicago, 1958, pp. 140–1, 293.

6 *The Mysore Population Study*, United Nations, New York, 1961, p. 144.

7 A brilliant account is to be found in TAEUBER, I., *The Population of Japan*, Princeton University Press, Princeton, 1958.

8 HARKARY, O., *Impact of Family Planning Programmes on the Birth Rate*, unpublished.

9 For fuller accounts see SCRIMSHAW, N. S., and REVELLE, R., in *Technology and Economic Development*, Penguin, 1965, pp. 55–90, and 'Agriculture', *Science and Technology for Development*, vol. III, United Nations, New York, 1963, pp. 3–171, 241–9. The latter source is used in much of the remainder of this section, including quotations not otherwise attributed.

10 *Fertilisers 1968*, F.A.O., Rome, 1969, 9, pp. 17–20.

11 SEN, A. K., *Choice of Techniques*, 3rd edition, Blackwell, 1968, Appendix C.

12 OLDHAM, G., FREEMAN, C., and TURKCAN, E., 'Document TD/28/Supp. 1', *U.N. Conference on Trade and Development: 2nd Session*, Geneva, 1967, pp. 8–9. The following discussion draws heavily on this paper.

13 DHAR, P. N., and LYDALL, M., *Small Enterprise in India*, Asia, 1962.

14 SCHURR, S. H., 'Energy', *Technology and Economic Development*, Penguin, 1965, pp. 91, 94.

Chapter 4: How Poor are the Poor Countries?

1 BECKERMAN, W., *International Comparisons of Real Income*, Development Centre, OECD, Paris, 1966, p. 28. See also BECKERMAN, W., and BACON, R., 'International Comparisons of Income Levels: A Suggested New Measure', *Economic Journal*, vol. LXXVI, no. 303, September 1966, pp. 519–36.

2 A long list of characteristics of underdeveloped areas is found in LEIBENSTEIN, H., *Economic Backwardness and Economic Growth*, John Wiley, New York, 1963, pp. 40–41.

3 The classifications, though not the items enumerated, follow generally those in MYRDAL, G., *Asian Drama*, Penguin, 1968, Appendix 2, section 5, pp. 1,859–64.

Chapter 5: Social Perspectives

1 DILIM OKAZOR-OMALI, *Nigerian Villager in Two Worlds*, Faber, 1965.

Chapter 6: Political Perspectives

1 GROSS, B. F., 'From Symbolism to Action', in ASHFORD, D. E., *Morocco-Tunisia: Politics and Planning*, Syracuse University Press, Syracuse, 1965, p. xvi.

2 This area of problems was brilliantly surveyed by SHILS, E. A., 'On the Comparative Study of the New States', GEERTZ, C., ed. *Old Societies and New States*, Free Press, New York, 1963, from which these expressions are taken.

3 ZOLBERG, A., *Creating Political Order: The Party – States of West Africa*, Chicago University Press, Chicago, 1966, pp. 22–3.

4 The source for table 6.1 is: HAGEN, E. E., 'A Framework for Analysing Economic and Political Change', in ASTON, HAGEN, et. al., *Development of the Emerging Countries*, The Brookings Institution, Washington, D.C., 1964, p. 4. The data are from the period 1956–60.

5 Many political writers have experimented with classifications relevant to the theme of this book, e.g. COLEMAN, J. S., in ALMOND, G., and COLEMAN, J. S., eds., *The Politics of the Developing Areas*, Princeton University Press, Princeton, 1960, pp. 541–2; ALMOND, G., and POWELL, G.B., J. R. *Comparative Politics: A Developmental Approach*, Little Brown, Boston, 1966, p. 217; APTER, D. E., *Political Modernization*, University of Chicago Press, Chicago, 1965, p. 256; WOLF, C., JR, *United States Policy and the Third World*, Little Brown, Boston, 1967, pp. 116–17.

6 GROSSHOLTE, J., *Politics in the Philippines*, Little Brown, Boston, 1964, p. 161. The best analysis of the political consequences of such highly personalized – dyadic – political relations is LÁNDE, C., *Leaders, Factions, and Parties: The Structure of Philippine Politics*, Yale South East Asian Studies Program, New Haven, 1965, especially the Appendix: 'Group Politics and Dyadic Politics: Notes for a Theory'.

7 The source for table 6.2 is: RUSSETT, B. N., *Trends in World Politics*, New York, 1965, p. 127, table 8.1.

8 BRASS, P. R., *Factional Politics in an Indian State*, University of California Press, Berkeley, 1965.

9 This way of looking at politics in poor countries has been extremely fruitful and was the main contribution of the 'functionalist' school popularized in ALMOND, G., and COLEMAN, J. S., *The Politics of the Developing Areas*, Princeton University Press, Princeton, 1960.

10 HIRSCHMANN, A. O., *Journeys Towards Progress*, Twentieth Century Fund, New York, 1963, explores the tactics of this in Latin America.

11 See, for example, SHILS, E. A., 'The Military in the Political Development of New States', in HUNTINGTON, S., ed., *The Role of the Military in Under-Developed Countries*, Princeton University Press, Princeton, 1962, pp. 39–40.

12 FINER, S. E., *The Man on Horseback*, Pall Mall, 1962. Finer himself however thinks that the new states will 'as often as not' be ruled *directly* by the military, p. 238.

13 As is suggested by WATERSTON, A., *Development Planning: Lessons of Experience*, John Hopkins Press, Baltimore, 1965, pp. 343–50, in an otherwise extremely valuable book.

14 VINCENT, J. E., 'Local Cooperatives and Parochial Politics in Uganda', *Journal of Commonwealth Political Studies*, vol. VIII, no. 1, March 1970, pp. 3–17.

FURTHER READING

MOORE, BARRINGTON, Jr, *The Social Origins of Dictatorship and Democracy: Lord and Peasant in the Making of the Modern World*, Penguin, 1969.

Chapter 7: Economic Strategies

1 HIRSCHMAN, A. O., ed., *Latin American Issues*, Twentieth Century Fund, New York, 1961.

2 Cf. Introduction by STREETEN, P., to MYRDAL, G., *Value in Social Theory*, Routledge & Keegan Paul, 1958.

3 LEIBENSTEIN, H., 'Allocative Efficiency vs X-Efficiency', *American Economic Review*, vol. LVI, no. 3, June 1966, pp. 392–415.

4 CAMERON, R., 'Some Lessons of History for Developing

Nations', *American Economic Review, Papers and Proceedings*, May 1967, pp. 313–16. Also MYRDAL, G., *Asian Drama*, Appendix 3, vol. 3, Penguin, 1968.

Chapter 8: The External Economic Strategy:
Outward – or Inward – Looking?

1 'The Developing Countries in World Trade', *World Economic Survey 1962*, United Nations, New York, 1963, and *International Trade 1961*, GATT, Geneva, 1962. See also BALASSA, B., *Trade Prospects for Developing Countries*, Irwin, Homewood, 1964. A good analysis of the whole problem of the 'trade gap' is to be found in LINDER, S. B., *Trade and Trade Policy for Development*, Pall Mall, 1967.

2 The sources for table 8.1 are: Documents TD/34/Supp. 1 and TD/34/Supp. 1/Add. 1, UNCTAD, 2nd session, 1967.

3 NURSKE, R., *Problems of Capital Formation in Underdeveloped Countries*, Oxford University Press, 1953.

4 See 'Document TD/40', UNCTAD, 2nd session, Geneva, 1968. This also shows that they enjoy some advantages in certain goods that are more capital intensive, but where the technology is established and easy to acquire.

5 The source for table 8.2 is: *International Trade, 1966*, GATT, 1967.

6 Here again it should be noted that the effective tariffs are in general much higher than the nominal tariffs. See JOHNSON, H. G., *Economic Policies Towards Less Developed Countries*, Allen & Unwin, 1967, pp. 94–104.

7 The preceding paragraphs have drawn largely from two articles by SEERS, D., 'The Other Road', *International Development Review*, vol. IX, no. 4, and 'The Transmission of Inequality', unpublished paper.

Chapter 9: Strategy for Agricultural Development

1 HERDT, R. W., and MELLOR, J. W. 'The Contrasting Response of Rice to Nitrogen: India and the United States', *Journal of Farm Economics*, vol. 46, no. 1, Feb. 1964.

2 FIRTH, R., ed., *Themes in Economic Anthropology*, Tavistock Publications, 1967.

FURTHER READING:

BROWN, LESTER R., *Seeds of Change*, Praeger, 1970.

HUNTER, GUY, *Modernizing Peasant Societies*, Oxford University Press, 1969.

HUNTER, GUY, *The Administration of Agricultural Development: Lessons from India*, Oxford University Press, 1970.

MELLOR, JOHN, *Economics of Agricultural Development*, Cornell University Press, 1968.

MELLOR, JOHN, *et. al.*, *Developing Rural India*, Cornell University Press, 1968.

WHARTON, CLIFTON R., Jr, ed., *Subsistence Agriculture and Economic Development*, Aldine Publishing Co., Chicago, 1969.

DE WILDE, J. C., *Experiences in Agricultural Development in Tropical Africa*, Johns Hopkins, 1967.

The State of Food and Agriculture, FAO (annually).

It is all but impossible to give a satisfactory short reading list for this topic but the above works cover some of the points in chapter eight in greater detail and provide further guides to the literature.

Chapter 10: Manpower and Education

1 COOMBS, P. H., *World Education Crisis – a Systems Analysis*, Oxford University Press, 1968.

2 For a fuller description see SEERS, D., ed., *Cuba: The Economic and Social Revolution*, University of North Carolina Press, Chapel Hill, 1964, pp. 190–219.

3 For two contrasting approaches see BALOGH, T., 'A Proposal to Relate Education Directly to Production', and FOSTER, P. J., 'The Vocational School Fallacy in Development Planning', HANSON, J. W., and BREMBECK, C. S., eds., *Education and the Development of Nations*, Holt, Rinehart & Winston, New York, 1966. Educational reform is usually only part of what must be done to relate education to rural development. Rural opportunities must be opened up and incentives provided as discussed elsewhere in this book.

4 *Yearbook of Labour Statistics* 1966, I L O, Geneva, 1966.

FURTHER READING:

BLAUG, M., ed, *The Economics of Education*, vols. 1 and 2, Penguin, 1969.

JOLLY, RICHARD, *Planning Education for African Development*, East African Publishing House, Nairobi, 1969.

TURNER, H. A., *Wage Trends, Wage Policies and Collective Bargaining: The Problem for Underdeveloped Countries*, Cambridge University Press, 1965.

Towards Full Employment (Report of an inter-agency mission to Colombia, led by Dudley Seers), I L O, Geneva, 1970.

Chapter 11: Financing Economic Development

1 TAWNEY, R. H., *Religion and the Rise of Capitalism*, Penguin, 1966, a passim, especially pp. 233–34.

2 *Third Five-year Plan*, Government of Pakistan, Rawalpindi, 1965, p. 5.

3 KALDOR, N., *Indian Tax Reform*, Ministry of Finance, New Delhi, 1956, pp. 103–5.

4 *The Times*, 18 April 1968, p. 28. Average of high and low prices for the new 1967–8 account.

5 *Development Assistance: Efforts and Policies*, OECD Development Assistance Committee, Paris, 1968.

6 *Third Five-year Plan*, Government of Pakistan, Rawalpindi, 1965, pp. 5, 8.

7 *Fourth Five-year Plan: 1969–74*, Government of India, 1970, p. 83. This is for repayments of principal only. Interest probably eats up a further 10–15 per cent of new aid.

8 YOUNGSON, A. J., *Possibilities of Economic Progress*, Cambridge, 1957.

9 THORNER, D., *Agricultural Cooperatives in India*, Asia, Bombay, 1965.

10 SEERS, D., 'Big Companies and Small Countries: a Practical Proposal', *Kyklos*, vol. XVI, no. 4, 1963, pp. 599–607.

11 HIRSCHMANN, A. O., *The Strategy of Economic Development*, Yale University Press, New Haven, 1958.

Chapter 12: Planning and Development

1 WATERSTON, A., *Development Planning – Lessons of Experience*, OUP, 1965.

2 GORHAN, W., 'PPBS: its Scope and Limits. Notes of a Practitioner', *The Public Interest*, No. 8, 1967.

3 HIRSCHMANN, A. O., 'The Principle of the Hiding Hand', *The Public Interest*, No. 6, 1967.
4 WATERSTON, A., 'Public Administration for What? A Pragmatic View', *Meeting of Experts on the United Nations Programme in Public Administration*, United Nations, New York, January 1967 (mimeo); and 'What Do We Know about Development Planning?', *International Development Review*, vol. VII, no. 4, December 1965. See also LEYS, C. T., 'The Analysis of Planning', in *Politics and Change in Developing Countries*, Cambridge, 1969.

Chapter 13: Trade and Investment

1 See *Programme for Expansion of Trade in Tropical Products*, GATT, Geneva, 1963; it is calculated that the total elimination of such taxes would increase the world volume of exports of the goods concerned in percentages ranging from 4 to 6 per cent.
2 The Cotton Textiles Arrangement has been mentioned in Chapter thirteen p. 305. Documents TD/20 and TD/20/Supp. 3, UNCTAD, 2nd session, Geneva, 1967, provide a summary of the existing quantitative restrictions on trade in goods of special interest for the poor countries.
3 See 'Document TD/21', UNCTAD, 2nd session, Geneva, 1967.

Chapter 14: Aid

1 *Effective Aid*, ODI, 1967, p. 104.
2 The source for tables 14.1, 2, 4 & 5, is: *Development Assistance Efforts and Policies: 1969 Review*, OECD, Paris 1970, table 111.1.
3 'Document TD/L. 37', *Report of the U.N. Conference on Trade and Development, Second Session*, United Nations, New York, 1968.
4 *Development Assistance Efforts and Policies: 1967 Review*, OECD, Paris, 1968.
5 The sources for table 14.6 are: *British Aid Statistics, 1963–67*, HMSO, 1968 and *Development Assistance Efforts and Policies: 1967 Review*, OECD, Paris, 1968.

6 'British Development Policies: Needs and Prospects', *O.D.I. Review*, No. 2, 1968.

Chapter 15: The Total Relationship

1 An earlier version of this paper appeared in the *Journal of World Trade Law*, Vol. 4, No. 2, under the title 'Other ways in which rich countries affect development'.

2 'Partners in Development'. Report of the Pearson Committee (Praeger, 1969). Another target is that net aid should amount to 0.70 per cent of each donor's GNP by 1975 'or soon thereafter but in no case later than 1980'. The Pearson Report discusses other issues but it gives an excessive emphasis to aid, indeed to the economic aspects of the rich/poor relationship. ('Partnership' is perhaps a rather misleading way of describing this, even as an objective capable of achievement.)

3 The author discusses the definition of 'development' more fully in a paper for the Society for International Development World Conference in New Delhi, November 1969, since printed in *The International Development Review*, December, 1969.

FURTHER READING:

DOMERGUE, MAURICE, *Technical Assistance Theory, Practice and Policies*, Praeger Special Studies in International Economics and Development, Praeger, New York, 1968.

Partners in Development: Report of the Commission on International Development, Praeger Publishers, New York, 1969.

A Study of the Capacity of the United Nations Development System, vols. I and II, United Nations, Geneva, 1969.

Seventh Report from the Estimates Committee – Overseas Aid, HMSO, 1968.

Overseas Aid. Observations by the Minister of Overseas Development, Cmnd 3976, HMSO, 1969.

BIOGRAPHICAL NOTES ON CONTRIBUTORS

OSCAR BRAUN received his degree in Economics in 1965 from the University of Buenos Aires and pursued postgraduate studies at Nuffield College, Oxford. In 1967 he became Research Fellow at the Institute of Development Studies and in 1968 took a teaching post at the University of Rosario. At present professor at the University of Buenos Aires, and Visiting Fellow at the Centro de Investigaciones Económicas of the Instituto Torcuato Di Tella. Publications include: 'A model of economic stagnation' (in collaboration with J. L. Joy), *Economic Journal*, December 1968; and 'Desarrollo del capital monopolista en Argentina', Editorial Tiempo Contemporaneo, Buenos Aires, 1970.

H. E. CAUSTIN. Formerly Resident Representative of United Nations Technical Assistance Board, Libya, and Resident Representative of UNDP, Nigeria. Visiting Fellow of the Institute of Development Studies 1966–8. Special Consultant to the Administrator of UNDP 1969.

RICHARD JOLLY is a Fellow of the Institute of Development Studies, with special interests in employment, education and manpower. Since graduating in economics from Cambridge, he has spent about half his time in government work in various developing countries and the other half in study, teaching or research on development problems in the Universities of Cambridge, Sussex, Yale and Makerere College, Uganda. He has been a Community Development Officer in Baringo District, Kenya; Adviser on manpower to the Government of Zambia; and a member of advisory missions to various countries in Latin America, Africa and the Middle East. He is author of *Planning Education for African Development* and part-author of *Cuba: The Economic and Social Revolution*.

LEONARD JOY. Fellow of the Institute of Development Studies. Taught at Makerere College, Kampala; Cambridge and the London

School of Economics. An L.S.E. trained economist who specialized in agricultural economics and then in agricultural development. Member of various technical assistance and consulting missions in East and West Africa, the Pacific, Latin America and Pakistan. Has published on agricultural and economic development issues as well as on the economics of nutrition, and irrigation. Currently researching in the application of social science analysis to policy making in an area of North India.

COLIN LEYS. Born in Wales, 1931. Taught at Balliol College, Oxford; Kivukoni College, Dar es Salaam; Makerere University College, Kampala; University of Chicago and University of Sussex. Fellow of the Institute of Development Studies 1967–70; currently Visiting Professor, University of Nairobi. Author of *European Politics in Southern Rhodesia*, 1959; *A New Deal in Central Africa* (with R. C. Pratt), 1960; *Politicians and Policies*, 1967; *Politics and Change in Developing Countries* (editor), 1969.

MICHAEL LIPTON, 33, is a Fellow of the Institute of Development Studies. Former posts include Reader in Economics, Sussex, and Fellow of All Souls College, Oxford. Interest in development started while working on Gunnar Myrdal's *Asian Drama* in 1960–61. Specializes in Indian agriculture, has worked for eight months in an Indian village, and is presently directing a programme of international comparative village studies. Publications include *Assessing Economic Performance*, 1968 and (with Paul Streeten) *The Crisis of Indian Planning*, 1969 and several papers and articles.

PETER MARRIS was a district officer in the Colonial Service in Kenya for two years, before joining the Institute of Community Studies in 1955. He has done research in both East and West Africa – most recently a study of the development of African businesses in Kenya – as well as in Britain and in the United States, where he studied the evolution of anti-poverty programmes.

DUDLEY SEERS. Director of the Institute of Development Studies at the University of Sussex. Leader of UN Mission to Zambia 1964; leader of the ILO Mission to Colombia, 1970. Consultant and adviser to Governments of Barbados, Jamaica, Trinidad, Zambia, Malta, Burma, etc. Director-General of Economic Planning Staff, Ministry of Overseas Development, 1964–7. Publications include: (editor) *Cuba: The Economic and Social Revolution*, 1964; (contributor) *The Theory and Design of Economic Development*, 1967; *The Teaching of Development Economics*, 1967; *Crisis in the Civil Service*, 1968; *Labour's Last*

Chance, 1968; *Unfashionable Economics*, Essays in Honour of Lord Balogh, 1970.

PAUL STREETEN is Warden of Queen Elizabeth House, Director of the Institute of Commonwealth Studies, and Fellow of Balliol College, Oxford. He has also taught at the University of Sussex, and been Deputy Director-General of Economic Planning at the Ministry of Overseas Development. His publications include *Economic Integration*, *Value in Social Theory*, and *Unfashionable Economics*. He also contributed to Gunnar Myrdal's *Asian Drama*.

INDEX